Distributive Justice and Taxation

Providing a thorough examination of distributive justice, *Distributive Justice and Taxation* presents and discusses different theories of what constitutes a just society, and how goods should be distributed in such a society.

The distribution of goods in society has direct and serious consequences on the lives of the people. There are therefore important questions to be asked regarding the justice of that distribution: Is it just that some people inherit large fortunes while others inherit nothing? Do rich people have additional access to political power because of their wealth? If so, is that just? And should the ambition for economic policies be to combat poverty, or to reduce inequality? This book explores these questions and a number of others through the analysis of related theories, spanning from strong egalitarian theories on the left to right-wing libertarianism. The chapters also explicitly examine the case of taxation – one of the most important and controversial measures of distribution of goods in society. Placing emphasis on the case of Norway and using data from both the UK and USA as a point of comparison, the work details and explores the key features of the tax system. It concludes by presenting and evaluating arguments for and against taxes such as income tax, wealth tax, and inheritance tax.

This book is essential reading for those interested in distributive justice, as well as students and scholars of philosophy, law, political science, and economics.

Jørgen Pedersen is Professor of Practical Philosophy at the Department of Business Administration, Western Norway University of Applied Sciences, Norway.

Routledge Frontiers of Political Economy

Capitalism, Institutions and Social Orders
The Case of Contemporary Spain
Pedro M. Rey-Araújo

Power and Influence of Economists
Contributions to the Social Studies of Economics
Edited by Jens Maesse, Stephan Pühringer, Thierry Rossier and Pierre Benz

Rent-Seeking and Human Capital
How the Hunt for Rents is Changing Our Economic and Political Landscape
Kurt von Seekamm Jr.

The Political Economy of State Intervention
Conserving Capital over the West's Long Depression
Gavin Poynter

Intangible Flow Theory in Economics
Human Participation in Economic and Societal Production
Tiago Cardao-Pito

Foundations of Post-Schumpeterian Economics
Innovation, Institutions and Finance
Beniamino Callegari

Distributive Justice and Taxation
Jørgen Pedersen

For more information about this series, please visit: www.routledge.com/books/series/SE0345

Distributive Justice and Taxation

Jørgen Pedersen

Routledge
Taylor & Francis Group
LONDON AND NEW YORK

First published 2021
by Routledge
2 Park Square, Milton Park, Abingdon, Oxon OX14 4RN

and by Routledge
52 Vanderbilt Avenue, New York, NY 10017

Routledge is an imprint of the Taylor & Francis Group, an informa business

British Library Cataloguing-in-Publication Data
A catalogue record for this book is available from the British Library

Library of Congress Cataloging-in-Publication Data
A catalog record has been requested for this book

ISBN: 978-0-367-32124-6 (hbk)
ISBN: 978-0-367-67959-0 (pbk)
ISBN: 978-0-429-31675-3 (ebk)

Typeset in Bembo
by codeMantra

Contents

Illustrations

Figures

Tables

Preface

When I started writing this book, I wanted to present and discuss the most important theories of distributive justice. I had a deep admiration for the literature on distributive justice, and I thought it was important to convey these theories because they can make people better equipped to take a stand on some of the most pressing issues of our time. I still hold that view today, but as I continued to work on the book, it became clear to me that despite the fact that taxation is a key question of distributive justice, it is normally not given the position it deserves. Thus, I decided to write a book on distributive justice and taxation.

My hope is that the book can be used by the readers to clarify what a just society is and what role taxation should play in such a society. When I say "clarify", I don't necessarily mean that the reader should let themselves be convinced that my understanding of distributive justice and taxation is the correct one (even though that would be nice). The hope is also that the perspectives and arguments brought forward here can contribute to better justified judgement and opinions on some of the important issues that the book addresses.

This book is a translation of the original Norwegian book *Rettferdig fordeling og rettferdig skatt*, published in 2019. Since the publication of the Norwegian version, I have added substantially, and tried to improve the text. The major changes have come in Part 3, and Chapter 11 on the wealth tax is new compared to the original. The book's aim is to connect theories of justice to taxation. In order to do so, I employ distribution and taxation in the Norwegian context as an illustration. However, I also supply data on distribution and taxation from other contexts, particularly that of the UK and the US. I believe that this combination of a normative and a comparative approach can allow a better conversation on issues of inequality, justice, redistribution, and taxation.

Many people have helped me writing this book. First, I would like to thank Sveinung Sundfør Sivertsen who translated the book from the Norwegian original. Sveinung helped me clarify many statements and came up with a number of good suggestions. I hope I have been able to take some of them on board. I am also extremely grateful to Steinar Bøyum and Robert Huseby who read previous versions of the text and helped me clarify my thinking and writing. Without your comments, my understanding of these issues would have been much poorer. I would also like to express my gratitude to Cornelius Cappelen and Richard Sørli. I have learned a lot from the courses we taught together, and have benefitted tremendously from our conversations concerning the issues treated in this book.

The major part of this book was written while I was a post doc at the institute of philosophy at the University of Bergen. I would like to thank the institute for excellent assistance. In particular, I appreciated the many conversations on economic issues with head of administration, Steinar Thunestvedt. The practical philosophy group at the institute has provided an excellent arena to present and test out ideas and drafts. I am deeply grateful to all those who participated and commented upon some of my early writings.

A number of friends and colleagues have commented on previous drafts: Trond Erlien, David Chelsom Vogt, Bjarte Vatlestad, Ole Koksvik, Jesse Tomalty, Bjørn Sandvik, Eirik Andre Strømland, Preben Sørheim, Torjus Midtgarden, Trygve Lavik, Johannes Servan, Espen Gamlund, and Matthew Coffay. Thank you all for your important questions and criticism.

Thank you also to Hannah Gitmark, to my Norwegian editor Kristin Eliassen, to two anonymous referees, and to Andy and Emma at Routledge for their assistance with bringing this English version into existence.

Finally, to the most important persons in my life: Anne, Synne, and Thale: This book is dedicated to you.

Introduction

Inequality, justice, and redistribution

This book is about inequality, justice, and redistribution. My main goal is to present and discuss different theories of justice, and tie these to the question of what constitutes just taxation.

How goods are distributed in society has major consequences for the lives of individuals. Political decisions affecting this distribution are made continually. Should we increase child benefit? Increase the fuel tax? Introduce or abolish the inheritance tax? Frequently, decisions on such questions are made with a view to what constitutes a just level of inequality. Many agree that if inequalities in the distribution of goods are large, this is unjust, and something to be acted on. However, there is disagreement about whether inequality is a problem, why it might be a problem, what, if anything, counts as too much inequality, and why, if at all, we should respond to inequality by redistributing goods.

If redistribution is justified by an appeal to reducing inequality, we call this an egalitarian justification. From an egalitarian perspective, it is the *difference* between what some have and what others have that is problematic (Scanlon 2018:1). The argument of democratic equality is sometimes presented as an egalitarian justification for combating inequality. This argument begins by noting that citizens in democratic societies are free and equal, and must therefore be ensured equal opportunity to influence the political processes and to achieve political positions. Large economic inequalities are seen as problematic in this regard because those with large economic resources can achieve greater political influence than others, or so it is claimed.[1]

Another common justification for redistribution is to reduce or eliminate poverty. If reducing poverty is the main justification for redistribution, it is not the *difference* between people that is held to be problematic. To illustrate, assume that there are two groups of people in a society. Half of them earn €200,000 a year (the rich), the other half 20,000 (the poor). The poverty line is set at 30,000. If every individual in this society were to double his or her annual income, there would be no more poverty, but there would still be substantial inequality.

We must therefore distinguish between egalitarian and non-egalitarian justifications for redistribution. In addition, we must distinguish between differences in *opportunity* and differences in *outcome*. Democratic equality requires that differences in *outcome* must not become so large that those with the most resources can achieve greater political power. The ideal of equality of opportunity, by contrast, demands (only) that people be ensured equal opportunity, but accepts large differences in outcome.

Democratic equality and the ideal of equality of opportunity are examples of important ideals of justice. They provide different justifications for why different kinds of inequalities are problematic. For those who emphasize democratic equality, the central question is whether money can in fact be used to achieve political power. If one believes that it can, one can try to reduce the problem by taxing wealth, thus reducing the accumulation of money with which political power can be bought. For those who emphasize the ideal of equality of opportunity, by contrast, an important question is whether those who inherit money have greater opportunities than those who do not. If one believes that they do, one can try to reduce the problem by taxing inheritance. In the following chapters, I will discuss these and several other ideals of justice.

How one justifies redistribution affects which practical political solutions one will endorse. If one thinks that concentration of wealth is a democratic problem, then taxation of wealth will seem like a good solution. A wealth tax helps limit the accumulation of wealth, thereby also reducing the danger that this wealth will be used to achieve political influence. If, by contrast, one's main concern is to combat poverty, what matters is generating tax revenue that the state can use to reduce poverty; how that tax revenue is generated does not matter (compare Fleischer 2017:268–269).

Justifications for redistribution are often presented as parts of more comprehensive theories of just distribution. What is a just distribution? Different theories hold different views on what it means to say that goods are justly distributed. In the two first parts of the book, I will present various theories of what constitutes a just distribution, and discuss their strengths and weaknesses. In the final part, I will employ one of these theories to discuss justice in taxation.

Normative and comparative benchmarks

In order to employ theories of justice to matters of taxation, it is useful to put things in context. Thus, in the final part of the book, I will be discussing tax policy in the context of the Norwegian economy. This is to illustrate how a theory of justice can be applied to assess a country's tax system and its overall distribution. In this section, I give a rough idea of the Norwegian political economy. Furthermore, I explain why we need both a normative and a comparative approach when we discuss inequality, justice, and taxation. Finally, I explain why we should understand inequality as a multidimensional concept, and argue that we need to consider both inequality of income and inequality of wealth in our discussion.

Following the French economist Thomas Piketty, we can describe the Norwegian political economy through six characteristics: a mixture of state and privately owned businesses; a strong welfare state with universal benefits; progressive taxation; strong labour unions involved in centralized bargaining with employers and governments; laws that ensure employee representatives on companies' boards; and finally, virtually free higher education (Piketty 2020).[2]

According to Gøsta Esping-Andersen's famous typology, Norway is a social democratic welfare state where the citizens receive generous benefits such as childcare, health care, and education. These services are primarily provided without means testing (Esping-Andersen 1990; Schemmel 2015:397).[3] Historically, a special condition of trust between labour unions and capital interests where the former could trust that wage constraint would result in further investments was a key factor. This allowed an institutional framework where private enterprise and a powerful working class could coexist. The result is often seen as a remarkable success where full employment could be combined with welfare state reforms but without ensuing inflation (Esping Andersen 1990:162–190).[4]

Furthermore, the Norwegian economy is special due to the impact of the oil economy. Since the discovery of large oil reserves in 1969, Norway has been able to stimulate the economy and ensure full employment in a way not open to most other countries. Moreover, with the establishment of the Government Pension Fund Global (or the oil fund), which now holds more than kr10,000 billion (or close to €1,000 billion), the financial situation of Norway is likely to be exceptional in years to come.[5]

As a result of these factors, Norway is commonly held to be one of the richest and most egalitarian countries in the world and regularly figures on the UN's list of countries where the citizens are most happy (United Nations 2019). Furthermore, Norway has been ranked as one of the countries in the world where it is best to become old (Global AgeWatch 2015), and are generally ranked top in many similar studies.

Given these favourable conditions, we might wonder whether there is any reason to worry about justice or inequality in Norway. Is there any basis at all for claiming that there is injustice in a society as rich and happy as the Norwegian one? The answer is yes, because we ought to assess levels of inequality not only by comparing different countries, but also by reference to normative ideals.

If, for example, we compare the set of tasks and responsibilities for which the Norwegian state is responsible with the libertarian ideal of a minimal state, Norway is obviously unjust. Libertarianism emphasizes the freedom of the individual and is strongly opposed to all forms of redistribution of goods and mandatory schemes for social security.[6] Held up to this ideal, the Norwegian state intervenes to an unacceptable extent in the lives of individuals, most notably through collecting taxes for redistribution. If, instead, we compare the Norwegian society with the egalitarian ideal defended by John

Rawls, the result is less clear. Rawls is often seen as a defender of the welfare state. However, recent scholarship has questioned this understanding, and focused on Rawls' critique of social systems characterized as welfare states.[7] In line with this, I shall argue that Rawls' theory demands a far greater state intervention to avoid capital concentration than what is the case in Norway today.

When discussing inequality, justice, and redistribution, we can employ two different benchmarks: the comparative approach and the normative approach. The comparative approach discusses matters of justice by comparing empirical realities, such as countries. For example, a Norwegian politician might state that Norwegians should not worry about rising inequality because the level of inequality is lower than it is in the US and the UK. The politician might go on to substantiate this claim by providing descriptive statistics. She might choose to employ the Gini-coefficient to facilitate the comparison. The Gini-coefficient assigns the number 0 to the state in which everyone has the same income and/or holds the same amount of wealth, and the number 1 to the state in which a single person has all the income and/or holds all the wealth in the economy. Globally, in countries with the least inequality, the income Gini-coefficient lies somewhere between 0.2 and 0.3, while in countries with the most inequality, it lies somewhere between 0.6 and 0.7. Norway has an *income* Gini of 0.25, whereas the equivalent in the UK is 0.32, and in the US is 0.37 (*Global Finance* Magazine 2018). This situates Norway among the Organisation for Economic Co-operation and Development (OECD) countries with the lowest income inequality.

We might think that this demonstrates that Norway is more just than the UK and the US. However, that would be false for two reasons. First, because in order to say that a lower income Gini is better in terms of justice, we need to specify the normative ideals that can be used to justify this claim. That is, we need to settle on a normative theory that allows us to say that lower income inequality is better compared to higher inequality. Second, the conclusion is false because we need to understand the complexity of the concept of inequality. Inequality is not straightforwardly understood. To see this, consider the following formulation by the Swedish economists Calmfors and Roine:

> Inequality is a genuinely complex and multidimensional concept. There is no obvious measure that would capture the "true inequality" in society. Should we, for example, care more about inequality in income or wealth or in consumption, or perhaps in some other dimension? Should we consider inequality between households or individuals or perhaps some other division of the population? Does it matter if inequality is driven by the poor falling behind or the rich becoming even richer? Should we measure income inequality at a fixed point in time or consider lifetime incomes?
>
> (Calmfors and Roine 2018:6)

Thus, the statement by the politician does not distinguish between different *forms* of inequality, and assumes that income inequality captures the "true inequality".[8] In fact, this mistake is commonly made in the Norwegian debate.[9] The most basic distinction we need to employ in order to avoid the simplistic picture of inequality is the distinction between inequality of income and inequality of wealth. Using the Gini measure for wealth, Norway's score is 0.80, whereas the wealth Gini for the UK is 0.73 and the US is 0.86 (*Global Finance* Magazine 2018).

There is some uncertainty associated with wealth inequality,[10] but according to two sociological studies from the University of Oslo, wealth inequality in Norway may be on a level with the US (Hansen 2012; Wiborg 2017; see also UNCTAD 2012:66). According to Norwegian economist Kalle Moene, Norway actually has a higher number of super-rich per million inhabitants than does the US.[11] The social democratic model appears to create a larger upper class than does the American model (Moene 2015a, 2015b).[12] Norwegians thus tend to perceive their country as more equal than (most) others, while the truth of the matter is that we are probably highly unequal in terms of wealth.

We should also note that the Gini coefficient is not the only measure of inequality. In fact, this measure is often criticized for being too sensitive to changes in the middle of the distribution, and not sufficiently oriented towards the extremes. Thus, much inequality research focuses on how much the top 10% or the top 1% have of wealth or income. Focusing on wealth, the top 1% wealth share in the UK increased slightly and reached almost 30% in 2010 (Piketty 2014:344). Similar figures for the US show an increase in the top 1% share to a level above 30% (Piketty 2014:348). In the case of Norway, the figures are imprecise and uncertain, but show that the top 1% control around 25% of wealth in the same period (Aaberge and Stubhaug 2018).

Despite these relevant differences between countries, we should also note a general trend that is cross-cultural. Focusing on the top decile share, Piketty has studied the development of inequality over time and found a clear pattern across a number of countries: In 1910, there were massive inequalities of both income and wealth. These inequalities were drastically reduced following the two world wars, and the trend of low inequality continued for 30 years after 1945. Then, in the 1970s and the 1980s, inequalities of both income and wealth began to increase until reaching the level of inequality we see today (Piketty 2014, 2020:20–23).

Wealth inequalities are always greater than income inequalities and there is less reliable data when it comes to wealth inequalities compared to income inequalities (Chang 2014:332). This complicates the picture. However, the crucial distinction between income and wealth inequality reinforces the point made above: We need normative theory not only to assess whether a higher or lower level of inequality should be considered just, but also to take a stand on the question of whether income or wealth inequality should be considered most problematic. If, for example, we think inequality is problematic because it threatens democratic equality, we should probably worry more about wealth inequality.[13]

An important aim of this book is therefore to introduce normative theory into the public debate about inequality and taxation. The comparative perspective is insufficient. In order to fully evaluate the debate on inequality, we need theories of what constitutes a just society. In this book, I present a collection of normative theories that each provides different bases on which to build arguments about what kinds of inequalities are problematic. These theories represent the whole spectrum of political theories, from a defence of the minimal state on the right to one of socialism on the left.

Thus, much of this book is devoted to presenting and discussing different theories of what distribution should be considered just. However, we should not underestimate the value of the comparative perspective. Comparing countries can be important because one country can learn from another country when it comes to how it is possible to reach given ideals. For example, if one is convinced that some form of egalitarianism constitutes the better theory of justice, one might want to look to those countries that are considered egalitarian in order to find out what policies are useful to employ. The point is that we need both normative ideals and comparative perspectives in order to have good conversations about inequality, justice, and redistribution. Norway is normally regarded as one of the most egalitarian welfare states. A discussion of inequality and taxation in Norway provides an interesting test case for theories of distributive justice and a relevant comparison for other countries.[14]

The tax system as a tool to realize a just society

Much of the discussion on inequality in Norway and most other countries turns on questions about taxation. In Norway, the inheritance tax was eliminated in 2014, and the wealth tax has been scaled back in recent years. In general, these tax cuts are presented as necessary to ensure Norwegian jobs and competitiveness. At the same time, the OECD points out that Norway should reintroduce the inheritance tax for reasons of distribution (Dagens Næringsliv (DN) 14.05.2014). Moreover, the International Monetary Fund (IMF) points out that equality is good for economic growth, and that progressive taxation only inhibits growth to a limited extent (Ostry et al. 2014).

However, taxation is not the only factor affecting inequality. Some argue that the welfare state, and the fact that Norway has a compressed wage structure due to powerful unions, matters more than the tax system for equalizing inequalities of income (Moene 2014:15). Nevertheless, the tax system remains one of the most important means available to realize the ideal of a just society (Murphy and Nagel 2002:3).

Questions about tax tend to be complex and involve several academic disciplines. One has to evaluate the effects of a given tax on society, which is a central task of economics. If, for example, a high tax on inheritance leads people to work less because they cannot freely transfer funds to their children, this would count as an important argument against such a tax. However, evaluating a given tax also means evaluating whether it is just. If equality of opportunity were a basic ideal, then this would be an important argument for inheritance tax, because it goes against the ideal of equality of opportunity that some inherit large sums while others do not. Theories of justice are developed within political philosophy, which therefore has an important role to play in connection with discussions about whether a specific tax, or the tax system as such, is just. This role is, however, largely neglected. The extent to which political philosophers have participated in discussions of just taxation has been limited (Murphy and Nagel 2002:4; Halliday 2013:1111; Dietsch 2015:8). This in spite of the crucial role the tax system plays in realizing different ideals of justice. Therefore, I will explicitly tie the various normative theories to questions of just taxation.

Why is there a connection between theories of justice and taxation? There are many reasons why; I will highlight two. First, different theories of justice differ in their views on which tasks should be assigned to the state. Libertarians, for example, maintain that the state should only be assigned the task of guaranteeing the rights of individuals, including their property rights. From this view follows a minimal state that can only legitimately tax to protect the rights of its citizens. Egalitarians reply that the state must continually intervene to redistribute goods between citizens. This requires far more comprehensive taxation than what is allowed by libertarians.

Second, individual taxes are tied to an understanding of which inequalities are most problematic. To illustrate, tax on inheritance, tax on consumption, and tax on wealth are instruments that can be used to combat inequality, but they have different justifications. They are justified on the basis of what one takes to be problematic inequality, which in turn is grounded in a comprehensive theory of justice. Tax on wealth can, as already noted, be justified by the argument that too much concentration of wealth can have a negative impact on democratic processes. Tax on inheritance can be justified by the claimed negative consequences of transfers of money from one generation to the next, for example, by undermining the ideal of equality of opportunity. Tax on consumption can be justified by the claim that high consumption has negative consequences (Fleischer 2017:261).

The book's goals and structure

This book has two main goals. The first is to present and discuss some of the most important positions and debates in distributive justice, a field within political philosophy. This makes up the largest part of the text. The second goal is to apply one theory of justice to questions of just taxation.[15]

The book has three parts. In Part 1, I present and discuss the most important contemporary normative theories of distributive justice. These theories operate with different understandings of the importance of equality, of what constitutes just inequalities, of what role the state should play, and of what constitutes just taxation.

In *A Theory of Justice* (1971), John Rawls presented his theory of justice, called *justice as fairness*. This book marked the beginning of the debates about just distribution that we will investigate in Part 1. Rawls' point of departure is the assumption that citizens are free and equal, and that no citizen must be allowed to dominate and control any other. From this ideal Rawls criticizes capitalist welfare states because they permit too much concentration of capital, and defends inheritance tax and arguably a wealth tax as important tools to realize the ideal of free and equal citizens.[16] As such, this ideal represents a critical, left-wing corrective even to the comparatively speaking left-leaning Norwegian welfare state.

Robert Nozick defends *libertarianism* and the minimal state. Nozick's justification is based on the assumption that individuals possess inviolable rights, and that anything more expansive than the minimal state would necessarily violate these rights. The state can only legitimately protect citizens against arbitrary power, prevent theft, and insure that contracts are honoured. Any state that tries to go beyond this is illegitimate because doing so would violate the rights of the individual. Therefore, the state cannot redistribute goods, and Nozick sees taxation of income as forced labour because humans have inviolable rights, among which is the right to the fruits of one's own labour. According to libertarianism, the Norwegian welfare state is far too extensive.

Ronald Dworkin defends *equality of resources*. He introduces a crucial distinction around which his theory is built: people must be held responsible for their choices, but not for circumstances beyond their control. This means that a just society must equalize inequalities that are due to chance, such as talent or the family into which one is born, but not inequalities that are the result of free choice. To Dworkin, tax on inheritance and income are legitimate tools for the state, while wealth tax is not. This ideal is the closest we get to a defence of the Norwegian welfare state.

G. A. Cohen represents a modern version of *socialism*. He defends an egalitarian principle on which inequalities due to free and informed choice are acceptable, but adds that this principle alone may permit inequalities that can harm community. Therefore, the egalitarian principle must be supplemented by a principle which states that inequality must be combated to allow the existence of genuine communities. He emphasizes that a just society depends on individuals standing up for each other, and argues that the best off in such a society will accept very high income taxes for the most capable. Cohen's socialism is an alternative to both the Norwegian welfare state and Rawls' theory.

Amartya Sen and Martha Nussbaum defend the *capability approach*. This theory is not primarily concerned with specifying a particular ideal or principle of just distribution. Instead, adherents of the capability approach focus their argument on what we should distribute. Our focus, they claim, should be on what individuals are capable of being and doing. This will vary based on person and context. The capability approach does not say anything specific about what would constitute a just level of taxation, but offers instead an opportunity to better understand what it means to be worse off.

An important goal of this book is, as already mentioned, to employ different theories of justice to say something about how we should think about just taxation. The positions we will study are, however, not primarily concerned with taxation. They defend general principles of justice that speak to the just distribution of goods and burdens in society. Rawls is a good example of this. He says little explicitly about tax, but does provide a few suggestions in different parts of his writing.

In this part of the book, we therefore primarily concern ourselves with clarifying what the different theories claim just distribution to be, and only towards the end of each chapter connect this to questions of just taxation.

The writers whose work we shall look into are all North American philosophers within the analytic tradition of political philosophy.[17] They have developed their theories in dialogue with each other, which makes comparing them quite a lot easier. Nozick's book, for example, is a reply to Rawls, and Rawls has, in later treatments of *justice as fairness*, responded to some of Nozick's objections. In this first part of the book, I will present and discuss the different positions in part by comparing them. I will defend Rawls' position, but in so doing I will present an interpretation of Rawls' theory that is somewhat different to how Rawls used to be understood prior to the publication of his later writings.[18] Furthermore, I shall argue—contrary to some of Rawls' critics—that the distributive ideal that follows from his theory is an ideal with practical relevance and critical sting.

In Part 2, I discuss some of the most important controversies in the literature on just distribution. One central debate concerns the question of whether equality is inherently valuable, or only has value to the extent that it can contribute to the realization of other values. Sufficiantarianism, which was initially defended by Harry Frankfurt, holds that once everyone is ensured enough, further inequalities are morally unproblematic. This theory is followed by Derek Parfit's defence of prioritarianism, which involves giving priority to those who are worst off. Both of these theories deny that equality has any inherent value. I introduce and discuss these theories, contrasting them with the view that equality does have inherent value, and provide a list of egalitarian reasons for favouring equality.

Next, I turn to a debate on whether equality should be understood primarily as an ideal for how we distribute goods or primarily as an ideal for how we organize social relations. Following Rawls, I argue that the ideal of equality is not primarily about everyone being perfectly equal in terms of material resources. Instead, equality is about both avoiding some citizens being dominated and controlled by others and avoiding stigma and status hierarchies. I proceed to discuss whether the richest people in Norway have the opportunity to dominate and control others by means of their economic resources.

In Part 3, I turn to questions of taxation. I first discuss some foundational problems related to taxation. The first claim I discuss is the notion that it does not make sense to criticize a tax system for taxing "my money". This claim maintains that such an approach puts the cart before the horse because we cannot say anything about what constitutes "my money" until after we have defined a legitimate tax regime. Next, I discuss what role property rights play in discussions of just taxation. The ambition with this chapter is to lay out and discuss the political philosophical work that *has* provided a thorough discussion of justice in taxation: Liam Murphy and Thomas Nagel's *The Myth of Ownership*.

The following chapter is split into two parts. In the first part, I introduce a number of key issues for debates about just taxation. This includes the various purposes of the tax system, the potential conflict between efficiency and just distribution, the question of what it is that is to be taxed, whether the tax system as a whole should be proportionate or progressive, and finally, I briefly sketch what a Rawlsian theory of justice requires of the tax system. I show that some of Rawls' statements are puzzling and in need of interpretation and corrections.

In the latter part of the chapter, I turn to a brief sketch of the Norwegian tax system. I outline the rough characteristics of this system by focusing on the corporate tax, the income tax, capital tax, and indirect taxes such as the value added tax. I argue that the recent reduction of the corporate tax and income tax is understandable, but that the redistributive effect these taxes has must be replaced by other taxes or other mechanisms.

In the following chapter, I discuss the inheritance tax. I show that there are good arguments both for and against taxing inheritance. The ideal of equality of opportunity and desert speaks in favour of taxing inheritance. Family concerns and concerns for productivity are important arguments against too harsh taxation of inheritance. I argue in favour of a cumulative accession tax, which was first proposed by the English philosopher John Stuart Mill. This proposal entails setting a threshold to how much someone can inherit tax-free throughout their life, and progressively taxes everything above that threshold. This scheme allows one to balance the different considerations for and against inheritance tax. Drawing on empirical studies, I also show that the inheritance tax has few negative effects compared to other taxes.

In the final chapter, I discuss the pros and cons of wealth taxation. I outline the wealth tax that exists in Norway, and show how such a tax can be justified by combining arguments from Rawls and Piketty. I then turn to discuss a number of arguments against such taxation. I focus particularly on the claim that lower taxes on the rich will have a trickle-down effect on the economy, and be good for all members of society. I consider a recent criticism levelled at the European type of wealth taxes, and argue that the Norwegian wealth tax should be reformed. The exemption level and the rates should be significantly higher than they are today.

In the conclusion, I gather the threads of the various discussions in the different chapters, and argue that Norway does in fact allow too much inequality today, and that this, in combination with the increases in inequality we can expect in the future, gives reason to worry. There is too much inequality today, and if Norwegians are to stop this inequality from becoming even more problematic in the future, it is important to make use of the tax instruments that already exist, but also to continue to strengthen the welfare state, and make use of other instruments that can ensure a more equal distribution. The discussion is, I argue, of general interest, because if a comparatively egalitarian country such as Norway allows too much inequality, countries such as the US and the UK will have even graver concerns.

The what, how, and where of distribution

Before proceeding further, I will say a few words about three overarching debates in the philosophical literature on just distribution: What is it that is to be distributed (the equality of what-question), which principle of justice should govern the distribution, and where the principles should be operational. Let me explain.

The discussion about what it is that is to be distributed is a discussion of what benchmark or "currency" one should use when speaking of distribution. In the literature, this is known as the *Equality of what*-question, after an eponymous article by Amartya Sen (1979). The debate has, to a large degree, been dominated by philosophers concerned with equality, and the question that has been discussed is therefore *what* it is one should distribute if one cares about equality. It might come as a surprise that one cannot simply distribute money. After all, money is what one is concerned with when discussing justice in taxation. However, money is just a means to achieve more fundamental goals, and people are differently skilled at getting good things out of the money they have at hand. The debate has consolidated around three main answers to what it is that we should distribute: welfare, resources, or capabilities.

The debate about which distributive principle(s) best realize the end of justice is ultimately concerned with how the "what", which is to be distributed, is distributed, to put it somewhat abstractly. If, for example, we conclude that the best answer to the equality of what-question is that we should distribute resources, we can go on to ask by which principles of justice we should regulate the distribution of these resources. Examples of such principles for distribution is the principle of equality of opportunity, the principle of prioritizing the worst off, and the principle that everyone must be ensured sufficient resources.

The question of what range the theory has is about the unit to which one thinks these distributive principles should apply. Rawls, for example, thinks that the two principles of justice that he suggests should apply *within* countries, and that internationally, other principles of justice should apply. Others, in contrast, think that principles of justice have global reach. If, for example, one thinks that the principle of equality of opportunity is the best distributive principle, one may argue that all people, independent of which countries they live in, should be ensured equality of opportunity.

The what, how, and where of distribution point to different questions any theory of justice should address. These questions identify different parts of a theory of justice. Richard Arneson has suggested that we can compare a theory of justice to an engine (Arneson 2010:103; Robeyns 2018:111). Different kinds of engines can have different parts, but all engines need certain key parts for the thing in question to count as an engine. The same is true of theories of just distribution. All such theories must be able to say something about what it is that is to be distributed, which principle(s) should govern the distribution, and what range the distributive principle(s) should have.[19]

Here, however, I will limit myself to discussing just distribution within countries, and only relate this to international matters where needed. In other words, I will only briefly discuss the question of range.[20] I will also not offer any detailed discussion of the equality of what-question. This is an important debate, and a comprehensive theory of just distribution must contain a clear answer to the question of what it is that is to be distributed. However, it is also possible to meaningfully discuss distributive principles without a particular view on what should be distributed (Caney 2005:104; Hirose 2015:3). In the various chapters, I will therefore briefly address the equality of what-question, but will not give this debate any thorough discussion.[21] My primary focus will be principles of justice.

Further reading

Will Kymlicka's book *Contemporary Political Philosophy: An Introduction* was, for a long time, the standard introductory text in political philosophy. The book is not limited to distributive justice, but provides a thorough introduction to some of the theories that I will discuss in this book. Jeppe von Platz's excellent book *Theories of Distributive Justice* presents Hayek, Rawls Nozick, and Cohen as the major theories of justice. It goes more into depth on the foundational philosophical issues compared to what I do here. Michael Allinghams' *Distributive Justice* provides an accessible introduction and is written by an economist. More advanced readers, whether economists or philosophers with an interest in economy, should read John Roemer's *Theories of Distributive Justice* and Bertil Tungodden's *The Value of Equality*. Jeremy Moss' *Reassessing Egalitarianism* discusses, as the title implies, primarily egalitarian theories, but it does so very well. A number of the chapters in David Estlund's (ed) *The Oxford Handbook of Political Philosophy* are both very good and very relevant to the themes addressed in this book. *The Oxford Handbook of Distributive Justice* has recently been published, and contains among other things a number or articles on how distributive justice is relevant to questions of retributive justice, climate change, and migration.

In terms of shorter introductory articles, there are two I will mention: Jonathan Wolff's *Equality and Social Justice* provides an easily accessible discussion of important questions illustrated through good examples. Peter Vallentyne's *Distributive Justice* is more thorough, but also harder to follow.

There are also a number of good articles in the Stanford Encyclopedia of Philosophy. Examples include entries like *Justice* (David Miller), *Distributive Justice* (Julian Lamont and Christi Favor), *Egalitarianism* (Richard Arneson), and *Justice and bad luck* (Kasper Lippert Rasmussen).

Philosophy Bites has a number of good podcasts on distributive justice. Particularly relevant is Alex Voorhoeve *On Inequality* and T.M. Scanlon *On What Is Wrong with Inequality.*

Notes

1 There are two versions of the argument of democratic equality. One is sufficiantarian and the other limitarian. The former holds that to ensure democratic equality, we must ensure that everyone has enough. The latter holds that to ensure democratic equality, we must limit how much the wealthiest are allowed to control. It is the limitarian version that is egalitarian. I shall return to this.

2 I am here relying on a combination of Piketty's recent book and Kjetil Jakobsen, a Norwegian historian who read Piketty's French version and presented the book to the Norwegian audience (Jakobsen 2019).

3 Esping-Andersen (1990) distinguished between liberal, conservative, and social democratic welfare state regimes. Sweden is another social democratic welfare state that shares many of the same characteristics as Norway. The US and the UK is classified as liberal welfare states with lower levels of state intervention and more reliance on the market to supply social security compared to the social democratic model.

4 Esping-Andersen argues that no other country, apart from Switzerland, managed to secure full employment throughout the entire post-war era (Esping-Andersen 1990:163).

5 During 2019, the oil fund reached the 10,000 billion threshold for the first time.

6 I am here referring to right-libertarianism in the tradition of Robert Nozick.

7 Important contributions include O'Neill and Williamson (2012) and Thomas (2017).

8 We should distinguish *forms of inequality* such as income inequality and wealth inequality from *ways to measure* inequality such as the Gini-coefficient and top income/wealth shares.

9 Consider, for example, the following comment by the conservative Prime minister of Norway: "We are Europe's second most equal country and will continue to be so even if you removed the entire wealth tax" (quoted from Skarvøy and Henden 2017). This comment fails to distinguish between inequality of income and inequality of wealth, and as we shall see shortly, Norway is not among the most equal when it comes to wealth inequality.

10 In a large comparative study on inequality of wealth across ten countries, Roine and Waldenström conclude that Norway is the country with the most uncertain data on wealth inequality (Roine and Waldenström 2015:56).

11 Moene defines the super-rich as individuals with higher wealth than 100 million USD (Moene 2015:250).

12 For an excellent popular presentation of the essence of Moene's article, see Harald Eia's Ted talk (Eia 2017).

13 It is primarily people with great wealth that have the possibility to convert money into political power or influence.
14 I shall return to the relationship between the normative and the comparative approach in the final section of Chapter 5.
15 I have chosen to structure my presentation based on the central philosophers of distributive justice rather than by theme. I find this to be most appropriate, given the aim of understanding what the most important normative perspectives can contribute to a discussion of just taxation.
16 Note that Rawls explicitly defends taxation of inheritance but does not discuss wealth taxation. However, I claim in Chapter 11 that there is a Rawlsian case for wealth tax given the substantial inequality of wealth we see in many countries today.
17 The exception is Amartya Sen, an Indian economist and philosopher, who, since the beginning of the 1970s, has worked at different English and American universities.
18 This interpretation of Rawls focuses on his critique of the welfare state and his defence of an alternative social system; Property-owning democracy
19 Robeyns (2018) has suggested that we can also think of a theory's meta-ethical standpoint, and how a theory justifies the principles or claims they make, as other important parts of a theory of just distribution. The meta- ethical standpoint of a theory is, for example, a matter of whether the theory wants to discover what justice is or if it is more concerned with contributing to practical improvements. A theory can justify principles by, for example, using contract theory, as we shall see Rawls does in using the thought experiment of the original position. Seen under one, then, we can say that a theory of just distribution has at least five parts, and this way of analysing can be a fruitful way to see the particular elements that go in to a given theory.
20 I will touch upon questions of tax evasion and tax competition, which is central in much of current tax debates. However, I will not enter into the philosophical discussions about international distributive justice here. That is a limitation in this project. Nevertheless, there is no reason to exaggerate this limitation, as there is still a substantial role to play for the nation state, especially with regard to taxation (see Saez and Zucman 2019 a:195; Piketty 2020:991–995).
21 Chapter 5 is an exception, in that the capabilities approach is primarily an answer to the equality of what-question.

Part 1

Theories of justice

1 Justice as fairness

John Rawls

Introduction

John Rawls (1921–2002) is a liberal egalitarian thinker. He is liberal in his defence of a rule of law that secures individual rights and economic liberties. This puts him in the tradition of philosophers like John Locke, Immanuel Kant, and John Stuart Mill. At the same time, Rawls is egalitarian in his defence of a distribution of goods in which equality plays a central role. Marx criticized liberalism for ascribing a merely formal status to the political rights and liberties. Rawls takes this criticism seriously, and maintains that political rights must be secured substantially as well as formally. In practice, this means that inequalities must not grow too large to ensure everyone the same opportunity to exert political influence.

Rawls' book *A Theory of Justice* (henceforth *Theory*) was published in 1971.[1] It presents and defends the theory of *justice as fairness* that Rawls kept refining for the rest of his life. In 1993, he published *Political Liberalism*, and in 1999 *The Law of Peoples*. The year 2001 saw the publication of *Justice as Fairness: A Restatement*. In this chapter, I will present Rawls' position using his first and last book as my sources. However, when it comes to the distributive ideal, I will emphasize Rawls' last book, which in my view defends a theory of just distribution that is clearer and more radical than the one he defended in *Theory*.

I shall start by introducing Rawls' conception of society as a social cooperation, and his critique of utilitarianism. Next, I present and explain Rawls' two principles of justice, and show how he uses these to criticize welfare state capitalism. Taken together, Rawls' ideal of justice requires that the wealth of those who are best off in society is restricted, while those who are worst off must be ensured some wealth. I shall argue that tax on wealth and inheritance are important instruments to achieve justice according to Rawls' ideal.

Society as social cooperation

Rawls' goal in *Theory* is to formulate principles of justice for a society in which individuals are seen as free and equal, and where society is understood as a social cooperation to achieve common advantages. To Rawls, these two ideals are absolutely fundamental to modern democracies. Based on these ideas, he wanted to develop a theory of justice.

The way Rawls sees it, questions of justice arise from the conflicts of interests in a society with moderate scarcity of goods. In such a situation, people will realize that cooperation pays, because in that manner they can produce more than they would on their own. By dividing different tasks between them, so that some become specialists in producing one kind of good, and others specialists in producing another, the total amounts of goods in society increase. Cooperation thus yields a *social product*, and a theory of justice should, according to Rawls, tackle the question of how we distribute this social product.

Rawls sees society as an association of people where individuals have common interests, as in the example of division of labour. However, we may expect there to be disagreements between these individuals about how the collectively produced social product is to be distributed (Rawls 1999a:4). To avoid continuous conflict arising from such disagreement, it is in the interests of citizens to arrive at ways of regulating disagreements in the best possible way. Certain social institutions are therefore central to successful cooperation between the members of society: The Constitution, the justice system, the economy, and the family (Rawls 1999a:6). Rawls calls these institutions the basic structure of society.

This basic structure must be organized in such a way that it does not violate the fundamental rights of individuals. "Each person", Rawls writes, "possesses an inviolability founded on justice that even the welfare of society as a whole cannot override" (Rawls 1999a:3). We cannot allow ourselves to disregard this inviolability, even if doing so were to serve society as a whole. The goal of *Theory* is therefore to arrive at criteria that can be used to decide whether the basic structure of society is just. It is especially important to Rawls to arrive at a set of principles of justice that allow us to distribute the goods and duties that follow from social cooperation.

Critique of utilitarianism

With *Theory*, Rawls wanted to challenge utilitarianism that dominated Anglo-American political philosophy. Utilitarianism is a theory in moral and political philosophy, which in its political manifestation maintains that the actions of the most important political institutions should create the greatest amount of welfare for the greatest number of citizens. Rawls challenges utilitarianism, both on the question of what principle of justice should guide the distribution of goods and on the question of what should be distributed. Let us look at the first question first. The main problem with utilitarianism is that it allows for the maximization of the total amount of welfare in society, without regard to the fact that doing so may come at the expense of certain individuals or groups. Rawls thus sees utilitarianism as a theory that allows the welfare of some individuals to be sacrificed for the sake of the welfare of the rest.[2]

Rawls also thinks utilitarians are wrong about what it is that is to be distributed. What we should distribute is not welfare, but primary goods. It is by looking at these goods that one can compare individuals to discover whether they are well or badly off. Rawls presupposes that people normally prefer having more rather than fewer primary goods. Primary goods are (1) personal rights and freedoms, (2) the opportunity to achieve power and positions in their working life, (3) income and wealth, and (4) social bases of self-respect. Social bases for self-respect means that institutions must be so arranged as to allow people to feel secure that the position they have in society will be respected, and that pursuing one's conception of the good is a worthwhile endeavour. Civil rights are central to securing the social bases of self-respect (Freeman 2007:153). Rawls thinks that these primary goods are goods one will value and desire regardless of what one may otherwise value in life (Rawls 1999a:54).

The principles of justice in a well-ordered society

Rawls is thus concerned with articulating principles of justice for a well-ordered society. Note that these principles are not primarily supposed to apply to individuals in their everyday life. Rather, they shall apply to the basic structure of society, controlling duties and rights as well as regulating the distribution of social and economic goods (Rawls 1999a:53). These principles shall regulate core issues of our economic and legal institutions. The tax system is one example of what belongs to the basic structure of society.

Rawls defends two principles of justice

a Each person has the same indefeasible claim to a fully adequate scheme of equal basic liberties, which scheme is compatible with the same scheme of liberties for all; and

b Social and economic inequalities are to satisfy two conditions: First, they are to be attached to offices and positions open to all under conditions of fair equality of opportunity; and second, they are to be to the greatest benefit of the least-advantaged members of society (the difference principle) (Rawls 2001:42–43).

In what follows, we will first try to understand each of these two principles and what significance they have for distribution. Towards the end, we will clarify what is the overall ideal of distributive justice in *justice as fairness*.

Rawls calls the first principle—(a)—the Liberty Principle. The Liberty Principle ascribes every individual *equal* rights to fundamental freedoms. It comprises right to life, freedom, and security for one's own person, liberty of conscience as well as freedom of speech and assembly, property rights, and the right to vote. These are rights that are commonly secured and guaranteed in the constitution of liberal democracies. In addition to these liberties, the Liberty Principle also comprises rights that are more controversial, including that everyone must be ensured equal opportunity to hold public office and to influence elections. Rawls also maintains the importance of ensuring *fair value* of these political liberties. In other words, they cannot merely be guaranteed formally, but must be guaranteed substantially. Rawls' distinction between formal and fair value of equal political liberties is inspired by Karl Marx. Marx claimed—for example, in *On the Jewish Question*—that liberal capitalist societies ascribed to citizens formal liberties that would necessarily be undermined by the inequalities produced by capitalism. Rawls took Marx's criticism of merely formal liberties very seriously (Rawls 2001:148–150, 176–179).

The reasoning runs as follows: If everyone really is to be ensured equal opportunity to influence politics, one cannot allow too much inequality. With large inequality, there will always be a danger that the wealthiest use their economic power to achieve political power. Rawls is especially concerned that the very rich would unite on questions having to do with the advancement of their own interests and privileges (Rawls 1999a:198). However, even separately, the best off may achieve power by, for example, threatening to withdraw their investment in a local community if they are not given the conditions they desire. Alternatively, they could give large donations to political parties to ensure their own interests. Rawls thinks one can guard against the last kind of influence by introducing special arrangement such as public financing of political parties, limits on how much individuals can donate to candidates and parties as well as ensuring everyone equal access to the media. However, according to Rawls, such interventions are necessary but not sufficient to ensure the fair value of equal opportunity to affect politics. In addition to such special arrangements, one must prevent too great concentration of capital (Rawls 1999a:198).[3]

The second principle—(b)—is about socio-economic goods. The principle has two parts: The first part is frequently referred to as the principle of fair equality of opportunity, while the second part is referred to as the difference principle. The principle of fair equality of opportunity is similar to the general principle of equality of opportunity mentioned in the introduction. Even though this ideal is well known, the principle is "not altogether clear" (Rawls 2001:43), and most would agree that it should not be completely realized. For example, research indicates that parents who read to their children provide their children with several benefits. However, few think that it follows from this that the state should ban parents from reading to their children because of the inequalities thus created between those who are read to and those who are not.[4]

Rawls, however, has a particular interpretation of this principle. Here, we must make a distinction between formal equality of opportunity and Rawls' more demanding notion of fair equality of opportunity. Formal equality of opportunity is a well-known principle implemented through legislation in many countries. It requires that, for example, a company advertising a position must choose the best qualified applicant for the job. One cannot give the job to someone on the basis of a wish to hire a woman or a man. Such a principle contributes to justice because it ensures that a person's fate is determined by their qualifications, and not by their gender or family background. Many Norwegians like to believe that the principle of formal equality of opportunity is fully realized in Norway. However, the fact that people whose name sounds foreign are statistically far less likely than those whose names sound traditionally Norwegian to be called for job interviews or offered the lease on apartments for rent proves that Norwegians cannot take the realization of this formal ideal for granted. If a society really did have formal equality of opportunity, Peer's opportunity to realize his ambitions would depend on his formal qualifications, and not on his Norwegian-sounding name.

Rawls' notion of fair equality of opportunity is more demanding. It requires not only that positions are open to those best qualified, but also that people with comparable innate abilities and motivation have equal prospects of becoming best qualified (Rawls 1999a:63). When then minister of education in Norway, Thorbjørn Røe Isaksen, stated that "it is your skills and abilities that should decide, not what home you come from", he could be seen to express support for this ideal (Isaksen quoted in Bøyum 2016:50). Fair equality of opportunity also entails that one must correct for disadvantages that are due to social background. In practice, this means that everyone must be ensured equal access to education; that one must establish a right to basic health care for all; and that the state limits the concentration of capital if such concentration impacts fair equality of opportunity (Rawls 2001:174). We know that in most societies, children born in the middle or upper classes have better opportunities to take a longer education and achieve prestigious positions compared to those born in the lower classes. This is the kind of inequality the principle of fair equality of opportunity is supposed to correct. It is therefore a radical principle, and would require significant state intervention to be realized.

One can argue for equality of opportunity in different ways. One way would be to claim that ensuring everyone equal opportunity is good for economic growth. If everyone is ensured equal opportunity to develop their skills and abilities, they will be able to contribute optimally to the social cooperation. Rawls' argument for equality of opportunity is, however, *not* an efficiency argument. His argument is that fair equality of opportunity is necessary to ensure citizens' rights as free and equal (Rawls 1999a:73).

Rawls' ideal of fair equality of opportunity does not eliminate inequalities that are due to effort and talent. He thinks that people who have the same abilities and motivation should have the same prospects. However, if two people have the same abilities but different motivation, the one who works hard may end up with more than the one who does not. Second, differences in innate abilities will also entail that some end up with more than others. If, for example, Peer and Pål are born with similar family background, but Peer is born with an IQ of 150 and Pål with one of 75, chances are that Peer will be better off than Pål, even if they are ensured fair equality of opportunity. IQ is an important part of one's innate abilities.

Many would therefore think that one *deserves* that which one acquires by virtue of one's talent. Rawls does not agree. He thinks that the talent with which one is born is arbitrary from a moral point of view. Therefore, the principle of fair equality of opportunity cannot be the sole principle to regulate the basic institutions of society. It must be supplemented by the difference principle. To Rawls, people do not deserve the advantages they get from their innate abilities. However, if the work of those better endowed benefits the worst off, this difference in endowment is no longer unjust. Those who are talented will then perform their work in a way that benefits those who have not been as lucky in what Rawls calls "the natural lottery", that is, the random allocation of natural endowments (Rawls 1999a:64).

It is important to note how Rawls, with the help of the difference principle, attempts to reach a compromise between two views that have played important roles in questions of just distribution: Adherents of what we have termed outcome equality have argued in favour of equal material distribution between all members in society. Humans are morally equal, and equality of material goods is the best way of maintaining this moral equality, they claim. Opposed to this view is the view of most economists: The wealth in a society will increase if we allow those who produce the most to earn the most. With the difference principle, Rawls tries to bridge these two views. The principle allows inequalities in outcome if and only if doing so benefits the worst off compared to what their situation would be with strict outcome equality.

Rawls is concerned with the *absolute position* of the worst off. If by increasing inequality, the sum of primary goods of the worst off increases in comparison to what it would be with strict outcome equality, the new distribution will be preferable. Let me illustrate Rawls' argument: Imagine four economic structures, A to D, with the lifetime average income that would be produced for representative members of three different groups (Source: Wenar 2013) (Table 1.1).

In this illustration, a defender of outcome equality would choose economy A, while on the basis of Rawls' difference principle one would choose C. Note that it is not obvious what a utilitarian would choose. A simplified

Table 1.1 Four hypothetical economic structures

Economy	*Least-advantaged groups*	*Middle group*	*Most-advantaged group*
A	10,000	10,000	10,000
B	12,000	30,000	80,000
C	30,000	90,000	150,000
D	20,000	100,000	500,000

Source: Wenar (2013).

version of utilitarianism would choose D, based on the assumption that the total lifetime average income is highest in D.[5]

The difference principle therefore builds in an incentive argument: Differences in income and wealth can improve the prospects of those worst off, for example, by giving talented people the incentives to do work in which their talents can create assets for society, assets which may, in turn, be redistributed. The total size of the pie can be increased, either by talented people working harder, thus raising the total tax income, or by new jobs being created as a result of incentives motivating people to innovate (Cohen 2008:35). Thus, the difference principle is attractive because it formulates an egalitarian impulse while at the same time being oriented towards efficiency.

Rawls thinks that people can come to accept and give their support to the difference principle if they consider some of the basic assumptions we started out with in this chapter. Recall that, to Rawls, distributive justice is about distributing the social product that results from cooperation. Rawls claims that those who accept the idea of society as a social cooperation also have good reason to accept the difference principle. The idea is this: On the one hand, the well off see that they have been lucky: They see that talent, family background, and luck are random morally speaking, and that any advantage due to these factors therefore can justly be used to improve the prospects of those who are worst off. The best off will, within the frame of a basic structure regulated by the difference principle, to a certain extent restrain themselves. They know they could achieve greater advantages, while also recognizing that they, because of their natural endowments, have more primary goods than the worst off. The better off are therefore willing to accept the limitation that any additional increase in their primary goods must include an improvement of the prospects of the worst off. On the other hand, the worst off see that they would not be better off with any other distribution. The difference principle thereby realizes an ideal of reciprocity because those who are better off are not better off at the expense of those who are worst off (Rawls 2001:123).[6]

The principles of justice are lexically ordered. That means that the first principle (the liberty principle) must be completely satisfied before the next principle can come into force. In other words, one cannot justify violations of the liberty principle by pointing to improvements in economic or social conditions. The basis of this lexical ordering is that the principles can come into conflict. This may best be illustrated with an example. We could imagine a society that, by limiting the freedom of expression, would become more stable, increase its production, and thereby be able to provide tax exemptions to the worst off (Holtug 2003:398). Without a lexical ordering of the principles, this would be a possible interpretation. To Rawls, however, this is unacceptable. The liberty principle always has priority.

The lexical ordering also applies within the second principle. The first part must be satisfied before the second can come into effect. Fair equality of opportunity must be satisfied before the difference principle can be applied. However, the principles must be seen in relation to each other as a unit

(Rawls 2001:46). The difference principle is not the only principle relevant to questions of just distribution—contrary to the impression one might get from reading the discussion that followed the publication of *A Theory of Justice*. The other two principles also affect distribution, as explained above. Starting with the liberty principle, one can mount an argument against economic inequalities that hinder people from participating in politics on a par with others.[7] Large economic inequalities may also make it almost impossible for poor people to be elected to political office or to advance their political views. Moreover, starting with the principle of fair equality of opportunity, one can argue that large economic inequalities in society negatively impacts fair equality of opportunity.

Who are the worst off?

Provided that we now have a basic understanding of how the difference principle can be applied, how do we proceed to identify "the worst off"? Rawls admits that this is a difficult question and that there will always be some arbitrariness in categorizing. He nevertheless suggests two possible ways of proceeding. The first is to pick a particular social group, for example, unskilled workers, and then include anyone who has the same level of income as them, or less, in the group of the worst off. The second approach is to base the choice on income relative to others. For example, one could say that anyone with less than half the median income can be classified as a member of the group of the worst off (Rawls 1999a:84).

The question of who the worst off are can also be used to highlight an important general point in Rawls' understanding of what constitutes just distribution. When Rawls defines the worst off, he does so based on groups who work. One could object to this that there are a number of people who are not able to work, who are even worse off, and who therefore should form the basis for the category of the worst off. People with congenital physical and mental disabilities might be relevant examples. However, Rawls sees distributive justice as a question of how to distribute the fruits of social cooperation between people who are willing and able to work. Rawls thinks this question must be answered first, and that the question of what duties we have to those who do not participate in the production of social goods is secondary and must be answered apart from the fundamental question of just distribution (Freeman 2007:106–109).

Arguments for the principles of justice: the unofficial argument

With *Theory*, Rawls not only introduced a new theory, but also renewed the way political philosophers argue in favour of principles and positions.[8] We may say that his theory revolves around two principles of justice, while his arguments for these principles can be divided into an unofficial, an official, and an underlying argument.[9]

The first argument is unofficial, in the sense that it is not strictly speaking an argument for the principles of justice. Instead, it may be said to prepare the ground for the principles, thereby making them seem less extreme (Rawls 1999a:65).

What Rawls does in the unofficial argument is to compare the two principles of justice with what he calls the system of natural liberty, which largely corresponds to libertarianism. Such an ideal allows inequalities so long as everyone is ensured a minimum of liberty and formal equality of opportunity. This means that the distribution allows inequalities that are due to natural endowments and family background. As a theory of justice, the system of natural liberty has no ambition to distribute resources from those who are born with talent to those less talented, or from those who are born into resourceful families to those who are not. Rawls, however, does not think that natural endowment and family background should be accorded any weight in the just distribution of goods. These factors are, as we have seen, "arbitrary from a moral point of view" (Rawls 1999a:63).

This is a radical claim. Many believe that they deserve what they earn as a result of their talent, and it is precisely this assumption about desert that Rawls wants to challenge. The way he does that is by emphasizing that such contingent factors cannot justify that something is deserved. When people justify inequality, they tend to appeal to three factors explaining why they deserve more than others:

- Effort
- Talent
- Luck

Effort may mean the number of hours one is willing to put it, whether one is willing to undergo a demanding education, and so on. Talent relates to the traits and abilities with which one is born, and whether these are appreciated by the society in which one lives. Pure luck is about being in the right place at the right time, how exposed one is to illness, and so on. Rawls' point is that talent is something with which one is born, and therefore that we do not deserve what we earn as a result of our talents. Whether we are born into a resourceful family is a matter of luck, and the inequalities that arise from this luck ought to be equalized. When it comes to effort, Rawls is also very radical. He claims that whether we work hard or not is partly the result of our natural endowments, and partly the result of whether we are born into a family where hard work is encouraged. Both are arbitrary from a moral point of view and not something that can be used to justify the claim that some deserve more than others. Based on this, Rawls concludes that neither effort, nor talent, nor luck can be used as arguments for the claim that some deserve more than others.

That effort cannot justify some having more than others seems unreasonable. If I choose to work five hours a day and you choose to work ten, it seems reasonable—all else being equal—that you should end up with more than me. We shall discuss this more thoroughly in the coming chapters,[10] but it is important to note that Rawls does allow for legitimate inequalities due to talent and effort. The difference principle states that inequalities can be legitimate if they improve the position of the worst off. However, note the difference between the claim that inequalities due to talent are deserved and the claim that inequalities due to talent are just if it benefits the worst off.[11] Rawls does not accept inequalities justified by desert.

We may say that the unofficial argument forces us to rethink what the legitimate bases for inequality may be. If we accept Rawls' argument against desert, we will also be more inclined to accept the principles of justice. If we instead claim—as do libertarians—that our talent is part of us, and that we own our bodies, and what we produce by our own labour, we would reject the claim that talent is morally speaking arbitrary, and therefore also be sceptical of Rawls' suggested principles of justice. Rawls' unofficial argument has given rise to a number of interesting debates about justice that we will investigate further in the coming chapters.

Arguments for the principles of justice: the official argument

Imagine two people set on figuring out what constitutes just taxation. One is rich, the other poor. In such a situation, it will often be the case that the rich is in favour of lower taxes, while the poor is in favour of higher (or more redistributive) taxes. It will be hard to determine who is right, and the situation may appear to be a stalemate. What Rawls does is to tell us that we can resolve this stalemate by asking the rich and the poor what kind of taxation they would want if they did not know whether they were rich or poor (Wolff 2010). When trying to arrive at an answer to what is just, we must think impartially, and it is this thought that Rawls develops in the official argument for the principles of justice.

The official argument rests on a thought experiment inspired by the tradition of social contract theory in political philosophy. The most important representatives of social contract theory are Thomas Hobbes (1588–1679), John Locke (1632–1704), and Immanuel Kant (1724–1804). Common to all social contract theories is a formal model where the central components are a state of nature, a social contract, and a civil society. The state is seen as legitimate if citizens in the state of nature would have created it through a social contract. The state of nature—for most contract theories—is a thought experiment that is used to show citizens why they should support the state. Similarly, Rawls develops a thought experiment that he calls the original position, the goal of which is to allow us to choose principles of justice.

Rawls thinks that the two principles of justice would have been chosen in the original position. He suggests that we must imagine parties in the original position as being behind a "veil of ignorance" (Rawls 1999a:11).

We are to imagine a position where we, as free, equal, and rational parties, have no determinate knowledge about personal traits and place in society. The choices that are made in such a situation may therefore be characterized as impartial. Rawls writes the following about persons in the original position:

> Among the essential features of this situation is that no one knows his place in society, his class position or social status, nor does any one know his fortune in the distribution of natural assets and abilities, his intelligence, strength, and the like. I shall even assume that the parties do not know their conceptions of the good or their special psychological propensities. The principles of justice are chosen behind a veil of ignorance.
>
> (Rawls 1999a:11)

Rawls asks us to think of the parties making a choice from behind this veil of ignorance as tasked with securing the fundamental interests of free and equal citizens (Rawls 2001:84–85).

Of course, Rawls does not think that one can actually bring people behind a veil of ignorance. Instead, he sees the original position and the veil of ignorance as a thought experiment that can teach us something about what a just society would look like. The reason participants in this thought experiment are divested of all particular knowledge about their position in society is that such knowledge would allow them to choose principles that would favour people just like themselves, for example, people with the kinds of skills they themselves possess at the expense of those who do not have these skills. The veil of ignorance thus employs ignorance as a means to model impartiality. The point of the veil of ignorance is to create a starting position in which parties can make impartial choices while at the same time choosing from self-interest. The construction of the original position ensures this. Hence, the parties are not motivated by moral concerns, but are simply out to get the best possible outcome for those they represent.[12]

How will people in the original position think? Rawls holds that they will seek to minimize risk. He assumes that parties in the original position will seek to minimize the loss they, in the worst case, might be subject to rather than maximize the gain they, in the best case, may achieve. This is Rawls' maximin rule about decisions under uncertainty. It holds that we are:

> to identify the worst outcome of each available alternative and then to adopt the alternative whose worst outcome is better than the worst outcomes of all the other alternatives. To follow this rule in selecting principles of justice for the basic structure we focus on the worst social position that would be allowed when that structure is effectively regulated by those principles under various circumstances.
>
> (Rawls 2001:97)

This means that when choosing between alternatives, one should look at the worst possible outcome of each alternative, and then choose the alternative for which the worst outcome is least bad.

That the parties would choose the principles of justice in the original position is, to Rawls, a strong argument in their favour. This is because the parties choose the principles from an equal and symmetrical position. They choose without being either rich or poor. They choose without being partial. The veil of ignorance ensures impartiality through depriving the parties the opportunity to choose principles based on subjective self-interest. An important claim in Rawls is that the two principles are thereby objectively justified, since they are not based on subjective considerations (Rawls 1999a:510). Rawls understands objectivity as that which excludes the particular. Such an understanding, he argues, is also in line with our intuitions about objectivity.

Arguments for the principles of justice: the underlying argument

The third underlying argument is that the two principles of justice best embodies the idea of citizens understood as free and equal. It is only when the principle of equal opportunity to influence the politics of the state is in place that citizens in modern constitutional democracies can see each other as equals. By contrast, inequalities that hinder equal opportunity to influence the development of society will, according to Rawls, harm the individuals' self-respect, and cause the worst off to feel dominated and subjugated by those with real political power. Correspondingly, the principle of fair equality of opportunity is also grounded in the idea of free and equal citizens. If, for example, a person is denied social positions because of race, gender, or religion, this is a violation of the person's dignity as an equal person and citizen (Freeman 2007:91). Both kinds of infringement on a person's status as free and equal citizen can make those who are most subject to it apathetic or bitter, which in the long term may undermine democracy.

Notice that this is not just an argument about large inequalities being negative because they violate the ideal that all citizens should have equal opportunity to influence politics. It is also an independent, but related argument about large inequalities in income and wealth having negative psychological consequences for those who are worst off. If someone is allowed to dominate and control others, this may also harm the self-respect of the dominated. Submissiveness and servility are psychologically harmful and constitute "serious evils", as Rawls puts it (Rawls 2001:131). Moreover, the lack of equal opportunity to influence politics and social relations that allow some to dominate others may be mutually reinforcing. If the best off can both dictate the conditions in the workplace and also have significantly larger political influence than those who are worse off there is a serious risk of negative consequences, both for the political process and for the self-respect of some citizens (Moss 2014:21). We shall explore this point further in Chapters 6 and 7.

The fundamental question of justice: choice of social system

Rawls uses the two principles to settle what he calls the main problem of distributive justice: to determine which social system is the most just (Rawls 1999a:242; Freeman 2013:9). To Rawls, therefore, it is not sufficient to formulate abstract principles of justice. As his thinking matured, he became more and more concerned with specifying which institutional arrangements would best realize the principles. This effort culminated in *Justice as Fairness: A Restatement* (Thomas 2017:xviii). Here, Rawls distinguishes between five different types of social system or regimes: Laissez-faire capitalism, state socialism, welfare state capitalism, property owning democracy, and liberal socialism (Rawls 2001:136). All these regime types can be evaluated using the two principles of justice.

Laissez-faire capitalism, which has strong similarities with a system of natural liberty, is not concerned with ensuring fair value of the political liberties or fair equality of opportunity. Market outcomes are seen as just so long as formal equality of opportunity exists. State socialism violates the principle of fundamental rights by its lack of democratic procedures. Most interesting, however, is Rawls' discussion of capitalist welfare states. For a long time, there was a general assumption that Rawls held a comprehensive welfare state to be the institutional arrangement best suited to maintain the two principles. In his later works, however, Rawls points out that this rests on a misunderstanding (Rawls 1999a:xiv–xv, 2001:135 ff.).

The welfare state is seen by many to be a successful solution worth defending. It provides a safety net for those who need health services, ensures a minimum of means to those who have no income, and guarantees everyone the right to an education. The Nordic welfare states, which ensure extensive benefits, are celebrated the world over and used as models in countries wanting reforms. But are capitalist welfare states just? Rawls did not think so. Capitalist welfare states allow too much concentration of capital. Capitalist welfare states are unwilling to introduce mechanisms that would deny a few privileged the control over the means of production. Moreover, since economic resources are often convertible into political capital, Rawls argues that capitalist welfare states violate the most important principle of justice: to ensure basic liberties for all.

If welfare states are not just, what is the alternative? Rawls argues that both liberal socialism and property owning democracy can satisfy the principles of justice (Rawls 2001:138). Liberal socialism is characterized by publicly owned means of production and worker-controlled companies (Rawls 1999a:248). However, Rawls does not thoroughly discuss this kind of regime, and hence it is the property owning democracy that has gained the most attention, and which is generally viewed as the kind of regime Rawls is trying to defend.[13]

Rawls leans on the economist James Meade in his sketch of property owning democracy. In a property owning democracy, property is continuously distributed by means of state intervention to avoid concentrated economic power being translated into political power, and to ensure the equal status of all citizens. Meade writes:

> Extreme inequalities in the ownership of property are in my view undesirable quite apart from any inequalities of income which they may imply. A man with much property has great bargaining strength and a great sense of security, independence and freedom; and he enjoys these things not only vis-à-vis his propertyless fellow citizens but also vis-à-vis the public authorities. He can snap his fingers at those on whom he must rely for an income; for he can always live for a time on his capital. The propertyless man must continuously and without interruption acquire his income by working for an employer or by qualifying to receive it from a public authority. An unequal distribution of property means an unequal distribution of power and status even if it is prevented from causing too unequal a distribution of income.
>
> (Meade 1993:41)

The most important trait of property owning democracy is thus that it avoids significant concentration of capital. Therefore, it depends on arrangements that spread capital around, and ensure everybody access to capital. Adherents of property owning democracy should therefore defend progressive wealth tax and high taxes on capital income and inheritance, coupled with arrangements that allocate capital to everyone.[14] Negative income tax is an example of such an arrangement. Negative income tax means that everyone whose salary is under a certain level will receive transfers from the state so that they reach the desired level. Negative income tax is similar to universal basic income, but differs from this in setting as an absolute criterion that one is willing to work to receive the benefit. Such an arrangement could be combined with other schemes such as a state fund that pays monthly payments to all working citizens.[15] The goal of these measures is to ensure everyone a social minimum, not just to provide their basic needs, but also to enable them to participate on equal terms with everyone else, and to forestall the possibility of those better off controlling and dominating those who are worse off.[16]

Rawls also opens up for the possibility that workers, to a greater extent than at present, must be able to own the companies in which they work, and he argues for more democracy in the workplace. Rawls stands by property rights, and is less critical of the market than are traditional socialists.[17] What remains crucial is that the state has to ensure a far greater spread of capital than is the case in most modern welfare states.

The problem with capitalist welfare states, as Rawls sees it, is that they allow too much power to those who are best off. In capitalist welfare states, the worst off are treated as a group that has to be compensated for low income or other factors (Freeman 2013:22). Rawls claims that the logic of capitalist welfare states entails compensation for the worst off ex post. The logic of property owning democracy, in contrast, is to equip free and equal citizens with the resources they need for full participation from the beginning (Rawls 2001:139–140).

Property owning democracy therefore requires predistribution and not just redistribution: Predistribution is about limiting people's pre-tax income, while redistribution is about more well-known mechanisms such as tax on income and wealth. In other words, predistribution is about reforming the market so that one promotes a more equal distribution of economic power and market outcomes *before* the government collects taxes (Hacker 2011:35). An example of predistribution would be changing the laws protecting intellectual property rights so that these rights do not last as long as they do today. This would reduce pre-tax inequalities (Scanlon 2018:102). Wealth tax is an example of redistribution which reduces post-tax inequalities.[18]

Property owning democracy rests on a combination of predistribution and redistribution. The result is not necessarily harsher taxation overall, but a transition from tax mainly on income to tax on wealth and inheritance, where the goal is to avoid concentration of capital (O'Neill 2012c:12–13). The goal of both predistribution and redistribution is to ensure the spread of capital. Capital here also means human capital, something everyone is allowed to possess because property owning democracy requires full access to high-quality education for all (Rawls 2001:160–161; Scanlon 2018:102).[19]

The distributive ideal of *justice as fairness*

Seen together, the ideal of distribution that follows from *justice as fairness* is a radically egalitarian ideal. The inequality it allows must be kept within strict limits, especially in the case of inequalities of wealth. Rawls writes that the background institutions must:

> work to keep property and wealth evenly enough shared over time to preserve the fair value of the political liberties and fair equality of opportunity over generations. They do this by laws regulating bequests and inheritance of property, and other devices such as taxes, to prevent excessive concentrations of power.
>
> (Rawls 2001:51)

For our purpose—the design of a just tax system—this is perhaps the most important insight offered by *justice as fairness*: The ideal requires an upper and lower limit on the concentration of capital. It requires, in other words, what Kevin Vallier called a capital ceiling and a capital floor (Vallier 2018:144). The specific distributive ideal that follows from the two principles of justice requires society to avoid too large concentration of capital while at the same time ensuring that everyone who participate in social cooperation are secured sufficient capital.[20] This is to secure all citizens the basis for self-respect, and to avoid anyone dominating and controlling anyone else.[21] The basic structure must thus ensure a particular pattern of distribution by continuously intervening in and correcting the inequalities created by the market.[22] How such a distributive ideal affects the design of a tax system is a topic I will return to in Part 3.

We shall elaborate on this ideal of distribution by looking closer at Rawls' notion of a pure procedural background justice. Rawls writes:

> In a well-ordered society, in which both the equal basic liberties (with their fair value) and fair equality of opportunity are secured, the distribution of income and wealth illustrate what we may call pure background procedural justice. The basic structure is arranged so that when everyone follows the publicly recognized rules of cooperation, and honors the claims the rules specify, the particular distribution of goods that result are acceptable as just (or at least not unjust) whatever these distributions turn out to be.
>
> (Rawls 2001:50)

We have pure procedural background justice when the basic institutions of society are arranged so that the liberty principle and the principle of fair equality of opportunity are satisfied. Rawls' point is that, for justice to be established and maintained, one needs continuous state intervention to ensure that people have equal political rights and fair equality of opportunity.[23]

Rawls gives an interesting illustration of this point. American basketball is organized like a society with procedural background justice. At the end of each season, the table is flipped, so that the team at the bottom of the table gets to choose players first for the next season. The team that won is thereby last in line to secure the best players. This rule ensures a continuous intervention to equalize inequalities between the teams, thus securing a more exciting series and maintaining the interest of the audience as well as upholding the sporting ideal of fair competition. In the same way, Rawls thinks it necessary to have rules that ensure a continuous equalization to secure everyone the opportunity to participate on equal terms and to achieve fair equality of opportunity (Rawls 2001:50–51).

We can illustrate this by contrasting Rawls' ideal with the equality of outcome (or strict equality) and equality of opportunity. Against the ideal of equality of outcome, Rawls argues that as long as the fair value of political liberties and fair equality of opportunity are guaranteed, "the particular distribution that result is just whatever that distribution turns out to be" (Rawls 2001:54). The distribution may, in other words, deviate from outcome equality as long as the basic structure secures pure procedural background justice. However, Rawls' ideal also breaks with the common ideal of equality of opportunity. That ideal says that, as long as everyone is ensured an equal starting point, any inequality that may result is just. But this understanding of the principle of equality of opportunity disregards the fact that inequalities may also arise that conflict with the ideal of equal liberties. A society that allows all inequalities that follow from equality of opportunity opens up the possibility of the rich controlling the political process, and Rawls' liberty principle is supposed to exclude this kind of inequality. In other words, the distributive ideal that Rawls defends transcends the dichotomy between outcome equality and equality of opportunity to offer a new alternative.

Justice as fairness is thus a radically egalitarian ideal that demands state intervention to regulate concentration of capital. Capitalist welfare states are not just, since they allow some to control large quantities of capital, which may also give them political power. This way of interpreting Rawls is relatively new. In the first decades after the publication of *Theory*, many thought Rawls defended the welfare state. More recently, Rawls' criticism of the welfare state and the alternatives he proposes to it have become more central to the debates about his theory.

Some of Rawls' critics have argued that his ideal is abstract and has little to offer when it comes to levels of inequality (Piketty 2020:969). Others conclude that justice as fairness does not have a critical sting and is therefore without much practical relevance.[24] The interpretation I have given here shows that this is not the case. The critics, in my view, put too much emphasis on the difference principle. In order to understand Rawls and appreciate his position, it is, as I have argued, necessary to focus on the combined effect of the principles. This gives us an ideal that demands a capital ceiling and a capital floor, and this is a radical egalitarian ideal with plenty of critical potential.[25]

In the coming chapters, we shall discuss some of the criticism Rawls has been subject to, and investigate alternative positions that have been inspired by his work. We shall begin with one of the most important critics, Robert Nozick, a right-libertarian who argues that all states that engage in redistribution are unjust.

Further reading

Samuel Freeman's *Rawls* provides a thorough introduction to Rawls' position and how his thinking has developed over time. *The Cambridge Companion to Rawls*, edited by the same Freeman, provides thorough discussions of many of the debates influenced by Rawls' philosophy. Alan Thomas' *Republic of Equals: Predistribution and Property-Owning Democracy* reads Rawls in a way that closely matches the reading I have presented here. The articles in Martin O'Neill and Thad Williamson's *Property Owning-Democracy: Rawls and Beyond* has become an important point of reference in the discussion of property owning democracy and Rawls' criticism of capitalist welfare states. William A Edmundson's *John Rawls: Reticent Socialist* argues that Rawls' principles demand liberal socialism. A short, accessible presentation of Rawls' overall theory is given by Leif Wenar in his entry *John Rawls* in Stanford Encyclopedia of Philosophy. Mandle and Reidy's *The Cambridge Rawls Lexicon* contains over 200 dictionary entries and is a good source for those who want short, authoritative articles about key terms in Rawls.

For discussions of Rawls' views on taxation, see Linda Sugin's *Theories of Distributive Justice and Limitations on Taxation: What Rawls Demands from Tax Systems*, and O'Neill and Williamson's *Taxation*.

Finally, I recommend a podcast episode about Rawls on Philosophy bites: *Jonathan Wolff on John Rawls' A Theory of Justice*.

Notes

1 I will be referring to the revised edition, published in 1999.
2 I will return to utilitarianism in Chapter 6.
3 Thomas (2017:95) interprets Rawls differently when it comes to the question of necessary and sufficient means to ensure equal opportunity to influence. According to Thomas, Rawls thinks such a set of special arrangements sufficient on their own to ensure political liberties; if they work, the fair value of political liberties does not also require as extensive redistribution as it does on my interpretation. I shall return to discuss this in more detail in Chapter 7.
4 For a discussion, see Brighouse and Swift (2014:124–125).
5 We must, however, make two reservations when it comes to the utilitarian way of thinking about this choice. First, income does not necessarily translate into happiness, utility, or welfare, which is what is supposed to be distributed according to the utilitarian. Second, many utilitarians would appeal to a principle of diminishing marginal utility in evaluating such situations. This principle says that the utility one has from a good will diminish the more one has of that good. If you are thirsty, you will benefit more from the first glass of water than the second, and so on. The utility one derives from a unit of income will similarly diminish as the total income increases. Utilitarians, who base their reasoning on this principle, would presumably choose C in the above example.
6 For an excellent discussion of the central but complex idea of reciprocity in Rawls' work, see Gibbard (1991).
7 This understanding of Rawls is often neglected, but not new. As Daniels puts it, "it is the First Principle, rather than the Second, which carries the egalitarian punch" (Daniels 1975:280; see Edmundson 2017:55–56).
8 Generally speaking, we may say that the renewal of contract theory (to which we will shortly turn) represents an important innovation in Rawls' argument in political philosophy. Specifically, his focus on fairness, the priority he gives the worst off as well as his justification for objectivity in normative argument (explained below) are among the most important innovations in Rawls' thinking. For a more thorough discussion, see Sen (2009:62–65).
9 Samuel Scheffler (2003:9) has used the terms unofficial and official about the arguments I present here. I call the last argument underlying because Rawls appeals to it throughout his work, without presenting it as an explicit argument for the principles of justice.
10 We shall return to this question both in Chapter 2, where it is seen in light of Nozick's criticism, and in Chapter 3, where we look at Dworkin's position.
11 In Chapter 4, we will look at Cohen's criticism of the difference principle. Cohen claims that the principle allows unjust inequalities.
12 However, Rawls takes pains to point out that this is not the same as saying that the parties act from selfishness or self-interest. Rather, they are concerned with ensuring citizens interests as free and equal:

> In acting responsibly as trustees to secure persons' fundamental interests in their freedom and equality – in the conditions adequate for the development and exercise of their moral powers and the effective pursuit of their conceptions of the good on fair terms with others – the parties are not viewing those they represent as selfish or self interested.
>
> (Rawls 2001:85)

13 For discussions of property owning democracy, see Thomas (2017), Freeman (2013), and O'Neill and Williamson (2012). For a discussion of the history of this ideal, see Jackson (2012). Edmundson (2017) gives a recent defence of the claim that Rawls is in favour of liberal socialism.

14 Rawls' take on taxation is complex, and I shall return to this in Chapter 9. Rawls explicitly endorses inheritance taxation, but does not discuss wealth taxation.

15 See Thomas (2017) for a more thorough account of how citizens can be ensured a minimum of capital (provided they are willing to work). Note also that Mead supports universal basic income, while Rawls is against it. Rawls' opposition is tied to the main argument against universal basic income—that it is unjust for able-bodied adults to be able to live off the work of others. For a discussion of this and other arguments for and against universal basic income, see Cappelen and Pedersen (2015).

16 Property owning democracy must therefore keep economic inequalities within strictly limited bonds. As Ben Jackson has shown, some of the early republican thinkers express similar views. Rousseau, for example, maintained that: "Do you, then, want to give the state stability? Bring the extremes as close together as possible; tolerate neither very rich people nor beggars", and he subsequently added the famous sentence which states that no citizen should "be so very rich that he can buy another, and none so poor that he is compelled to sell himself" (Rousseau cited in Jackson 2012:34).

17 However, Rawls defends what we might call a thin conception of private property rights. We will return to his conception in Chapter 8.

18 Other mechanisms for predistribution involve the educational system, minimum wage, and worker representation on company boards (Piketty 2020:528–538).

19 For a recent discussion of the distinction between predistribution and redistribution, see O'Neill (2020). We shall return to this distinction in the conclusion.

20 I am indebted to Alan Thomas (2017) for this point; see also O'Neill and Williamson (2012b:9).

21 Beyond this, I will avoid assuming a position on what overall ideal of distribution follows from *Justice as Fairness*. This is a complicated question, not least because Rawls sticks to the lexical ordering of the principles while also claiming that they are a unified whole. Samuel Freeman claims that the difference principle is the most important principle, but also points out that the liberty principle and the principle of fair equality of opportunity affect distribution. From his interpretation, it follows that inequalities due to the difference principle cannot be accepted if they are in conflict with the liberty principle or the principle of fair equality of opportunity. Within the framework of a property owning democracy, the difference principle and the principle of fair equality of opportunity requires that the worst off are secured opportunities to achieve positions and posts and to control the means of production employed in their work (Freeman 2007:139–140). Alan Thomas provides an alternative interpretation. Thomas thinks the best interpretations of *justice as fairness* should disregard the lexical priority and consider the principles as a unified whole. Furthermore, the principles must be institutionalized in the proper background context, namely property owning democracy (Thomas 2017:95).

22 In the next chapter, we will discuss Rawls' focus on ensuring a pattern of distribution in the light of Nozick's criticism of Rawls.

23 Note that the difference principle does not play a decisive role in this argument. We shall return to the role of this principle in Chapter 4, where we will be discussing Cohen's criticism of Rawls.
24 Philip Pettit defended this claim in a lecture in Bergen on August 31, 2017. Pettit defends a similar view in Pettit (2012:123–127).
25 I will return to the interpretation of Rawls in Chapter 4, and investigate the critical potential in Part 3.

2 Libertarianism

Robert Nozick

Introduction

Libertarianism is a moral and political philosophical position that holds individuals to have full self-ownership as well as being able to achieve property rights over other things (Vallentyne 2012:152). Today, defenders of libertarianism are usually divided into two camps: right-libertarians and left-libertarians. These two positions are primarily distinguished by their view on how one achieves ownership over natural resources. A right-libertarian claims that individuals can achieve ownership over natural resources that are not already owned by someone else, such as land, minerals, etc., so long as no one is worse off as a result of the appropriation. By contrast, left-libertarians claim that everyone has equal ownership of natural resources, and that one cannot achieve private ownership of these without the consent of the original resource owners (the community) or by paying a significant compensation to them (Steiner and Vallentyne 2009:52). Put simply, we may say that left-libertarians think natural resources are owned in common, while right-libertarians think natural resources are owned by no one (if they are not already appropriated by someone).[1]

Historically, John Lock is an important inspiration for the development of libertarian views. Robert Nozick (1938–2002) is the most significant right-libertarian, and Friedrich Hayek and Milton Friedman are sometimes also counted as right-libertarians. Peter Vallentyne, Hillel Steiner, and Michael Otsuka are the most influential left-libertarians.[2]

Nozick's starting point is the assumption that humans own themselves and the fruit of their own labour. Nozick argues for the necessity of a free market, absolute property rights, and a minimal state. A minimal state is a state the sole task of which is to protect the citizens against misuse of power, theft, and fraud as well as to enforce contracts. The minimal state cannot have as one of its task the redistribution of resources. Nozick's main work of political philosophy *Anarchy, State and Utopia* was published in 1974. Here, Nozick points out that after Rawls' *Theory*, political philosophers must either work within the framework established by Rawls or justify their choice not do so (Nozick 1974:183). Nozick chooses to challenge Rawls' theory, replacing it with an alternative theory.

In this chapter, we shall primarily focus on Nozick, but also include Steiner and Vallentyne to illustrate important differences between the two libertarian positions. I start by presenting the primary ambition of Nozick's book: The defence of the minimal state justified by the need to secure individual rights. Then, I show how Nozick provides us with an approach that is radically different to that offered by Rawls. Nozick rejects the idea that one can start with a social product that must be distributed. The most important justification for this theory is the thesis of self-ownership, which has the implication that tax for the purpose of redistribution is a kind of state theft. I also show that Nozick sees the minimal state as an inspiring ideal, before I proceed to contrast Nozick's theory with Rawls'. By way of conclusion, I discuss the strengths and weaknesses of Nozick's libertarianism.

A defence of the minimal state

Nozick's book is divided into three parts corresponding to the three concepts in the title: Anarchy, State, and Utopia. In the first part, Nozick's goal is to show that the minimal state can be legitimate. Here, he argues against anarchists who claim that no state can ever be legitimate. In the second part, Nozick attempts to show that states more comprehensive than the minimal state cannot be legitimate because they infringe upon the rights of individuals. Here, Nozick argues against Rawls and other adherents of the idea that the tasks of the state extend beyond those of the minimal state. In the third part, Nozick tries to show that the minimal state is not only just, but also an inspiring ideal. We shall primarily focus on the argument in Part 2, because this part contains Nozick's theory of just distribution, or more precisely, his theory of justice in holdings (explained below).

The book opens as follows:

> Individuals have rights, and there are things no person or group may do to them (without violating their rights). So strong and far-reaching are these rights that they raise the question of what, if anything, the state and its officials may do...The nature of the state, its legitimate functions and its justifications, if any, is the central concern of this book.
>
> (Nozick 1974: ix)

Nozick understands rights as side constraints that are meant to secure to each individual a space of freedom from intervention by others. The rights in question are the right to life, freedom, and property as well as the right to self-defence, and to punish and demand restitution from those who infringe upon these rights. To Nozick, these are rights the individual has prior to the state. Nozick must therefore be said to be part of a natural law tradition where the importance of rights constitutes the starting point of the theory.

In Nozick's view, only the minimal state avoids infringing on these rights. In the first part of the book, Nozick argues against individualistically oriented anarchists who claim that individuals own themselves and the fruit of their labour. To individualist anarchists, no state is legitimate, because all exercise of state authority is a kind of tyranny. Nozick wants to refute this claim and show that the minimal state is legitimate. To justify this claim, Nozick draws on the social contract tradition in political philosophy (see Chapter 1 for a short presentation of social contract theory).

Nozick's point of departure is a state of nature where individuals have rights, but where it is unclear how they can separately safeguard or uphold these rights. They therefore voluntarily join forces in a protective association to defend their rights (Grimen 2010). Such a defensive union will be better able to defend the rights of individuals the larger and stronger it is. Therefore, the development will be in the direction of ever fewer and larger defensive unions, which over time develop into a minimal state. Such a minimal state is characterized by being the only entity that provides all citizens, within a limited territory, protection for their rights. In this way, Nozick offers what he calls an invisible hand-explanation of how a state can be established without infringing on the rights of individuals. The minimal state has emerged even though no individual intended to establish it.[3]

This is the core of the argument in the first part of Nozick's book. He claims to have refuted the anarchist assertion that no state can be established without infringing on the rights of individuals. In the second part, Nozick develops a critique of all those who argue that more comprehensive states than the minimal state can be legitimate. This theory rests on the thesis of self-ownership: Individuals own themselves, and the fruit of their labour therefore also belong to the individuals themselves. If a state, through force, demands that individuals pay tax beyond what the state needs to ensure the protection of the individuals, this right is infringed upon. In a dense passage that contains large parts of Nozick's project, he writes:

> Our main conclusion about the state are that a minimal state, limited to the narrow functions of protection against force, theft, fraud, enforcement of contracts, and so on, is justified; that any more extensive state will violate persons' rights not to be forced to do certain things, and is unjustified; and that the minimal state is inspiring as well as right. Two noteworthy implications are that the state may not use its coercive apparatus for the purpose of getting some citizens to aid others, or in order to prohibit activities to people for their *own* good or protection.
>
> (Nozick 1974:ix)

That is, the state cannot collect tax for the purpose of redistributing resources from those who have much to those who have little. To Nozick, taxing one individual to transfer those resources to another is the same as forced labour or slavery. In the following, we shall primarily focus on Nozick's justification for his claim that a redistributive state infringes on the rights of individuals. However, it is important to note that the kind of libertarianism

Nozick defends also rejects moralistic legislation, for example, banning sexual contact between persons of the same gender, and paternalistic laws that oblige individuals to protect themselves.

Entitlement theory

Nozick calls his theory of just distribution of goods an entitlement theory. Entitlements are those things we may rightfully lay claim to, and when we have a rightful claim to something, we may speak of an entitlement to that thing (Grimen 2010:62). Here, Nozick is, among other things, concerned with refuting Rawls. Rawls claimed, as we have seen in Chapter 1, that the market has to be regulated by the principle that any inequality must be to the benefit of the worst off (the difference principle). Nozick notes that the difference principle demands a particular pattern of distribution, namely a pattern that benefits the worst off. However, to Nozick, what matters is *how a given distribution has come about*, not what particular pattern it may happen to have. He thus defends a *historical theory* that focuses on how individuals have acquired their goods.

Distributive justice, as Nozick sees it, is not a neutral term. Most assume that distributive justice is a question of how one can distribute goods. That, however, presupposes that one *should* redistribute goods, and this is an open question, and not something we can take for granted. Nozick asks us to consider closely the fact that what someone gets as a result of such redistribution must be produced by someone else. Goods do not simply enter into the world by themselves ready to be redistributed. This means that, if we are to have any goods to redistribute, we must take these goods from people who have rights to them (Nozick 1974:149–150).

The entitlement theory offers three principles that clarify what one may rightfully lay claim to:

- The principle of justice in acquisition
- The principle of justice in transfer
- The principle of rectification

The principle of *just acquisition* concerns goods not owned by anyone. Individuals may acquire property rights over natural resources not owned by anyone by, for example, possessing and cultivating a piece of land. This kind of acquisition must, however, be subject to what Nozick calls a Lockean proviso. English philosopher John Locke argued that individuals could acquire property rights over objects not already owned by others by shaping them with their labour. However, such acquisition must, according to Locke, be subject to a limitation: Others must not be worse off as a result of the acquisition. Locke uses the expression "enough and as good proviso".[4] If one discovers a piece of land not owned by anyone, that is, Locke and Nozick argue that one can acquire private property rights over that piece of land so long as no one is worse off as a result, compared to the situation where the piece of land is neither used nor acquired by anyone else.

The principle of *justice in transfer* is Nozick's second principle. To Nozick, a just transfer is a voluntary transfer. If I cultivate a piece of land and then voluntarily exchange the potatoes I have grown there with the clothes you have sewn, the end result is just ownership on both sides (provided we have both acquired what we use to produce potatoes and clothes in accordance with the principle of just acquisition). Nozick illustrates this by introducing a thought experiment that has become famous in political philosophy: The Wilt Chamberlain example. Chamberlain was a famous American basketball player in the 1960s and 1970s.

Nozick asks you to choose a distribution you think is just, for example, a perfectly equal distribution. This distribution he calls D1. Then, imagine that Chamberlain signs a contract with a team that gives him 25 cents from each spectator that watches the games he plays. In the course of a season, one million people in total see Chamberlain's matches. He ends up with $250,000 at the end of the season, making him considerably richer than everyone else. Spectators who have watched Chamberlain play have voluntarily given him 25 cents extra for each match, and have enjoyed seeing him play. We now have a new distribution, D2. Is this new distribution just? Nozick's answer is an unequivocal YES. If D1 was just, and the transfers to Chamberlain were a result of voluntary actions, D2 is also just. In this way, Nozick argues that the pattern of distribution is never what determines whether that distribution is just. Such distributions require a continuous unjust redistribution of resources, and must therefore be rejected (Nozick 1974:161–163).

The principle of rectification is applied if the principles of just acquisition or just transfer have been violated. If a person has acquired goods through, for example, stealing, there will be a need for rectification. The need for rectification thus arises when a person possesses goods that have not been justly acquired.

This illustrates how Nozick's is a historical theory. When we evaluate whether a given distribution is just, we must evaluate how the distribution has come about. If it has come about without the violation of anyone's rights, it is just. In other words, an overall distribution is just if each person's goods are justly acquired. Whether this distribution is equal is beside the point. In theory, all property could be held by a single person, and the distribution would still be just on Nozick's theory as long as that property had been acquired justly.

A distribution or, to use Nozick's terms, a person's holdings are just if they do not violate any of the three principles:

> The holdings of a person are just if he is entitled to them by the principles of justice in acquisition and transfer, or by the principle of rectification of injustice...If each person's holdings are just, then the total set (distribution) is just.
>
> (Nozick 1974: 153)

The entitlement theory is thus developed to show that the state cannot legitimately redistribute resources. Many react to the fact that Nozick's theory thereby permits widespread poverty. We shall return to this kind of objection, but it is important to keep in mind that Nozick does not mean that we should not help the poor. What he objects to is the use of force by the state to take, through taxation, goods from individuals that those individuals rightfully own.

The sole task of the minimal state is to protect the rights of individuals. To see how radical this proposal is, it may be useful to compare this ideal with the state as we know it in most liberal, constitutional democracies, and the tasks we are used to thinking of as being the responsibility of the state. Roughly speaking, the state as we know it can be said to fulfil six tasks.[5] First, it is the task of the state to ensure the security of the citizens: Defence protects us from threats from abroad, while the police and the justice system protects us from threats from within, that is, from other citizens. Second, there are the services offered by the state to the citizens, like roads and firefighting. Third, in most western countries, the state constructs safety nets that are there if we need them: Provides paid sick leave, social security, and unemployment benefits. Fourth, the state takes care of the education of citizens. Fifth, the state takes upon itself to control the lives of individuals: The state enforces the use of seatbelts, censors movies, and criminalizes the use of narcotics. Last, but not least, the state also has the task of redistributing resources from those who have much to those who have less. All these tasks must be financed, and this normally happens by way of taxation.

To Nozick, the state can only legitimately undertake the first of these six tasks. It is not the task of the state to build roads. People have the right to choose whether to drive a car or not, and hence the state cannot force people to contribute to building roads through taxation. Firefighters may also be organized through private insurance systems. Next, it cannot, as Nozick sees it, be the task of the state to construct social safety nets. Doing so involves a kind of coercion that is incompatible with the freedom to choose: The state cannot force someone to insure against illness or unemployment, and the state cannot force an individual to help pay for his or her safety net. Public education is also out of the question, again because it must be financed, and one cannot force people to pay taxes to ensure that these kinds of institutions exist. Next, under no circumstance can the state coerce individuals into doing what purportedly is in their own best interest. Mandatory use of seat belts and prohibition of drugs are examples of paternalistic interventions into the lives of individuals that are incompatible with Nozick's libertarianism. Finally, the state cannot redistribute resources from one person to another. Compared to the state as we know it, Nozick's ideal state really is a minimal state.[6] Nozick's crucial claim is that no other state can exist without violating individual rights.

What kinds of arguments does Nozick provide for the entitlement theory? Kymlicka claims that Nozick puts forth two arguments (Kymlicka 2002:105).

An intuitive argument—the Wilt Chamberlain argument—which is meant to show that what follows from free market-based choices is just. Moreover, a principled argument that is meant to show that individuals own themselves and may rightfully lay claim to the fruits of their own labour. The first argument has been tremendously influential in political philosophy, and we shall return to it below. The second argument is philosophically speaking most interesting of the two, and also that which puts us in a position to compare Nozick's position to *justice as fairness*. We shall therefore start by clarifying the thesis of self-ownership, before returning to discuss it towards the end of the chapter.

Self-ownership

Nozick subscribes to Locke's view of humans as self-owners. Locke, who is one of the most important sources of intellectual inspiration for modern theories of self-ownership, claimed in his famous *Second Treatise of Government* that "every man has a property in his own person; this nobody has any right to but himself. The labour of his body and the work of his hands we may say is properly his" (Locke 1988, quoted in Cohen 1995a:209).

These rights, which libertarians interpret as side constrains or trumps, provide each individual with a sphere that no one can infringe upon without the consent of the individual. The individual has the right to self-determination over their own bodies, for the body belongs to the individual and no others. Theories that are built on self-ownership thus draw up boundaries to how individuals may be treated. Nozick explains what owning oneself means with the help of a thought we have already encountered in Rawls: It can never be right to sacrifice one person for another, or for the community as a whole. The individual has inviolable rights that cannot be put aside.

Let us illustrate the self-ownership thesis with an example: Assume that eye transplantation technology has progressed to the point where one can transplant eyes from one person to another without any risk of complication. Given that some are congenitally blind, should we redistribute eyes from those who have two well-functioning eyes to those who are blind? Some might volunteer, for example, if one twin is born seeing and the other blind. But if there are not enough volunteers, is it permissible to redistribute eyes using force? Should we, for example, hold a national lottery to determine whose eyes will be redistributed?[7] Most will say no to this suggestion. And they will do so citing the fact that we own our own bodies, and must be allowed to decide for ourselves how this body (or parts of it) is used.

Nozick holds that rights understood as side constraints is the right way of accounting for the fact that every individual is a distinct, separate individual that must be treated with respect. This is also, thinks Nozick, the best way of implementing Immanuel Kant's imperative to treat others never merely as means, but always also as ends in themselves.[8] The implied target here is utilitarian theories that (allegedly) allow the rights of an individual to be sacrificed to the benefit of the majority.

Applied to the question of redistribution, Nozick's understanding of the self-ownership thesis states that I have the rights to the fruits of my labour. Taxation is therefore a form of state theft that cannot be allowed even if it benefits the majority of citizens. But Nozick goes further. When the state taxes, it takes some of my time, namely the time I have to work to pay tax. If the state takes part of my time, it forces me to work. By forcing me to work, tax on labour is in effect forced labour (Nozick 1974:169). Put differently, if the state forces me to work, it becomes a part owner in me, and this violates full self-ownership.

In spite of this, the state must tax to protect the freedom of individuals and private property. What will the libertarian tax, and what rates will be used? Duff has argued that libertarians in general are open to different tax bases. He claims that both tax on income, wealth, and consumption are compatible with libertarian thinking. However, there seems to be agreement that flat or proportional taxes are the most just if personal income is to be taxed (Duff 2005:34). Flat taxes are the best way of taxing, if the goal is that the tax is to be proportional to the advantages gained by the individual from the existence of the state.[9]

Peter Vallentyne holds a different view. He has recently argued that only two tax bases are acceptable for libertarians. First, libertarians can accept taxation to finance the costs that result from someone violating rights. Those who enforce these rights can finance their operations by taxing those who violate rights. Second, libertarians can accept taxation of those who extract more than their share of natural resources. Any other tax, like tax on income, capital income, or wealth, is incompatible with the libertarian understanding of self-ownership and therefore unjust (Vallentyne 2018:98–110). An important nuance provided by Vallentyne's discussion is the need to distinguish between different kinds of libertarianism: Some kinds argue that all forms of taxation are unjust.

Finally, some libertarians advocate for special rules for the democratic procedure when it comes to matters of taxation. For example, it has been suggested that the state's opportunity to tax should be subject to strict constitutional limits. The constitution must first ensure that tax is only imposed to finance the protection of people's rights, and nothing else. Second, the loss incurred by the individual through the imposition of tax must be smaller than the advantages that follow from the existence of an entity that protects rights (Mack 2002:26). We shall return to a more thorough discussion of tax and the constitution in Part 3. There, I shall also extend the discussion of libertarianism and tax by looking at arguments against progressive taxation.

The minimal state as an inspirational ideal

Nozick is also concerned with showing that the minimal state is more than simply just: It is also an inspirational ideal. The minimal state provides a frame within which different people with different views on what constitutes a good life can realize their life plans in different ways. The minimal state provides room for freedom. People who live in a minimal state are free to assemble in groups to live out their version of the good life. In principle, we can imagine a group of people who want to distribute their goods with perfect equality, and another group who wants to distribute their goods so that those with the most abilities and will to work come out on top. Such groupings could exist within the framework of the minimal state. The crucial point is that members of such groups *voluntarily* choose to be part of the group (Nozick 1974:320–321).

A libertarian may therefore perfectly well claim that we have a moral duty to give to the poor, while denying that the state can legitimately force people to give to others through collecting taxes. Nozick assumes that the minimal state will provide conditions under which private initiatives will arise designed to care for the worst off. Many would share this view. They would think that they have a moral duty to help their neighbour if the neighbour has slipped on ice and broken something, while at the same time denying that anyone has the right to force them to help.

Nozick thus thinks that the state cannot exert force through redistribution. However, a community within the frames of the state may well do that. An example used by Nozick is the Israeli kibbutzim, which are a kind of delimited socialist communities. Within these communities, one can demand that everyone share alike, but membership must be voluntary (Nozick 1974:321). Thus, the minimal state is a framework within which one is free to experiment with different utopias. This also amounts to a criticism of traditional visions of utopias in which everyone agrees to a single way of life. Nozick thought that such uniform utopias would lead to repression, and suggested that the minimal state could be interpreted as a meta-utopia that would allow the realization of many different utopias (Nozick 1974:312).

Rawls vs. Nozick

To better understand the two theories we have looked as so far, we shall begin by comparing the basic values inherent in each of Rawls' and Nozick's theories, before we proceed to discuss some weaknesses in Nozick's position.

At the heart of Nozick's view is the self-ownership thesis. How does Rawls' relate to this thesis? Rawls does not discuss self-ownership explicitly, but there are passages that can be used as a basis to criticize it. Rawls writes:

> The difference principle represents, in effect, an agreement to regard the distribution of natural talents as in some respects a common asset and to share in the greater social and economic benefits made possible by the complementarities of this distribution.
>
> (Rawls 1999a:87)

The talent with which one is born is thus not an individual resource, but in certain sense a common one. That we are born with different talents is one of the factors explaining why we produce much more by cooperating than by acting alone. One has talent for shoe production, another for baking, and when these talents are utilized in social cooperation, the social product is many times larger than it would have been without cooperation. What talent one has from birth is arbitrary from a moral point of view, and it therefore follows that an individual does not *deserve* what is produced due to talent. This is radical, and contrary to the foundational assumption of libertarianism, namely the thesis of self-ownership. From this thesis, it follows that if I own myself, I own my talent, and if I own my talent, I also have full ownership to whatever is produced by means of my talent.

In extension of this, libertarians often defend those who have succeeded economically by arguing that it is fair that they get to keep what they have created by means of their talent and hard work. "To each according to what he makes for himself", as Nozick writes (Nozick 1974:160). However, this also means that large economic inequalities may also be legitimized. The problem with this argument is that it frequently overlooks the fact that a person's success in economic life is often due to knowledge, technology, and infrastructure that has been created over long periods of time rather than the feat of a single person made possible by the combination of their extraordinary talent and hard work. Take Bill Gates, who for a long time has been one of the wealthiest people on earth. Libertarians will maintain that Gates has the right to keep what he has made, without levying distributive taxes. However, Gates has not only been dependent on an institutional framework to succeed in his businesses, he has also drawn heavily on knowledge built up over a long time as well as on technological advances heavily subsidized by the US government (Williamson 2012a:298). Thus, when libertarians argue that the extremely wealthy have full rights to their wealth and cannot be taxed more heavily, there are good reasons to look closely at the examples they use.

Whether talent is not only an individual but a common asset, and whether we deserve what we earn by means of our talent—these are difficult questions. Frequently, the libertarian position is legitimized by showing that most people share the view that individuals own themselves and the fruits of their labour. Samuel Scheffler has discussed a similar problem with the following example:

> If I have a less successful career as a philosopher than you do because your superior philosophical gifts enable you to refute all my arguments… people would not regard that as unfair. Nor would most think it unfair if a naturally gifted professional athlete were offered a more lucrative contract than his less talented teammate.
>
> (Scheffler 2003:33)

I think Scheffler is right that most people perceive talent as something that belongs to the person and that people will accept inequalities that follow from talent. That, however, does not mean that such inequalities are just and should be left out of redistributive efforts.

Rawls thinks that the fruits of talent cannot go to the talented individual unless this is to the benefit of the worst off. This, as we saw in Chapter 1, is a specific argument against desert. Rawls' discussion of hard work must also be understood as a discussion of desert. The question is whether one deserves the fruits of hard labour. If one person works hard and another is lazy, then if the hard-working person ends up with more than the lazy one, this must surely be a just kind of inequality? Rawls notes that the will to work hard is also greatly affected by the family and social circumstances into which one is born and raised (Rawls 1999a:64). Because family and social circumstances are arbitrary from a moral point of view, it is problematic simply to claim that I deserve to keep whatever may come from my own hard work.

Does this mean that Rawls thinks that whether one is hard-working or lazy should have no influence on how much we are left with? No. However, Rawls thinks that we cannot reliably disentangle the fruits of talent from those of hard work. He writes:

> The effort a person is willing to make is influenced by his natural abilities and skills and the alternatives open to him. The better endowed are more likely, other things equal, to strive conscientiously, and there seems to be no way to discount for their greater good fortune. The idea of rewarding desert is impracticable.
>
> (Rawls 1999a:274)

The way Nozick reads Rawls, this quote means that individuals cannot be held responsible for their own choices. This seems to question a fundamental premise of liberal thinking: That individuals make free choices, and that the choices they make must be the basis for what goods they end up with. Rawls' thesis becomes a traditional egalitarian and deterministic thesis. Nozick interprets the word "affects" as something approaching a complete determination (Cohen 1989:914). In Nozick's reading of Rawls, persons are understood as completely determined by their innate natural endowments and skills, and the opportunities that are open to them. Nozick therefore criticizes Rawls' theory for not assigning any significance to the responsibility people have for their own choices. As Nozick sees it, this has serious implications. He writes:

> So denigrating a person's autonomy and prime responsibility for his actions is a risky line to take for a theory that otherwise wishes to buttress the dignity and self-respect of autonomous beings...One doubts that the unexalted picture of human beings Rawls' theory presupposes and rest upon can be made to fit together with the view of human dignity it is designed to lead to and embody.
>
> (Nozick 1974:214, quoted from Cohen 1989:915)

Rawls thereby risks painting a picture where those who choose to work hard ultimately have no control over, and therefore cannot be credited with or legitimately reap the fruits of, their own actions. These actions are determined by innate abilities and other circumstances outside of their control. With this deterministic understanding, we lose our conception of free action, and with that, our human dignity. Human dignity is, as we have seen, central to both Rawls' and Nozick's attempts at challenging utilitarianism.

The problem is that a charitable interpretation of Rawls does not fit with that given by Nozick. The word "affects" can reasonably be understood as "affects" rather than "fully determined by", as Cohen points out. Rawls' point is not that innate factors fully determine our actions, but that it is impossible, practically speaking, to disentangle that which is the result of hard work for which we should be rewarded, and that which is the result of natural endowments and hence a matter of luck for which we do not deserve reward (Cohen 1989:914–915). This is different to saying that effort is irrelevant to reward, which is what follows from Nozick's reading.

Rawls' project may therefore be interpreted as a project intended to eliminate the perception of desert. This follows from what I in Chapter 1 called the unofficial argument for the principles of justice.

Here, it may be objected against Rawls that instead of fighting against the arbitrariness in the natural distribution of talent and commitment to work, we should accept that this is the way nature is arranged and adapt to that. Rawls disagrees:

> The natural distribution (of talent JP) is neither just nor unjust; nor is it unjust that persons are born into society at some particular position. These are simply natural facts. What is just and unjust is the way that institutions deal with these facts.
>
> (Rawls 1999a:87)

What we can do is to create institutions that allow us to tackle what is arbitrary in the best way possible.

One of the reasons why Rawls and Nozick end up with divergent conceptions of justice is their point of departure. Rawls starts by claiming that distribution is a question of the distribution of a *social* product, something that in a sense belongs to the community (Wolff 1991:119). Nozick questions this basic premise. He claims that it is unclear what Rawls means when he says that what we distribute is a social product. Is this a claim about how the total product should be distributed or about how the part of the total that is due to cooperation is to be distributed? Is social cooperation what creates the distributional problem or would we have this problem also without cooperation? And, perhaps most importantly, given that there is social cooperation, is it actually impossible to separate out the contribution of individuals? Nozick thinks that it is possible to separate out the contribution of individuals, which is a precondition for any theory focused on entitlement (Nozick 1974:183–189).

Discussion

After having clarified these differences between Rawls and Nozick, we will now turn to a more systematic discussion of Nozick's contribution. First, we shall discuss the two first principles of justice defended by Nozick, before looking at some of the practical-political implications of his theory.

Let us first look at something that is not quite clear in Nozick. He is vague when it comes to how one can justify the appropriation of natural resources. The vagueness consists in whether Nozick defends or rejects the Lockean theory of the acquisition of natural resources. Locke claimed that people acquire natural resources by mixing their own labour with these resources. When we pick an apple from a tree no one owns, we mix our labour (the work needed to remove the apple from the tree) with the resource (the apple), thereby adding something (the apple no longer hangs on the tree), and the resource thereby becomes our own (we now own the apple). Nozick criticizes this "mixing of labour" theory. First, he explains how Locke may be interpreted: What Locke means, writes Nozick, is that we own our labour, and when we acquire something not already owned by anyone we do so because this thing is permeated by something we own. Nozick questions how mixing something one owns with something owned by no one gives one property rights to that thing. He illustrates his point by asking whether we can acquire the ocean by pouring tomato juice into it (Nozick 1974:174–175).[10] The vagueness in Nozick consists in the fact that despite this criticism of Locke, it remains unclear whether he adopts the Lockean theory of acquisition of natural resources.[11]

Then the principle: As we saw above, what separates right-libertarians from left-libertarians is their view on the justification of the acquisition of things not already owned by anyone. The main difference is on the question of what compensation others are due if someone acquires natural resources or something else not already owned by anyone. Let us imagine that I was the first person to find oil in the North Sea, and that I did so before anyone else had acquired territorial rights to this area, and prior to anyone else using these areas or knowing about the oil. Based on Nozick's way of thinking, the oil would then be a natural resource not owned by anyone. I can acquire the property right to the oilfield I discover without having to compensate anyone because no one is worse off, and I leave enough for others. This follows from the Lockean "enough and as good proviso". Left-libertarians, by contrast, see natural resources as something owned in common. If I acquire the oil in the North Sea, both me and my descendants who use this natural resource must pay a significant compensation to the community. Moreover, I must pay this compensation not only when I acquire the resource, but also for as long as I continue to reap benefits from it. In this way, the community will receive a continuous income because of my acquisition of the oil in the North Sea.

Left-libertarians thus claim that since the earth's resources like land, water, and minerals originally belong to everyone, everybody has the right to continuous compensation from those who have taken these resources into possession. On this basis, left-libertarians can justify a redistributive structure very different to that suggested by Nozick. Some left-libertarians defend the welfare state on this basis. A tax-financed welfare state is possible because those who possess and reap the fruits of common resources can be taxed. Seen in this way, the welfare state does not conflict with the idea of self-ownership.

What this contrast with left-libertarianism shows is that Nozick's justification for the first principle of just acquisition is problematic. Too much goes to those who first acquire natural resources. If this criticism is correct, and I think it is, then Nozick's point that any state more comprehensive than the minimal state would violate the principle of self-ownership is also incorrect. If so, there is no necessary conflict between self-ownership and the welfare state, contrary to Nozick's claim.

This is also relevant to Nozick's claim that redistributive income tax is equivalent to forced labour. Michael Otsuka has introduced an example to illustrate this point. Imagine people who get all their income from clothes woven using their own hair, and who are not dependent on any kind of assistance. If these people are subject to a 50% income tax, this would be a clear violation of their right to self-ownership, claims Otsuka. They are illegitimately deprived of the fruits of their labour. In a less hypothetical case where the persons producing something have to utilize natural resources, it is far from clear that the state violates anybody's rights by taxing them. If, for example, one acquires land to farm, one can legitimately tax this originally common resource for the purpose of redistribution. In that case, the redistributive tax is a compensation for that part of the farming production that stems from the natural resource (Otsuka 2006:2–3).[12] Hence, Otsuka's example shows that the thesis of self-ownership is compatible with a redistributive state.

What then about the principle of justice in transfer? Political philosophers of the egalitarian sort have used a lot of energy refuting the conclusions Nozick draws from the Wilt Chamberlain example. The crucial claim defended by Nozick in the famous example is that if someone has acquired something in a just way and then trades it with others, the result of this trade will also be just. Or, even more precise: "Whatever arises from a just situation by just steps is itself just" (Nozick 1974:151). "Just steps" is then tied to voluntariness, so that a transfer where the starting point is just and the transfer voluntary, the transfer is necessarily also just. What we must question is whether voluntary transfers are necessarily just.

One way of questioning the assumption that voluntariness is sufficient for justice is the following: Even if both parties enter into the transfer on a voluntary and informed basis, the transfer may have consequences for a third party. These consequences may make the transfer unjust in spite of being voluntary. Nozick claims that those who are not party to the transfer are not affected by it. Cohen, however, has shown that this is untrue. He points out that Nozick's claim about third parties being unaffected:

> is false, in one relevant sense. For a person's effective share depends on what he can do with what he has, and that depends not only on how much he has but on what others have and on how what others have is distributed. If it is distributed equally among them he will often be better placed than if some have especially large shares. Third parties, including the as yet unborn, may therefore have an interest against the contract.
>
> (Cohen 1995b:26–27, see also Wolff 1991:87)

Hence, persons who are not party to the transaction may be unjustly affected by it, which shows that voluntariness is not sufficient to make a transfer just.

Another argument against the sufficiency of voluntariness connects with the point about equal political power that we looked at in Chapter 1: The parties who chose D1 appreciated a society in which equality rules. In such a society, no one has more power than anyone else due to their financial resources. In a society where significant inequalities may arise as a consequence of voluntary transfers, this could change. Some might become significantly more wealthy and powerful than others. Persons who are not parties to the contract may thereby indirectly suffer from a contract that, in itself, does not appear to harm them, because the equality they appreciate no longer exists.

We ought therefore not follow Nozick in thinking that voluntariness is sufficient for justice. If we accept Nozick's argument, we must also accept considerable poverty and large inequality that may result from allowing voluntary transfers to determine distributions. If Nozick's argument about the sufficiency of voluntariness falls, his criticism of patterned theories of distribution also suffers. Provided that voluntariness is not sufficient to make a distribution just, we must accept that patterned theories have an important role to play for justice.[13] If we accept that kind of argument, which I think we should, we can, for example, argue that a distribution must be patterned in the sense that it ensures everyone sufficient goods to live a decent life. In later chapters, we shall return to what patterns best preserves justice.

A positive feature of Nozick's theory is that it acknowledges the importance of historical conditions. We have to ask how a distribution has come about to be able to decide whether it is just.[14] But what practical implications does a theory like this have? Take property ownership in the US as an example. We know that a large part of today's USA was populated by different indigenous populations before Europeans colonized the continent. Europeans frequently acquired their property through conquest and force. Does this mean no American citizens rightfully possess what they own? This is a problem with theories of justice that are historically sensitive: We have no clear answer to how far back into history we must go to figure out whether a given distribution is just.

Nevertheless, Nozick has something important to say to anyone who cares about inequality. Many egalitarians have a tendency to disregard the fact that what is distributed must first be taken from someone. The large pot from which we redistribute goods to create equality is a pot in part due to goods being confiscated. Redistribution has a cost; giving to one person means taking from another. This point is frequently overlooked because redistribution in specific cases comprises many people and complex decision procedures (Wolff 1998:99). However, we must remind ourselves that the strength of this argument depends on whether we understand the goods to be distributed as a social product, or if we accept Nozick's claim that we must be able to separate out the contribution of the individual.

One last point is that Nozick bases his theory on a single value: The thesis of self-ownership. The right to liberty is, to Nozick, a consequence of the self-ownership thesis, and he subsequently employs this value to answer all the topics a political philosophy must address: If the idea of a redistributive tax is in conflict with the thesis of self-ownership, tax is ultimately regarded as forced labour. Alternatively, take the example of paternalistic legislation: If a law mandating seat belt use is in conflict with the thesis of self-ownership, then it is illegitimate and must be repealed. In this way, freedom is made the only value that matters.[15] The strength of this approach is that it gives us a simple decision procedure when deciding important political questions: Does it break with the individual's right to self-determination? If yes, then it is illegitimate. The problem with this approach is that freedom is not the only value that matters when we make political decisions. Other values also play a role, and when reading Nozick, there is sometimes a danger of forgetting this important point.

This point, which is one of the most important conclusions to Jonathan Wolff's excellent book on Nozick (Wolff 1991:4, 139–142), was first pointed out by Bernard Williams. Williams claims that Nozick's theory of justice seems like an "enormous exaggeration of at best one aspect of our moral ideas" (Williams quoted in Wolff 1991:140). What we get is thus an image of what follows if we assume a single value and deduce all decisions from this value. What may be lost in the process is a more complex balance between different values. The need to weigh different values against each other is one we shall treat more extensively in the next chapter.

Further reading

Jonathan Wolff's book *Robert Nozick: Property, Justice and the Minimal State* is thorough, pedagogical, and critical. G.A. Cohen's book *Self-Ownership, Freedom and Equality* discusses the libertarian self-ownership thesis and the Wilt Chamberlain argument in a way that makes it an unavoidable reference in the debate. Jeffrey Paul's book *Reading Nozick: Essays on Anarchy, State and Utopia* contains several of the most important early contributions to the discussion about Nozick. *The Cambridge Companion to Nozick's Anarchy, State and Utopia* presents different aspects of Nozick's political philosophy by philosophers, both sympathetic and critical to his theory. Two of the best short texts I have read about Nozick are by Thomas Nagel. In *Review: Libertarianism*

Without Foundations and the Foreword to the second edition of *Anarchy*, Nagel contextualizes, presents, and criticizes Nozick with unparalleled clarity. Eric Mack's Stanford Encyclopedia of Philosophy article "Robert Nozick's Political Philosophy" defends Nozick against part of the criticism put forth by Nagel. Barbara Fried's article "Wilt Chamberlain Revisited: Nozick's 'Justice in Transfer' and the Problem of Market-Based Distribution" presents an important critique of Nozick's claim that the market maintains justice. In the essay "Nozick", David Schmidtz and Christopher Freiman provide an updated assessment of Nozick's contribution. Of particular interest is their discussion of historic and patterned principles of justice.

For specific discussions of taxation, see David Duff's *Private Property and Tax Policy in a Libertarian World: A Critical Review* and Peter Vallenetyne's *Libertarianism and Taxation.*

Notes

1 Note that Otsuka (2003:22) differs from the other left-libertarians by claiming that the world is unowned.

2 It is important to note however that libertarianism is not limited to the Lockean tradition we shall discuss here. F.A. Hayek and Milton Friedman are economists strongly in favour of a spontaneous market order. Their approach is more influenced by Adam Smith and David Hume. Hayek remains critical to the social contract approach favoured by Lockeans. Nevertheless, libertarianism has been strongly influenced by Locke. For a discussion of non-Lockean libertarianism, see Levy (2019). We shall return to Hayek in Chapter 9.

3 For a more comprehensive account and discussion of whether the minimal state can in fact emerge without infringing on anyone's rights, see Grimen (2010).

4 It is important to note that the interpretation of the Lockean proviso is highly contested. On one interpretation, the proviso implies that one cannot acquire natural resources unless there is more than enough left for others to acquire the same good. Nozick argues for a weaker interpretation that implies that there must be sufficient left of the resource for the usage, if not acquisition, of others. To clarify the distinction of acquisition, imagine an area where there are a number of wells needed to allow people to find water. If I acquire a well, Nozick's proviso will require that there is enough water left in the other wells to satisfy the needs of others. This is the weak proviso. The strong proviso says that I may only acquire a well if there are enough other wells to allow everyone else also to acquire wells as I have done. Nozick's argument appears to be that allowing acquisition and private property brings sufficient benefits to justify the weak proviso (Wolff 1991:106–110).

5 My presentation here is indebted to Jonathan Wolff (1991:10–11)

6 The youth fraction of the Norwegian Progress Party, which is a libertarian right-wing party, defends an ideal which is similar to Nozick's minimal state; see Ruud (2018).

7 The example is from Wolff (1991:7). Nozick writes about redistribution of body parts (1974:206), while Cohen makes this into the example of an eye-lottery.

8 For a critique of Nozick's view that Kant's thoughts about means and ends support the thesis of self-ownership, see Cohen (1995a:209–228).

9 Libertarians often also argue for special institutional arrangements in tax policies. For example, it has been argued that one should have two-third majority for important decisions about the tax system, and/or that such decisions must be voted over in a referendum (Duff 2005:36–38).

10 This illustrates that Locke is not a libertarian but a natural law theorist with strong religious leanings. To Locke, the mixing of labour argument rests on the fact that the agent improves the world according to Gods plan. Thus, to Locke, pouring tomato juice into the ocean is not a way to gain property right over something, as it does not improve on anything. Thanks to an anonymous reviewer for pointing this out.
11 For more on this criticism, see Fried (1995) and Paul (1982).
12 Otsuka's project is to "reclaim Locke from the libertarian right" (Otsuka 2003:2, 2006:1). His defence of left-libertarianism is perhaps the most egalitarian of the left-libertarians, expressed in his egalitarian principle for just acquisition. It runs: "you may acquire previously unowned worldly resources if and only if you leave enough so that everyone else can acquire an equally advantageous share" (Otsuka 2006:4). See Vallentyne (2012) for a different argument that shows that tax and self-ownership need not be the kind of opposites claimed by Nozick.
13 Moreover, not only for justice, but also for freedom; the title of the essay in which Cohen discusses this is "Robert Nozick and Wilt Chamberlain: How Patterns Preserve Liberty". The title is chosen as an answer to the part of Nozick's book that presents the Chamberlaine argument; that part is called "How Liberty Upsets Patterns" (Nozick 1974:160).
14 See Spinner-Halev (2012) for a discussion of historic injustice.
15 Provided that what is at stake is the question of what the state may legitimately impose on the individual.

3 Equality of resources

Ronald Dworkin

Introduction

Ronald Dworkin's (1931–2013) contribution can be read as an answer both to Rawls and to Nozick.[1] Dworkin develops an objection made by Nozick against Rawls. The objection can be formulated as follows: Before we use the resources of society to improve the position of the worst off, we must find out why they are badly off. We must, in other words, find out whether they may be said to be responsible for their situation. Some may be badly off as a result of not being able to work. However, others may be out of a job as a result of their own choice. Do these two have the same right to the resources of society? Is it fair to tax those who work hard to better the position of those who are equally naturally endowed, but who choose to stay on the couch playing computer games? The difference principle does not ask how the worst off have ended up where they are. As Dworkin sees it, subsidizing slackers is not only counter-intuitive but also wrong, because it conflicts with the spirit of equality. What follows from the principle of equality is that those who work hard should be able to reap the fruits of this labour, and that slackers must take the consequence of their slacking (Wolff 2007:127–128).

Dworkin's theory rests on a distinction between choice and circumstance (sometimes, choice and chance).[2] What matters is that people should be held responsible for their choices and compensated for circumstances outside their control. Dworkin thinks this distinction captures a deep intuition shared by many. Most people will perceive inequality due to the number of hours one works to be just and therefore a kind of inequality that should be preserved. Furthermore, most people will perceive inequality due to race or gender as unjust, and therefore a kind of inequality the state should actively equalize.

Here, I will first show how Dworkin positions himself on the equality of what-question. Dworkin defends equality of resources. Then, I demonstrate how Dworkin uses a thought experiment that includes an auction and an insurance scheme as starting points to arrive at some fundamental principles of justice, and show how these principles are meant to maintain the distinction between choice and circumstance. Dworkin employs this distinction to argue that people ought to be compensated for outcomes due to brute luck, but bear the responsibility for results due to calculated risk. With this starting point, I go on to show what implications Dworkin's theory has for questions of taxation. Finally, I discuss the criticism Dworkin directs at Rawls and Nozick, and evaluate *justice as fairness* against Dworkin's *equality of resources.*

Equality of resources, not welfare

In the introduction, I noted that one of the important questions in political philosophy is the question of *what* it is that is to be distributed (the equality of what-question). I distinguished between three different answers to this question: Welfare, resources, and capabilities.[3]

Why is the equality of what-question important? Imagine a father who has two children, and wants to draft a will. One of his sons, Peer, is used to an extravagant lifestyle with large consumption. The other son, Paal, is an artistic type with relatively modest material needs. If the father is an adherent of welfare equality, he should take into consideration the differences between the two sons when deciding how to distribute his funds. Welfare equality can be interpreted as the claim that everyone should have their preferences satisfied to the same degree. If the father wants Peer and Paal both to have their preferences equally satisfied, he should give more money to Peer than Paal, because he may reasonably assume that they can both live equally well—according to their preferences. If, on the contrary, the father is an adherent of resource equality, he may well share the funds equally between the two brothers. The point is that what it is that is to be distributed matters (Dworkin 2000:12–13).

In 1981, Dworkin published two articles. In "What Is Equality? Part 1: Equality of Welfare", he developed a critique of the idea that welfare is the best answer to the equality of what question. In the second article "What Is Equality? Part 2: Equality of Resources", he defended his own view: *Equality of resources.* These two articles provided important contributions both to questions of what should be distributed and to questions of which principles of justice should regulate the distribution.[4]

Dworkin starts by criticizing welfare egalitarians. Welfare egalitarians claim that the thing that should be equalized is individual well-being. Dworkin discusses different welfare theories; but here, I will simplify matters by only discussing the so-called success theory. The success theory says that persons' welfare depends on whether they are successful in satisfying their preferences. An egalitarian welfare theory therefore maintains that one must compensate those who to a lesser extent than others are able to achieve success in satisfying their preferences. From this, it follows that the answer to the equality of what-question provided by welfare egalitarians will be that justice is achieved when people have equal amount of welfare or, what amounts to the same, that they are equally successful in satisfying their preferences. In the following, equality of welfare and equality of preference satisfaction will be treated as two ways of saying the same thing.

Adherents of welfare equality claim that their theory has intuitive appeal, and is the correct answer to what we should distribute if we care about equality. It is welfare not money or other material things we actually care about. Money may well have value, but only instrumentally as a means of achieving welfare (Dworkin 2000:14). If our sense of justice alerts us to the fact that a person is treated unjustly, it is natural to focus on her well-being rather than on how much money or resources she has available (Arneson 2000b:503–504).

We will consider three objections Dworkin raises against welfare. The first objection concerns offensive preferences. The criticism is that if people have preferences that involve discrimination of others, it seems absurd to say that they should be compensated if they fail to satisfy these preferences. However, the welfare theory states that people should be compensated for their failure to satisfy their preferences, and so these people should be compensated. That makes the theory seem absurd: We cannot, for example, compensate racists for not being able to achieve their preference of living in a racially pure society (Dworkin 2000:21–25).

Second, Dworkin criticizes success theories because they do not take into consideration the fact that some people *choose* to develop expensive tastes. Dworkin illustrates this criticism with a famous example that we will pursue in later chapters: Louis consciously develops preferences for extremely expensive wine and rare bird eggs.[5] A welfare egalitarian, who thinks that it is just to ensure that people are equal in terms of preference satisfaction, would have to say that the community must ensure that Louis is able to satisfy his expensive preferences, or so claims Dworkin. According to Dworkin, this is a completely unreasonable view which makes welfare egalitarianism untenable. If people choose to develop expensive preferences, for example, by participating in wine tasting courses, it would be wrong to subsidize their wine shopping to help them satisfy their preferences.[6]

Third, and more generally, Dworkin points out that the term "welfare" is so general and abstract that it is difficult to know how one can use it to measure equal distribution. Welfare means different things to different people, and we must therefore specify it further to know what we are talking about. That is, the term must be hashed out in a (detailed) theory of welfare, and Dworkin claims that this results in the theory losing its appeal (Dworkin 2000:285). The objections about expensive taste and offensive preferences are examples of how the welfare theory loses its appeal when it is specified in the shape of a success theory. When the abstract term welfare is specified in this way, one sees how counter-intuitive it is to aim for equality of welfare.

Dworkin thus rejects welfare egalitarianism, and opts for resource equality. Resources include not only income, but property, health, and social intelligence. Income and property are examples of impersonal resources that can be owned by individuals, while health and social intelligence are examples of personal resources that a person can utilize to acquire impersonal resources (Lippert-Rasmussen 2009:681; Moss 2014:59).

Auction and insurance

How can we achieve an equal distribution of resources? How can we compare the different kinds of resources held by different people? If one person has high income, is very intelligent, but has very poor health, while another person has an average income, low intelligence, and very good health, it is difficult to say who has the most resources. Thus, there is a problem of how to compare different sets of resources (Lippert-Rasmussen 2009:681–682).

To solve this problem, Dworkin introduces a thought experiment where two market mechanisms—auction and insurance—are introduced to solve the problem of comparison of resources. Imagine a group of shipwrecked people who land on an island with several different natural resources. They decide to distribute the resources equally between themselves. Everyone gets an equal number of shells that they can use to bid in an auction of all the resources on the island. An equal distribution of resources is achieved when no one, at the end of the auction, envies the set of resources acquired by anyone else. Dworkin thus introduces what he calls the envy test for equal distribution: "No division of resources is an equal division if, once the division is complete, any immigrant would prefer someone else's bundle of resources to his own" (Dworkin 2000:67).

The auction contributes to render comparable resources that are otherwise hard to compare. But it is also designed to ensure that people take responsibility for their choices:

> people should pay the price of the life they have decided to lead, measured in what others give up in order that they can do so. That was the point of the auction as a device to establish initial equality of resources.
>
> (Dworkin 2000:74)

The auction helps distribute what we may call *external* resources such as land and tools, bananas and coconuts. But people will still have different *internal* resources. Some will be talented and healthy, while others will be less fortunately equipped with advantageous abilities. After the auction is over, the shipwrecked are equal with regards to their external resources, but unequal when it comes to internal resources (Lippert-Rasmussen 2009:681). As an example, a person with a disability will be able to bid on resources on a par with others, but have special needs, and therefore not end up equally well off as others. Hence, a person with a disability may rightly envy others who are in a better position because of this distribution of resources. To equalize inequalities that arise from inequalities in internal resources, Dworkin introduces the idea of a hypothetical insurance scheme. Imagine asking people how much they, purely hypothetically, would be willing to pay for insurance, for example, against certain genetically determined disorders. Similarly, we ask people what they would pay not to have a low level of talent. Ideally, we would ask everyone what they would insure against; but since this is difficult in practice, Dworkin thinks that we can determine an appropriate insurance premium based on how average people would insure.

Using the insurance scheme as a starting point, we can then imagine a tax system that builds on the same way of thinking. The claim is that the immigrants on the island would choose a system where they would pay higher insurance premiums the higher their income (Dworkin 2000:100–101). Dworkin therefore thinks that the island immigrants will choose a progressive tax as a suitable means of solving the problem that some are born with more talent than others. The point Dworkin wants to make with the insurance scheme is that it is just to have a tax scheme that ensures equalization of circumstances such as one's natural endowment and health.

Using the hypothetical insurance scheme, Dworkin attempts to provide an impartial argument for a redistributive state; people are born with abilities that are more or less in demand in a market. This is unjust and something we should try to rectify. The argument asks us to envision two different worlds:

1 A world where everyone has the same risk of ending up with abilities for which there is little demand, and where those who are born with abilities for which there is little demand must themselves bear the consequence of this.
2 A world where everyone has the same risk of ending up with abilities for which there is little demand, but where there is an opportunity to dampen the consequences of this by taking out insurance.

Dworkin prefers world number 2 where resources associated with natural endowment are distributed through an insurance scheme, which, in practice, is a tax system (Dworkin 2000:106). This ensures that one equalizes inequalities that are due to circumstances for which individuals are not responsible.

Principles of justice

Dworkin's distinction between choice and circumstance has been extended and formed the basis for a number of political philosophical theories and empirical investigations.[7] What these extensions of the theory have in common is that they distinguish between factors for which individuals should be held responsible, *responsibility factors*, and factors for which they should not be held responsible, *non-responsibility factors*. Starting with these, we can formulate two Dworkinian principles of justice:

Principle of equality: Outcome inequalities not due to responsibility factors are unjust and should be eliminated (or sharply reduced).

Principle of responsibility: Outcome inequalities due to responsibility factors are just and should not be eliminated.

The principle of equality can be justified by noting that it is unjust if some people make more than others do only because they have a different class background, a different gender, or have certain innate abilities highly valued by the market. The principle of responsibility can be justified by appeal to the idea that people should be held responsible for their own choices.

A central question for any theory that includes a principle of responsibility is what counts as responsibility factors. Dworkin has discussed this with Cohen, and we shall briefly consider the most important arguments in this debate. Dworkin distinguishes between cravings and preferences. Cravings are outside the control of persons, while preferences are within their control. People who, for example, need to attend the opera on a regular basis, but wish they did not have this need, should be able to classify the need for opera as an innate disadvantage for which they should be compensated by the community through, for example, having their visits to the opera financed (Dworkin 2000:82). The same is true for people who hate the taste of tap water. If they wish they did not have this preference, they should be compensated for the costs they incur in satisfying this preference by buying bottled water (Dworkin 2000:288).

So far, Cohen and Dworkin agree. The difference between them becomes clear in their discussion of a different example. Assume that a person has a strong wish to become a photographer (Dworkin 2000:288). The problem is that photography requires expensive equipment. Dworkin thinks this person should not be compensated by the community, while Cohen disagrees. Cohen thinks that the aspiring photographer should be compensated. Dworkin thinks that the wish to become a photographer is something for which the person must be held responsible, while Cohen disagrees. How do they arrive at different conclusions about this?

Dworkin argues that as long as the photography-interested person views photography as something valuable and with which the person identifies, it must be counted as chosen. It is not an interest the person has been afflicted with, but one that follows from a set of notions such as their taste, opinion, and judgement (Dworkin 2000:291). The person cannot perceive photography as a burden so long as the person identifies with and is happy to be a photographer. Therefore, the person must take responsibility for the hobby and the costs that go with it.

Cohen, however, thinks that the photographer may have an involuntary interest in photography, which implies that the person should be compensated, even if happy about their interest in photography. The person may, for example, have grown up in a very photography-interested family. Cohen therefore distinguishes between different kinds of expensive taste, depending on whether the person who has this taste can be held responsible for having it. One is not entitled to compensation if one *consciously* chooses to develop a preference for something. The photography-interested may, however, have been afflicted with the interest without consciously having chosen it, and if that is the case, the community should cover the costs involved (Cohen 2011:21). The difference between Cohen and Dworkin thus consists in Dworkin thinking that such fundamental things as what our interests are, and what we perceive as important, must to a large extent be ascribed to choice, and thus as something we can be held responsible for, while Cohen thinks that many of these things are things we do not choose and hence cannot be held responsible for. Put simply, Cohen is more egalitarian because he holds that the community must compensate individuals to a larger extent.

Dworkin and Cohen have been criticized for using unrealistic examples. The trouble with unrealistic examples is that it is not always easy to see what they imply about the real world. A more realistic example might be tobacco. If a person has smoked all their life and then develops chronic obstructive pulmonary syndrome (COPS), we might wonder whether the community should cover their health care costs. Is it reasonable to hold people responsible for having developed health issues from smoking? On the one hand, there are many examples of people who succeed in quitting smoking as a result of strong will. People have a choice, and therefore there might be good reason to hold them responsible for smoking. On the other hand, many who smoke start smoking at an age where it would not be reasonable to hold them fully responsible for their choices. If, for example, one starts to smoke as a 13-year-old, and grows up in an environment where everybody smokes, it is more difficult to quit smoking than if one did not grow up under such conditions.

In the smoking example, it does not help us much if the smokers wished they did not have the need to smoke. Many wish to quit, but the mere fact that they wish to quit does not seem to justify not holding them responsible. Smoking thus seems to be a borderline case between preference and craving, which makes it particularly difficult to evaluate whether one should be held responsible. This illustrates two things: First, more realistic examples than those used by Cohen and Dworkin are often also more complex. Second, there are practical problems connected with theories that place significant weight on responsibility. We shall return to discussions of this last point towards the end of this chapter and in Chapter 7.

Two kinds of luck

The insurance scheme is also supposed to solve a more general problem. Dworkin is concerned that an adequate theory of justice must equalize those inequalities that are due to pure or "brute luck", but allow those that are due to calculated risk or "option luck":

> Option luck is a matter of how deliberate and calculated gamble turn out –whether someone gains or loses through accepting an isolated risk he or she should have anticipated and might have declined. Brute luck is a matter of how risks fall out that are not in that sense deliberate gambles.
>
> (Dworkin 2000:73)

Brute (bad) luck follows from situations outside of our control: If you are struck by lightning that is outside your control, you should therefore be compensated for any costs that may follow. This implies that natural endowment, one's social background, and other things that happens which one could not foresee all count as brute luck. Option luck, by contrast, is within your control, and thus something you must take responsibility for. A much discussed example is the following: If I choose to ride a motorbike without a helmet, crash, and require operations to my head as a result, I would, on Dworkin's way of thinking, not have the right to have my health expenses covered by the community.

However, insurance offers us a link between brute luck and option luck. If there is insurance against getting struck by lightning, and I live in a place where there are frequent thunderstorms, and choose not to take out a lightning insurance, what started out as brute luck is transformed into option luck as a result of my taking a calculated risk. In other words, insurance offers us an opportunity to take responsibility for our own lives so that we are better equipped to face the consequences of brute luck.

Dworkin gives the following example: Assume that two people with good eyesight have the same risk of going blind, and that the risk is known to both of them. They both have the opportunity to take out an insurance against going blind. If both end up in the same accident and both go blind, it follows from Dworkin's position that we should not redistribute from the one who took out an insurance to the one who did not: "For the availability of insurance would mean that, though both had had brute bad luck, the difference between them was a matter of option luck" (Dworkin 2000:77). This means that people must be held responsible for their choice not to take out insurance against brute luck if such insurance schemes exist (and everyone has equal opportunity to take out an insurance).[8]

What follows from this when it comes to distributing resources? Is it just that there may arise inequalities as a result of option luck? According to Dworkin, we must first consider the difference that will arise between those who voluntarily take risk and those who do not. If Paal chooses a life without risk and Peer chooses one filled with risks, there is no reason to redistribute from Peer to Paal if Peer happens to be lucky in his risk-taking. This follows from what we have said above about how individuals must bear the consequences of their choices (Dworkin 2000:74).

Let us look at two people who both choose to take risk, where one wins and the other loses. When one chooses to gamble, it is reasonable that one has to bear the consequences. Those who lose cannot put forth any demand for compensation from those who win:

> If winners were made to share their winnings with losers, then no one would gamble, as individuals, and the kind of life preferred by both those who in the end win and those who lose would be unavailable…the effect of redistribution from winners to losers in gambles would be to deprive both of lives they prefer.
>
> (Dworkin 2000:75)

In this case as well, then it follows that the inequality that arises as a result of voluntarily chosen risk is just and should be kept. Hence, if we follow

Dworkin, it cannot be the task of the state to redistribute between two people where one wins and the other loses, for example, a bet. However, this conclusion presupposes that everyone has the same opportunity voluntarily to take risks. If Peer bought stocks with his mother's inheritance that then skyrocketed, while Paal did not inherit and therefore could not buy stocks, the resulting inequality is not necessarily just.

Dworkin therefore argues in favour of an "ambition-sensitive" theory; he wants to maintain those inequalities that are the result of people's choices. Those who "choose to invest rather than consume, or to consume less expensively rather than more, or to work in more rather than less profitable ways must be permitted to retain the gains that flow from these choices" (Dworkin 2000:89). Dworkin holds that a distribution should not be "endowment-sensitive", that is, affected by differences in natural abilities. Distribution cannot depend on people's degree of talent, because talent is not chosen and is, to use Rawls' terminology, arbitrary from a moral point of view. Dworkin thus incorporates a consideration for responsibility in his egalitarian theory. This means that Dworkin's egalitarianism contains an element typically belonging to the political right. As Cohen writes: "Dworkin has, in effect, performed for egalitarianism the considerable service of incorporating within it the most powerful idea in the arsenal of the anti-egalitarian Right: The idea of choice and responsibility" (Cohen 2011:32).

The view that brute luck should not determine how well off people are, is shared by a number of egalitarian thinkers. The state should, for reasons of justice, seek to compensate brute bad luck whether this bad luck is a matter of congenital disability, a lack of skills (valued by the market), or of being the innocent victim of an accident.

This does not mean that all inequalities should be equalized. People can accumulate resources depending on their effort, lucky investments, etc. This may also mean that inequalities increase over time. It follows from Dworkin's fundamental distinction that, ideally, income tax should aim to equalize inequalities due to talent, but preserve differences due to choice, for example, of profession (Dworkin 2000:91). In practical politics, however, this cannot be accomplished in a precise and detailed way. Whatever talent a person may have must be cultivated, and that demands effort. Effort and talent will always affect each other reciprocally. Ideally, we would want to isolate what is due to talent, but that is not possible. Dworkin writes:

> We cannot hope to identify such a component, even given perfect information about people's personalities. For we will be thwarted by the reciprocal influence that talents and ambitions exercise on each other.
> (Dworkin 2000:91)

Talent is developed into a valuable ability through effort, while effort is put in through exercising one's talent.[9] In spite of this difficulty, Dworkin is clear that income tax must bear much of the burden of redistributive tax, justified by the idea that talent by itself can be legitimately taxed.

Dworkin therefore asks how one might avoid that differences over time develop into class differences. Should there, for example, be limits to how much can be transferred from one person to the next, thereby equalizing intergenerational inequalities?

Dworkin answers this question by arguing that inheritance is a matter of brute luck, and that the state must come up with a system to equalize the inequalities that follow from this particular kind of luck (Dworkin 2000:347). Hypothetically speaking, we can imagine taking out an insurance against not inheriting. Based on this idea, we can design a tax system that is sufficiently progressive to hinder the formation of classes.[10] Dworkin goes on to suggest that the income generated through inheritance tax should not be used to cover needs for health services and unemployment benefits. These will be covered by income tax. Instead, the state should use this kind of tax for targeted measures to hinder systematic inequalities in society. He mentions improved public education as an example of a measure that may have this function (Dworkin 2000:347–349).

However, Dworkin is not an adherent of wealth tax. This must be understood on the background of the choice/responsibility component of his theory. If people choose to save rather than spend their money, this is precisely the kind of choice Dworkin thinks should not be equalized through tax measures (Dworkin 2000:479). Dworkin therefore does not think wealth tax is an ideal tax.[11]

Thus, strict equality will not be just on Dworkin's view. He claims that his theory is superior to alternative egalitarian theories (like Rawls'), because it incorporates a sensitivity to the choices people make while simultaneously aiming to equalize inequalities in natural endowments.

Dworkin's critique of Rawls and Nozick

Here, I will summarize and further clarify Dworkin's position by contrasting it with Rawls' and Nozick's theories.

Dworkin criticizes Rawls' theory, and in particular the difference principle, on three counts: First, Dworkin's claim that Rawls' theory insufficiently compensates for congenital disadvantages. Second, Rawls' theory is insufficiently concerned with efficiency. Third, Dworkin, as we have seen, thinks Rawls' theory is insufficiently concerned with holding people responsible for their own choices.

To the first issue: Two people will be equal to Rawls if they have the same share of primary goods. Dworkin argues that this disregards the fact that a person with a disability will need access to more primary goods to be equal to a person who does not have a disability. A person born without legs will, for example, need expensive equipment to live a life equally dignified to that of a person born with legs. A person with a congenital disability has a disadvantage which is not the result of their own choice, but Rawls' difference principle is, according to Dworkin, unable to compensate for this. The

Table 3.1 Four hypothetical structures 2

Economy	*Least-advantaged group*	*Middle group*	*Most-advantaged group*
A	10,000	10,000	10,000
B	12,000	30,000	80,000
C	30,000	90,000	150,000
D	29,000	100,000	500,000

Source: Wenar (2013).

difference principle calls for equality unless inequality is to the advantage of the worst off. The talented should not have more primary goods than those without the same talent, unless the absolute position of the worst off improves with this inequality. Those with disabilities are to be ensured equal access to primary goods. Dworkin criticizes the principle because it does not say anything about those with disabilities being ensured more primary goods to lead a good life (Kymlicka 2002:71).

The second objection is that the difference principle is unreasonably focused on the worst off, and therefore insufficiently oriented towards efficiency (Dworkin 2000:114). The core of this objection can be summed up by returning to the table we used as an example in the presentation of Rawls (here, economy D has been slightly altered to illustrate the point) (Table 3.1).

The question is whether it is obvious that economy D, because the minimal reduction inflicted on the worst off group, is untenable.[12] Dworkin does not think so, and criticizes the difference principle on a general basis because it presupposes that just distribution starts with groups rather than individuals. *Equality of resources*, as opposed to *justice as fairness*, is a position that claims that "equality is in principle a matter of individual right rather than one of group position" (Dworkin 2000:114).

Dworkin's third criticism brings us back to the introductory assertion that a theory of justice must be sensitive to responsibility. His criticism of Rawls here is that the difference principle does not capture inequalities due to conscious choice. Assume that two persons are equally endowed with natural resources, abilities, and social background. Peer chooses a hard-working life as a fisherman and gradually accumulates a number of goods. Paal is a sports fan and chooses to spend all his leisure time in front of the TV. Paal works in a factory, but only works enough to acquire the bare necessities. The difference principle will only allow inequality between Peer and Paal if it is to the advantage of the worst off, namely Paal. If Paal does not gain anything by the inequality (that arises from Peer's hard work and Paal's laziness), then the state must redistribute income so that Peer and Paal end up equally well off. The state must, in other words, take part of Peer's income and give it to Paal.

This redistribution is, according to Dworkin, unfair. It implies that Peer must pay for Paal to lie on the sofa, watching TV. When inequalities arise from individual choice, it is not reasonable to redistribute from the one who chooses to work hard to the one who is lazy. Dworkin thus thinks that Rawls' position is insufficiently sensitive to choice and responsibility (Dworkin 2002:122).[13] Another way of putting this is to say that there are inequalities that are just, even if they do not help promote the worst off, and which it is not the job of the state to equalize.

Dworkin also addresses the Wilt Chamberlain argument. How will a position like *equality of resources* deal with the inequality that arises from Chamberlain's contract? At first pass, Dworkin points out, there does not appear to be any reason to redistribute from Chamberlain to the community. Granted, it is likely that Wilt's income is primarily a result of his talent, and only secondarily how he has cultivated this talent. Still, no one, or almost no one, would have taken out insurance against not being endowed with Chamberlain's talent. An insurance like that would simply be too expensive to be a reasonable investment (Dworkin 2000:111).

What if we add more information than originally allowed by Nozick, asks Dworkin. We may, for example, assume that Wilt plays basketball, not in an imaginary society where the only kind of inequality is what arises from Wilt's contract, but in a society like that in Philadelphia in the early 1970s. In such a case, the inequalities will be large, much larger than allowed by the kind of insurance scheme that Dworkin argues for. We would therefore have to establish a tax system for redistribution, and in such a system, Chamberlain would have to contribute. Indeed, he would have to contribute substantially more than most others. This follows from Dworkin's justification of a progressive tax system (Dworkin 2000:112). According to Nozick, Wilt may legitimately keep what is due to his talent. To Dworkin, the point of the insurance scheme is to arrive at a way of redistributing resources that dampens the importance of natural endowment.[14]

Discussion

A common way to argue for Dworkin's positions has been to hold that most people share the intuition that the inequality due to choice is fair, while inequality that is due to circumstance is unfair. However, I believe that this argument has been given too much weight. As Scheffler points out, it is more correct to say that these ideals both fit and conflict with most people's views. For example, surveys have shown that most people are willing to tolerate a larger degree of inequality due to talent than what is allowed in Dworkin's ideal. Furthermore, many will probably also be sceptical to the idea that people are to be allowed to keep all the resources that is due to choice (Scheffler 2003:6).

The most common objection to Dworkin's responsibility-based theory of justice—on which we shall elaborate further in Chapter 7—is that it is too hard on those who make wrong choices. If you make the wrong choice, you have to bear the consequences, even if it ruins your life. Richard Arneson has expressed this worry:

> The responsibility (Dworkins view of equality) assigns to individuals is to stark and unforgiving. Suppose that someone starts with an initial equality of resources and voluntarily makes a foolish, self-harming choice. The choice is bad, and then one has bad option luck; the result is that one's life from then on will be horribly grim absent further aid. In this situation, equality of resources condemns further aid to the individual, which would subtract from the equal shares owed to others. But I submit that in this case, the "punishment" the individual suffers is disproportionate to her "crime", and distributive justice must be interpreted to require further provision of aid, contrary to the equality of resources ideal.
>
> (Arneson 2002, quoted from Dworkin 2002:113–114)

According to this line of criticism, Dworkin's position is too concerned with responsibility. Giving too much weight to responsibility has unjust and exaggerated consequences for those who make bad choices.

A related criticism is directed not necessarily against Dworkin's theory, but against the problems associated with implementing a theory that gives responsibility such a central role. It is one thing to say that if two people who have the same upbringing and are equally talented, then they are responsible for the results that are due to their choices, for example, of how much or how hard they work. But in the real world, there are no such two people. Murphy and Nagel have criticized Dworkin and others who stick to choice and responsibility as justifications for inequality:

> The trouble with this ideal picture is that in the real world, people do not enter the market equipped with equal resources or equal skills or equal talents. They have some responsibility for what they make of their situation through their employment, investment and expenditure decisions, but it is responsibility against the background of unequal starting points or circumstances of choice.
>
> (Murphy and Nagel 2002:68)

Transferring the concern for responsibility from the idealized theory and into the real world is potentially unjust. This is a serious problem, also because it is much easier to implement the responsibility element than the element of equality of resources (Wolff and De-Shalit 2007:13). In the real world, it will be impossible to figure out whether two people have had the same resources. But it will not be impossible to implement policies that hold people responsible for how many years of education they choose to undergo by, for example, giving higher wages to professions that require longer educations.

If we hold people responsible for their choices in spite of very different starting positions, this will be deeply unjust, and also in violation of Dworkin's ideal.

Michael Otsuka has argued that there is a fundamental tension in Dworkin's defence of resource equality. This tension is especially clear when Dworkin discusses tax on inheritance and gifts. We have seen that it is crucial to Dworkin's thought experiment that the island immigrants have an equal number of shells in advance of the auction. To Otsuka, this raises the question of what happens if one of the immigrants, who, for example, adheres to an ascetic lifestyle, gives half of his shells to another immigrant. If that happens, one cannot arrive at a distribution where no one envies the share of anyone else. Otsuka therefore thinks that Dworkin must forbid gift-giving between the island immigrants. This shows the tension an equality-oriented theory like Dworkin's must deal with. A theory like this must always deal with the tension between certain liberal freedoms (like the freedom to give things away to other people), and the ideal of resource equality (Otsuka 2002:51–54).

Another problem is that Dworkin's theory in principle can allow inequalities that are sufficiently large to undermine democratic institutions. We can imagine a situation where Peer and Paal make different choices, with the result that Paal gets filthy rich and Peer gets poor. According to Dworkin, there is nothing about the distribution itself that makes it unjust. Dworkin follows Nozick in saying that we must look at how a distribution has come about, not whether it fits a desired pattern. If the distribution is the result of choice alone, it is just according to Dworkin.[15] This is problematic if our ideal of justice is not to conflict with the fundamental ideal that citizens in modern democracies must be free and equal with equal opportunity to influence the political process. That is, there is a danger that Dworkin's ideal will lead to a situation where Paal can dominate Peer. Thus, while Rawls' principle is situated in, and especially appropriate for, modern constitutional democracies, Dworkin's ideal is abstract and potentially in conflict with democratic institutions. This is, in my view, a central weakness in Dworkin's theory.

This point is particularly salient in the different views on taxation held by Rawls and Dworkin. Dworkin is in favour of income tax and tax on inheritance as primary redistributive taxes, and rejects wealth tax. Rawls' tax scheme, in contrast, can be interpreted to ascribe a central role to wealth tax precisely to protect democratic equality.[16] In my view, this illustrates how Dworkin's theory insufficiently deals with inequalities that may be problematic in a society where everyone must be ensured equal opportunity for political influence. Rawls' theory is attractive precisely because it emphasizes the importance of money not being used to increase people's political power.

What about Dworkin's criticism of Rawls? Is Dworkin right that Rawls' theory is insufficiently sensitive to responsibility, and that it follows from the difference principle that the community must subsidize slackers? I do not think so. The interpretation of Rawls that I presented in Chapter 1 says that we must keep inequality within strictly defined limits. We must limit how much the best off can have, while at the same time supplying capital to the worst off. This ideal in no way removes responsibility. Whether one ends up in the top percentile or not will depend on individual choices. But the position does not allow responsibility to play a too dominating a role. The basic structure is to ensure that the most talented are not able to become sufficiently wealthy to dominate and control others. In my view, Rawls' theory thus incorporates responsibility in a satisfactory manner.

In the following chapter, we will move toward the left of the spectrum to look at Cohen, who is deeply influenced by Dworkin, but develops his own distinct form of egalitarianism.

Further reading

Dworkin has written about many other topics besides distributive justice, and some of the introductions to his thinking are primarily about these other contributions. However, the book *Dworkin and His Critics* contains five good articles about Dworkin's understanding of equality as well as a reply by Dworkin himself. Of particular interest is the sharp and detailed answer Dworkin gives to Cohen's contribution to this book. Arthur Ripstein's *Liberty and Equality* provides a good overview of Dworkin's understanding of distributive justice. Among other things, this text highlights Dworkin's thinking about the relationship between freedom and equality. Lippert-Rasmussen's *Equality, Option Luck and Responsibility* commands an important place in the debate about Dworkin's theory, and among other things provides an elaboration of the understanding of different types of luck. In 2002, the journal *Ethics* published a special issue dedicated to Dworkin's book *Sovereign Virtue*.

For a discussion on Dworkin and taxation, see David Duffs *Tax Policy and the Virtuous Sovereign: Dworkinian Equality and Redistributive Taxation*. For a discussion on Dworkin and inheritance tax, see Daniel Halliday's *Inheritance and Hypothetical Insurance*.

Notes

1 This way of framing the understanding of Dworkin is indebted to Wolff (2007).
2 In the article "Equality of Resources" (1981), Dworkin writes about distinction between a person and that person's circumstances. Cohen (1989) criticized this, and pointed out that the relevant distinction is between choice and circumstances. In (Dworkin's?) later writings, and in the secondary literature, it is this latter distinction (between choice and circumstances) that has come to dominate (Scheffler 2003:19, fn.35).
3 I am here supposing that Rawls' primary goods can be grouped as resources. See Arneson (2010:101) and Moss (2014:54–65).
4 The articles were published in *Philosophy & Public Affairs*, and later as chapters in the book *Sovereign Virtue*. In the following, I shall cite from the book.
5 The example is originally from Kenneth Arrow, but was made famous through Dworkin's use of it. Arrow used plover's eggs, the eggs of a wader, and a rare

kind of wine (pre-phylloxera claret) as examples of expensive taste. Dworkin appropriated the example, tied it to Louis, and the Louis example became hotly debated and tied to the question of what it is that should be distributed (see Dworkin 2000:48–59; Cohen 2011:19–21).

6 In addition to those who choose to develop expensive taste, as we shall shortly see, Dworkin also wants to disqualify people who *identify* with expensive tastes as something that require compensation.

7 In Chapter 7, we will discuss Luck egalitarianism which is derived from Dworkin's theories. In addition to Dworkin, see Arneson (1989, 1990) and Cohen (1989). Furthermore, opinion polls and economic experiments have also shown that the ideal that we should keep inequalities due to choice, but compensate for inequalities that are due to circumstance, has significant public support. For example of opinion polls, see Schokkaert and Devooght (2003), and for economic experiments, see Cappelen et al. (2007).

8 For a discussion of this example, see Otsuka (2002:43 ff.).

9 For further discussion of talent and effort, see Nagel (1991:118–119).

10 For a discussion of how Dworkin grounds his justification of the inheritance tax in hypothetical insurance schemes, see Halliday (2018:95–100).

11 Nevertheless, one may, as Duff has pointed out, justify a wealth tax based on the resource equality that Dworkin defends. This may be due to two conditions. First, the rejection of wealth tax presupposes that income and inheritance is taxed prior to being saved. If this is not the case, Dworkin's position may allow taxation of wealth as the second best solution. Second, wealth tax may be necessary if a society is class-divided and individuals may reasonably be supposed to have insured against ending up among the worst off in that society. In general, however, Dworkin is against wealth tax (Duff 2016:27–28).

12 For a similar criticism, see Sen (1979:208–209), and for nuances, see Nagel (1991:68).

13 Note that commentators disagree about the centrality of the distinction between choice and circumstance in Rawls' theory. Will Kymlicka (2002) claims that Rawls anticipates the distinction between choice and circumstance, but that he is unable to produce a theory to match. Samuel Scheffler (2003) argues that the distinction does not play a central role in Rawls. In my view, Scheffler is right.

14 Dworkin follows Nozick on an important point: He distinguishes between "continuous" and "discontinuous" theories of justice (Dworkin 2000:323). *Equality of resources* is a continuous theory because it makes the distribution dependent of people's choices, but not their circumstances. In contrast, discontinuous theories employ special standards for politics and disregard the idea that choice is crucial to determining the justness of a distribution. It may therefore seem like Dworkin follows Nozick in rejecting end result principles: The distribution may have any pattern whatever: What matters is not the pattern, but how it has arisen. If it is the result of choice and not circumstance, it is just. In principle, therefore, justice in Dworkin's conception is compatible with very large inequalities.

15 Where the theory clearly departs from Nozick's libertarianism is in Dworkin's view of talent as an arbitrary factor that must be equalized. Nozick, we remember, sees talent as something that can give rise to legitimate claims according to the thesis of self-ownership. We can also see the central difference (between the two) by pointing out that Dworkin ascribes a crucial value to equality, and attempts to unite equality and responsibility (Dworkin 2002:7), while Nozick is less concerned with equality.

16 I shall elaborate on this in Chapters 9 and 11.

4 Equality and community

G.A. Cohen

G.A. Cohen (1941–2009) has been one of the most influential political philosophers of the last few decades on the question of distributive justice. Of all the liberal egalitarians, Cohen is the most critical of the idea that a society based on a market economy can be just. He defends socialism, and has been one of the most important contributors to a renewed interest in Karl Marx. Cohen has delivered important contributions on three fronts of political philosophy: He was the leading representative for the so-called September Group of analytical philosophers interested in Marx, and thereby also an important contributor to what has later become known as analytical Marxism. Next, he has played an important role as a critic of Rawls, Nozick, Dworkin and Sen. And, finally, he has delivered a distinct contribution to a theory of equality. Here, he defends luck egalitarianism inspired by Dworkin's distinction between choice and circumstance, while also providing a defence of socialism.

We have already touched upon Cohen's critique of Nozick and Dworkin. In this chapter, we will start by taking a closer look at Cohen's criticism of Rawls. As a starting point, we will use Cohen's book *Rescuing Justice and Equality* (2008), in which he pursues the double goal of the title: Both our conception of justice and of equality must be rescued from Rawls, and the influence of Rawlsians, to allow the establishment of a just society based on genuine equality. Although these two rescue operations are tightly interwoven, here I will limit myself to discussing how Cohen claims to rescue our conception of equality. As we shall see, solidarity and community are important values that Cohen thinks are missing in Rawls.

Next, we turn to Cohen's answer to the question of what egalitarians should be concerned with equalizing. Cohen's answer is that equal access to advantage can mean both resources (as per Dworkin's position) and welfare, and that a theory of distributive justice must use a broad measure for what is to be distributed. This perspective is elaborated in Cohen's most well-known and cited article, "On the Currency of Egalitarian Justice". Then, we will consider Cohen's defence of socialism as given in his book *Why Not Socialism?*. Here, Cohen argues for two principles of justice: An egalitarian principle that allows inequality due to circumstances within control, and a community principle which states that inequality must be combatted to allow the existence of genuine communities. Finally, I discuss Cohen's criticism of Rawls and consider some important tensions in Cohen's position.

Cohen's criticism of Rawls: rescuing our conception of equality

In the first part of *Rescuing*, Cohen carries out an immanent critique of Rawls.[1] This means that he asks what actually follows from Rawls' fundamental ideal of justice. To Cohen, what follows is an endorsement of the claim that justice requires equality. His criticism of Rawls is that Rawls is too permissive of deviation from equality. Cohen's criticism is directed at the difference principle. As we saw in Chapter 1, Rawls claims that talented people do not *deserve* to be rewarded for their talents, because talent is the result of pure luck. Therefore, the talented may only reap the rewards of their talent if doing so betters the position of the worst off. Above, we called this Rawls' incentive argument. It allows inequality to the extent that inequality is necessary to better the position of the worst off. An example would be to offer especially talented people economic rewards for taking jobs that contribute to a total increase of productivity in society. If, for example, there is a lack of medical doctors, one could increase the pay of medical doctors to attract more people to the profession.

Cohen, however, thinks that the principle can only be used to justify inequality if one presupposes that the talented people have attitudes that conflict with the egalitarian spirit of the difference principle. He therefore asks why talented people that support an egalitarian ideal should demand higher pay to contribute to society. The result of such demands is inequality, and Cohen wants to show that this kind of inequality is not compatible with justice.

Cohen thus claims that the difference principle can be used to justify a kind of inequality that conflicts with the egalitarian spirit that the principle presupposes. To illustrate, consider a dialogue imagined by Jan Narveson (and cited by Cohen). The dialogue plays out between a person who belongs to the group of the well off and a person who belongs to the group of the worst off:

> Well-off: "Look here, fellow citizen, I'll work hard and make both you and me better off, provided I get a bigger share than you."
>
> Worse-off: "Well that's rather good; but I thought you were agreeing that justice requires equality?"
>
> Well-off: "Yes, but that's only as a benchmark, you see. To do still better, both of us, you understand, may require differential incentive payments to people like me."
>
> Worse-off: "Oh. Well what makes them necessary?"
>
> Well-off: "What makes them necessary is that I won't work as hard if I don't get more than you."
>
> Worse-off: "Well, why not?"

> Well-off: "I dunno…I guess that's just the way I'm built."
> Worse-off: "Meaning you don't really care that much about justice, eh?"
> Well-off: "Er, no, I guess not".
>
> (Narveson quoted in Cohen 2008:27)

What Cohen wants to illustrate with this dialogue is that the well off person does not have to demand a higher pay to work as hard as possible. The difference principle, when interpreted as implying that it is *necessary* for talented people to be paid more to do their best, was one of the most effective arguments for inequality in the Thatcher-Reagan era. And Cohen claims that this argument for inequality was difficult to counter for people on the left. Because of this, it was very important for Cohen to show why it is inadequate as a justification for inequality.

Cohen only accepts what he calls a strict interpretation of the difference principle, namely the interpretations that holds that only the inequality that is to the greatest possible advantage to the worst off is justified. However, when the difference principle is employed as it is by the well off person in the dialogue above, it is actually to the detriment of the worst off. Why? Because it justifies an unnecessary inequality. The well-off person *could* have worked just as hard without any extra compensation. If that was the case, there would be no inequality, and to a true egalitarian, this will obviously be preferable. We can therefore distinguish between a strong and a weak interpretation of the difference principle:

> Strong interpretation: Only inequalities that are to the greatest possible advantage to the worst off are justified.
> Weak interpretation: Inequalities are justified if they make the worst off better off by motivating talented people to do work they otherwise would not do.

Cohen thinks that Rawls' texts support both interpretations. The weak interpretation opens up the possibility that people who are primarily motivated by self-interest can demand higher pay for work they could have done without such higher pay. This, in turn, opens up for large inequalities, and hence the only permissible interpretation of the difference principle is the strong interpretation. This interpretation allows some inequality, but only if this is strictly necessary to get people to do especially demanding work. Under the strict interpretation of the difference principle, no one demands extra pay for egoistic reasons, because everyone has an egalitarian attitude and are willing to work hard without extra pay. From solidarity with their fellow citizens, they will do their best without demanding something more in return:

> On the lax interpretation of what the difference principle demands, it is satisfied when everyone gets what she can through self-seeking behavior

> in a market whose rewards are so structured by taxation and other regulation that the worst off are as well off as any scheme of taxed and regulated market rewards can make them. On my view of what it means for a society to institute the principle, people would mention norms of equality when asked to explain why they and those like them are willing to work for the pay they get.
>
> (Cohen 2008:74)

In a society where the citizens are truly egalitarian, one will therefore hear people say things such as "I know I could push for a higher salary, but because I am concerned with equality, I do not do so". Only a strict interpretation of the difference principle is defensible according to Cohen: On this interpretation, people have internalized a norm of equality in line with the spirit of the principle, and as a consequence, the worst off are considerably better off than they would be under the weak interpretation of the difference principle.

The weak interpretation of the difference principle, in Cohen's opinion, smuggles in a premise disguised as a fact: That talented people will only do their best if they receive additional rewards. Cohen questions this premise. It may well be that in capitalist societies, we are used to thinking that talented people must be rewarded extra to do their best. That, however, is not an unquestionable fact on which one can base an argument of justice.

An important point to Cohen is that Rawls is inconsistent. According to Cohen, Rawls presupposes that for the difference principle to regulate society, there must be something like ties of civic friendship between citizens. However, the incentive argument presented in the weak interpretation of the difference principle "can justify inequality only in a society where interpersonal relations lack a communal character in the specified sense". (Cohen 2008:47). Again, we can return to the dialogue between the person who is well off and the person who is worst off to illustrate. When the well off says "I won't work as hard if I don't get more than you", the well off person expresses an argument whose use would be prohibited in a society committed to maintaining ties of civic friendship. For, in a society with genuine community, such an argument would have no weight. In a society with genuine community, one would on the contrary expect talented people to do their best without any extra reward.

Thus an important difference between Rawls and Cohen is brought into view. Distributive justice cannot, to Cohen, be limited to the basic structure of society. To Rawls, it is primarily the basic structure—the constitution, the legal system, and the market—that is to be regulated by the principles of justice. Individual choice is outside their scope. Cohen claims that this limitation is problematic. Focusing too much on the basic structure may lead one to neglect the importance of how people relate to one another. To Cohen, a genuinely egalitarian society cannot be based on individuals who are primarily motivated by self-interest. Instead, an egalitarian theory should criticize the tendency of the market to emphasize competition between individuals, in which others are understood as means we use to reach our own goals. An egalitarian theory must, in Cohen's view, require a shift in the way people think and act. Because of this, Cohen is deeply critical of how Rawls justifies inequality with the weak interpretation of the difference principle. According to Cohen, a just society requires "both just rules and just personal choice within the framework set by just rules" (Cohen 2000:3).

It is important to emphasize that Cohen is not advocating the replacement of Rawls' concern for a just basic structure with a personal moral based on an egalitarian ethos. Private actions and attitudes that arise from an egalitarian ethos are instead intended to promote the way public institutions can facilitate justice by pulling in the same direction. Cohen writes:

> Private action enhances public when, to illustrate, a willingness on the part of the more fortunate to work hard at high tax rates enables government to set those rates under an expectation of high tax revenue and, therewith, the capacity to redistribute radically. Government tax policy is not then set against the grain of self-interest, and its range of options is thereby propitiously widened.
>
> (Cohen 2008:375)

In other words: In the bringing about of a just society, the contributions from a just basic structure and an egalitarian ethos will be mutually reinforcing. But what is an egalitarian ethos?

Cohen does not give a detailed or systematic account of what he means by an "egalitarian ethos". However, the following elements are important: When an egalitarian ethos manifests itself, people will be willing to set aside their own interests and work for the community without expectation or demand for extra rewards. Cohen sums up such an attitude by pointing to an egalitarian rule: It says that "no one should seek such compensation as makes him all things considered (far) better off than anyone else" (Cohen 2008:370). He also provides a historic example of an egalitarian ethos manifesting itself:

> During World War II in Britain, a social ethos induced people to sacrifice personal interests for the sake of the war effort, and everyone was expected, as a matter of justice, to "do his bit", to shoulder his just share.
>
> (Cohen 2008:353)

Another implication of an egalitarian ethos is that people will accept very high tax rates (Cohen 2008:70), and that citizens will think altruistically when they vote (Cohen 2008:175). Last, but not least, an egalitarian ethos implies relating to others not as competitors, but as fellow citizens, to whom we have duties like those we have to family members.[2] An ethos is thus an informal set of effective social norms (Carens 2015:53), and an egalitarian ethos exists when equality is one of the most important norms in society.

Cohen's currency

In *On the Currency of Egalitarian Justice* (1989), Cohen discusses the question of what it is that people who care about equality should distribute.[3] Or, using Cohen's terms: What currency should count for egalitarians?

To understand Cohen's reply to this question, we need both to recapitulate some of what we have said and to introduce a central argument from Richard Arneson, one of Cohen's most important intellectual allies. We need, in short, to recall the discussion of expensive tastes. As we saw earlier, Dworkin's criticism of welfare egalitarianism pointed out that it would be unfair to compensate Louis for his expensive tastes to allow him the same level of welfare as others with less expensive tastes. Louis consciously developed his preferences for expensive wine and rare bird's eggs, and expensive preferences are not something for which the state should compensate.

Arneson introduces an important distinction. To answer what it is that should be distributed, we need to distinguish between outcome and opportunity theories. Equality in welfare outcome would require Louis to be compensated, since everyone must be ensured equal satisfaction of their preferences. A theory that required equal opportunity for welfare, however, would say that inequality in welfare outcomes is just if they are the result of choices. Since Louis *chose* to develop expensive preferences, he cannot demand compensation. Put differently, it is Louis' own fault that he can now only be happy if he drinks expensive wine. Dworkin could, according to Arneson, have argued for equal *opportunity* for welfare, and thereby have solved the problem. The argument about expensive taste thus shows that equality of welfare outcomes cannot be the right currency for egalitarians. It does not, however, show the same about *equality of opportunity to achieve welfare*. Arneson's claim is that this is precisely the thing those who are concerned with equality should distribute: Egalitarians must be concerned with giving everyone equal opportunity to welfare (Arneson 1989, 2000:506–508; Wolff 2007:130–131; Cohen 2011:13).

Cohen thinks Arneson's turn to equality of opportunity for welfare represents an improvement compared to Dworkin's resource equality. However, he still thinks that an adequate answer to the question of what it is that we should distribute must incorporate both resources and welfare. He therefore claims that *equal access to advantage* is what egalitarians must aspire to (Cohen 2011:13). That is the right currency and the right answer to Sen's "equality of what"-question.

Cohen illustrates this by introducing an example. Tiny Tim is paralysed, but has an unusually strong right arm that is very painful to use.[4] Nevertheless, he is an extraordinarily happy person. Egalitarians will, Cohen thinks, compensate Tim for his need for a wheelchair, and do so without asking about his level of welfare. We do not, as egalitarians, need to know whether Tim is happy or unhappy to claim that the state must cover the cost of his wheelchair. This is a decisive argument against (pure) welfare egalitarianism because what matters is not Tim's welfare, but the fact that he needs a wheelchair. Tim also needs strong medication to relieve the pain in his arm. Egalitarians think these expenses should be compensated for or covered by the community. This is a decisive argument against (pure) resource egalitarians, because the resources needed to relieve the pain cannot be understood as a compensation for a lack of resources (Cohen 2011:15–16).[5]

We need a currency—or an answer to what it is that should be distributed—that is sufficiently broad to cover resources (needed to buy a wheelchair) and allow us to compensate pain (e.g., through subsidizing expensive medicines). Therefore, Cohen writes, equal access to advantage is what a just society must ensure, where advantage is understood as "a heterogeneous collection of desirable states of the person reducible neither to his resources bundle nor to his welfare level" (Cohen 2011:59, quoted from Miller 2015:135).[6]

Cohen admits that the example with Tiny Tim is strange. However, there are examples in the real world that capture the same intuition. People who suffer from arthritis are less able than others to move, and experience pain in connection with movement. In these kinds of cases, resource egalitarians are unable to explain why we should compensate for pain (expensive medicine), while welfare egalitarians are unable to explain why we should compensate for the difficulties of moving about (Cohen 2011:17).

Hence, on Cohen's view, egalitarians should strive for equal access to advantage.[7] Furthermore, an egalitarian theory must remove inequalities which are not due to individual choice (Cohen 2008:7–8). This is Cohen's egalitarian principle, and we shall return to how it may be interpreted. Beyond this, Cohen does not provide us with any detailed image of the ideal of equal access to advantage. The important point is that lack of resources and lack of welfare are two different kinds of inequalities, and that a satisfactory answer to the question of what we should distribute must address both kinds of lack or disadvantage (Cohen 2011:18).

The egalitarian principle forms the basis of Cohen's criticism of the market. According to Cohen, capitalist markets distribute advantages arbitrarily and in violation of justice. At the same time, the market coerces people into relating strategically to each other, thus undermining community.

Equality and community

Cohen's alternative involves a defence of certain aspects of socialist thinking. Cohen develops this alternative in his book *Why Not Socialism?*. To illustrate how socialists think about justice, Cohen asks us to imagine a camping trip: You, and I, and some friends go camping. We bring coffee, a canoe, fishing rods, and tackle, and a number of other things to make up a nice camping trip. These items are privately owned. During the trip, however, we share them between us without thinking about who owns what. We distribute different tasks between us, so that some fish, some cook, and some do the dishes.

We try to share our things equally, and we distribute tasks so that everyone has a chance to do what she or he likes. In such a setting, claims Cohen, we take equality and reciprocity for granted.

To show that people on a camping trip would in fact prefer ideals built on equality and community, Cohen gives a few examples: Assume that Harry is both good at and enjoys fishing. He gets lots of fish, but when the fish is to be distributed among the campers, Harry claims that he is entitled to the best pieces. Or assume that Sylvia goes for a walk in the woods and chances upon a large apple tree. She returns to the campers and demands to have fewer chores than the rest in exchange for giving us access to the apples she found. Both Harry's and Sylvia's demands for extra rewards annoy the other campers; Harry's because he demands rewards for doing something he is good at and likes doing, and Sylvia's because her claim is founded on pure luck. Both of their claims for reward conflict with community ideals based on equality and reciprocity (Cohen 2009:3–8).

According to Cohen, two principles are realized on the camping trip: A principle of socialist equality of opportunity and a principle of community. When both these principles are realized, we may speak of society as just. Cohen employs the two principles as starting points to justify the claim that a just distribution is fundamentally an equal distribution. It may therefore seem like Cohen is defending what we above called strict equality. However, he also claims that it cannot be the task of the state to compensate for the results of choice. If a person freely and voluntarily chooses not to work, it cannot be the task of the state to transfer advantages to this person.

The principle of socialist equality of opportunity is identical with the egalitarian principle. This principle is strongly inspired by Dworkin, and only allows inequalities due to taste and choice. If Peer and Paal have the same level of talent and are raised in the same kind of environment, one could allow inequalities that, for example, were due to Peer choosing to work twice as much as Paal. Inequalities due to talent and the inequalities that follow from one's socio-economic background, however, must be compensated for. The state must ensure redistribution from those with a high level of talent to those with lower levels of talent; the talent with which one is born is not something for which one is responsible. Correspondingly, those who have grown up in a nurturing environment must transfer advantages to those who have not grown up in a nurturing environment. The environment in which one grows up will have consequences for what skills one develops, and these skills will be rewarded by access to advantages. However, given that one cannot be held morally responsible for the environment in which one is raised, it is reasonable that those who grow up under favourable conditions transfer advantages to those who grow up under less favourable conditions. The principle of socialist equality of opportunity therefore corrects for inborn and social differences (Cohen 2009:17).

However, if the principle of socialist equality of opportunity is not supplemented by a second principle, it will allow a kind of inequality that may threaten community. It will, for example, allow inequality due to option luck, that is, risk taken voluntarily. Cohen uses gambling as an example. Peer and Paal both have €100 each. They agree to toss a coin for €50. Peer wins, and is left with €150, while Paal is left with €50. This kind of inequality is compatible with socialist equality of opportunity because that ideal allows inequalities due to choice.

However, Cohen thinks that in a market economy, the kind of choice due to option luck will potentially result in very large inequalities. Moreover, there is a crucial difference between the kind of gambling involved in a coin toss and choices made in the market. While gambling can be voluntary, the market economy *forces* us to make choices that involve option luck. As Cohen puts it, "the market... is a casino from which it is difficult to escape, and the inequalities that it produces are tainted with injustice for that reason" (Cohen 2009: 33). To illustrate, if Peer and Paal, with the same talent and background, choose different professions, they may end up with a very unequal distribution of resources. Say that Peer chooses to become a painter, while Paal chooses to become a carpenter. Due to unexpected changes in the weather conditions, Peer can only paint for six months each year, while Paal can work year round. As a consequence, Paal ends up making twice as much as Peer. Because the market economy is full of these kinds of coincidences, inequality will become significant:

Hence, Cohen objects both to inequalities that result from option luck and to inequalities that seem to arise from option luck, but which are really the result of forced risk-taking, and therefore unjust. Cohen therefore thinks that we must supplement the socialist principle of equality of opportunity with a principle of community.

The justification for the principle of community is that community is threatened by the large inequalities that can result from option luck. We cannot be part of a genuine community if you make ten times as much as I do. If you do, our living conditions will be too different to support genuine community. We will, in a certain sense, inhabit different worlds. Cohen illustrates this claim with the bus example. Assume that I am rich, live a comfortable life, and drive a car to work every day. You are poor, either as a result of bad choices (you do not want to work) or as a result of option luck (with bad outcome). You must take the overcrowded bus to work every day. If I have to take the bus one day, say because my partner needs the car, I cannot say to you: "It is terrible that I have to take the bus today". We live in different worlds due to inequality, and because of this, my complaint will be completely unreasonable to you (Cohen 2009:35–36). The example is meant to show that community dissolves in the face of too extreme inequality. A society with less community will, to many, be a less good society.

Community, then, is an important value to Cohen. He thinks we should equalize inequalities that threaten community. However, there is also another way in which one can care about community. Cohen distinguishes between communal reciprocity and market reciprocity. Communal reciprocity is realized if I offer you a service not for what I get in return, but because you need or want my services. You offer me your services for the same reason. Communal reciprocity is therefore a part of the egalitarian ethos discussed above. Market reciprocity is characterized by services being offered to achieve rewards. The motive for actions in the market is often a mix of greed and fear (Cohen 2009:45). Other market actors are seen as an opportunity for self-enrichment (greed), or as a threat to my own success (fear). To Cohen, the kind of interaction encouraged by the market is a terrible way of interacting with other people.

As Cohen sees it, we have good reason to try to change society in a direction where equality, reciprocity, and community are better cared for than what is the case under capitalism. A socialist community is Cohen's solution. The camping trip example is meant to convince us that the values realized there offer an attractive vision for how society could be arranged in a better and more just way. However, Cohen also tries to pose two other fundamentally important questions: Is organizing society in accordance with socialist principles *desirable*, and is societal change based on these principles *feasible*?[8]

Is socialism desirable and feasible?

Let us deal with the first question first. Some would claim that the ideals of the camping trip are not attractive ideals at all, not even in a small-scale situation like that trip. These people do not reject the ideal of the camping trip because they are in favour of more inequality, or because they are in favour of treating people merely as means. However, they think that humans have a *right* to make individual choices, even if this leads to more inequality and may result in others being treated instrumentally. If one thinks that the ideals of the camping trip are not compatible with this right to make individual choices, one also will not think these ideals desirable in society. In response, Cohen points out that the campers have the right to individual choice, and that there is significant room for such choice also on a camping trip organized by the above mentioned ideals (Cohen 2009:47–48).

A more relevant objection to the claim that socialism is desirable runs as follows: Even if the ideals may be desirable on a small scale, society is sufficiently different from a camping trip to make the realization of camping trip ideals on a large scale undesirable. On most camping trips, participants are likely to be friends, and one cannot be friends with everyone in society. Cohen replies that the point is not for everyone to be friends, but that reciprocity and community are ideals most people will subscribe to.

In his treatment of the second question, that is, whether socialism can be brought into being, Cohen makes the following remark:

> We socialist don't know how to replicate camping trip procedures on a nationwide scale [...] But I do not think that we now know that we will never know how to do these things: I am agnostic on that score.
>
> (Cohen 2009:75–76)

And, we might add, the fact that we do not know is not in itself a sufficient reason for not trying to change society in the direction of socialism.

Cohen's strategy in discussing the question of feasibility is as follows: To show that fighting for socialist values is not a matter of all or nothing. It will be good if one achieves *more* equality, reciprocity, and community, even if a completely socialist society cannot be realized. We need the socialist ideal, but we must not refrain from trying to achieve smaller, gradual advances while waiting for the more fundamental change.

The crucial problem is whether socialism would work if we were given the opportunity to realize a society based on such ideals. Our problem is thus a problem of *design*. Cohen here discusses a widely debated proposal often known as market socialism. One version of this proposal runs as follows: At birth, all citizens have the right to a share of the total value of the country paid out as stocks. They may then trade their stocks in a stock market, and in that way achieve more stocks than others. They may also take out dividends, but the stocks cannot be exchanged for money. In this manner, citizens cannot exchange their stocks for expensive luxury goods. When a citizen dies, all the stocks of that person are remitted to the state to be distributed to new citizens as their share of the total value of the country. The labour market is kept as it is, thus giving rise to certain inequalities, but the inequalities will not be exacerbated by a few people owning large shares of the country's values, as is the case in present-day market capitalism (Cohen 2009:70–71).

This suggestion is developed by the economist John Roemer. He claims that a system like this would be no less efficient than market capitalism. Many would question this assertion. When stocks cannot be converted to money, which may then be used to buy goods, it is likely that the motivation to work hard to increase one's share of capital would sink, reducing efficiency. However, let us not dwell on this question, and instead follow Cohen in simply assuming that Roemer is wrong about efficiency: Even if efficiency were to drop with this market socialist stock system, this does not mean that it is rational to stick with market capitalism. After all, efficiency is only one of several values. Many would be willing to give up some efficiency in exchange for equality and community.[9]

Discussion

I will here limit myself to discussing Cohen's criticism of Rawls, and then bring forth a tension between the two principles of justice defended by Cohen in *Why Not Socialism?*. In closing, I briefly discuss the implications of Cohen's position for just taxation.

Cohen's criticism of Rawls can be summed up in two statements[10]:

1 Rawls' theory allows for large inequalities.
2 Rawls is too focused on the basic structure while ignoring how people relate to each other.

With regards to 1, Cohen discusses the difference principle, while claim 2 is formulated as if Rawls' entire theory allows for large inequalities. Cohen is, of course, aware that the difference principle is not Rawls' only principle. Still, Cohen does not make a detailed analysis of what ideal of justice follows if one understands the difference principle as a part of a comprehensive theory of justice. Cohen's criticism therefore concerns *applications* of the principle more than the principle itself (to the extent that the difference principle was never meant to be understood in isolation).

At the same time, there is no doubt that Cohen is right about there being ambiguities in the way Rawls formulated the difference principle in *Theory*. The weak interpretation of the principle led many to think that Rawls' theory could be used to justify large inequalities. Some of Rawls' own statements supported such interpretations. Cohen, however, has shown that such an interpretation of the principle is not in the egalitarian spirit of Rawls' thinking. When this point is coupled with the need to see the two principles (in Rawls) as a connected whole, the result is that one must read Rawls as what Thomas calls a left-Rawlsian (Thomas 2017:70). In other words, those who claim that large inequalities can be justified within a Rawlsian framework are wrong.

Thomas (2017) argues in favour of a holistic interpretation of Rawls' theory that not only sees the principles as parts of a package, but also focuses on the context in which these principles are to be implemented. This context is property owning democracy. Property owning democracy implies a limitation on the amount of resources the wealthiest may possess, while at the same time ensuring necessary capital for the worst off. Inequalities must, in other words, be kept within strict boundaries. This follows from what we called procedural background justice. *Justice as fairness* understood as a comprehensive package implemented in the right context does *not* allow large inequalities. If, however, one were to focus too single-mindedly on the difference principle, one might draw the kind of conclusions drawn by Cohen—but that would mean mistaking part of Rawls' theory for the whole (Thomas 2017:xviii).

Then to assertion 2: Rawls is an institutionalist. He is concerned with how institutions are organized, and his form of institutionalism entails that institutions shape the attitudes of the citizens who live under them. Cohen's criticism presupposes that Rawls does not care that a just society also requires people to treat each other more justly. Thomas, in my view, makes a convincing case that Cohen is wrong about this. Cohen is wrong to understand Rawls as if he is developing principles that only apply to the basic structure and not to individuals: "The choice is [...] between applying principles of justice to individuals (and not to social structure) or to individuals via social structure" (Thomas 2017:81). Rawls pursues the latter strategy. Putting institutions at the centre does not mean excluding how individuals relate to each other.

This is a complex argument, and we need examples to understand what it means. Piketty has argued that when the tax level in the US was 80% for the top incomes, those with highest income did not have very strong incentives to negotiate for even higher pay; much of their salary (including any raise) would disappear in tax anyway. When the taxes were heavily reduced with Reagan in the 1980s, this changed, and top managers with high salaries had increased incentives to push for even more money (Piketty 2014:335, 512). In the same way, one could imagine that, if the background structure keeps inequalities within strictly defined boundaries where those who earn and own the most are only allowed to earn and own *some* more, but not much more, than others, the incentives will also change. Demanding much more than others will not get you very much more, and so people will change their demands. In time, one may hope that people also change their way of thinking by living under institutions that promote egalitarian relations. If that were to happen, we would have an example of institutions shaping peoples way of thinking and acting. This is an important point, and one to which we will return in the concluding chapter.

Does this mean that Rawls defends an egalitarian ethos? Thomas thinks yes, and he claims that the difference principle has a role to play in how the right institutions may shape people's perceptions and motivate them to action. Rawls' writes:

> The difference principle [...] does seem to correspond to a natural meaning of fraternity: namely to the idea of not wanting to have greater advantages unless this is to the benefit of others who are less well off. The family, in its ideal conception and often in practice, is one place where the principle of maximizing the sum of advantage is rejected. Members of a family commonly do not wish to gain unless they can do so in ways that further the interest of the rest. Now wanting to act on the difference principle has precisely this consequence. Those better circumstanced are willing to have their greater advantages only under a scheme in which this works out for the benefits of the less fortunate.
>
> (Rawls 1999a quoted from Thomas 2017:142)

On Thomas' interpretation of Rawls, a just society requires an institutional structure that only allows limited inequalities. This institutional structure can only be maintained and stabilized over time if citizens are motivated by an egalitarian ethos that includes reciprocal solidarity, and where the better off do their best without demanding extra rewards.[11] Cohen's two claims are thereby refuted. Rawls' theory does not allow large inequality, and Rawls is not exclusively concerned with the basic structure; he also has a theory of how people should relate to each other.

To sum up, and to make an explicit connection to the exposition in Chapter 1: Rawls is an adherent of pure procedural background justice. This means continuous interventions into the market to ensure the worst off capital and to limit how much the wealthiest may possess. The justification for this is given through the first principle and the principle of fair equality of opportunity. When we see Rawls' principles combined, it becomes clear that contrary to what many have claimed from only looking at the difference principle, the two principles do not allow large inequalities. From this arises the question of what role the difference principle plays. The answer to that question brings us to the egalitarian ethos. The difference principle expresses the egalitarian ethos, or that form of solidarity between citizens that is necessary for the basic structure to be maintained over time.[12] This is why it makes sense, from a Rawlsian perspective, to agree to Cohen's claim that a just society requires "both just rules and just personal choice within the framework set by just rules". Contrary to what Cohen thinks, this claim is compatible with Rawls.

We will now discuss Cohen's constructive contribution, that is, his defence of the two principles of justice as they are presented in *Why Not Socialism?*. What is the relationship between the two principles defended by Cohen? He writes: "The community principle constrains the operation of the egalitarian principle by forbidding certain inequalities that the egalitarian principle permits" (Cohen 2009:12). The bus example, given above, shows how this limitation is justified by appeal to the negative consequences of inequality in separating people into different worlds. Cohen therefore thinks that we must equalize differences that may threaten community.

There is a potential tension between the egalitarian principle and the principle of community. Or, put differently, there may be a tension between the luck egalitarian and the socialist elements in Cohen's thinking. The luck egalitarian element says that differences due to circumstances within control should be preserved, while the socialist element says that differences that threaten community must be removed. If the community principle is trump, in the sense that inequalities due to circumstances within control must be equalized to avoid dissolving community, it is difficult to see what role, if any, circumstances like how much one chooses to work can play in Cohen's socialist ideal society.

Let the following example serve as an illustration of this point: Assume a situation in which there is full equality. Peer and Paal, who have the same skills and social background, choose differently when it comes to how much effort they put into education and work. Peer studies hard and becomes a doctor. As a doctor, he makes a lot of money, and also chooses to work overtime. After ten years, he has accumulated a significant fortune. Paal also studies, but does not read much, and does not get into medical schools like he wanted. Instead, he becomes a nurse, works 37.5 hours per week, and after ten years has bought a flat, but is otherwise financially cramped. According to the egalitarian principle, the difference between Peer and Paal that is due to the number of hours put into studies and work is just, and not something the state ought to equalize. However, according to the community principle, the inequality between Peer and Paal may negatively impact community, and hence be used as a justification of redistribution from Peer to Paal.

This example illustrates a possible tension between the principle of bearing the responsibility of one's own choices and the principle of community. The way Cohen argues in *Why Not Socialism?*, it seems as if Peer would have to surrender a significant portion of his income even though the difference between Peer and Paal is purely the result of choice. What space remains for differences due to choice in a socialist society is therefore unclear. Put differently, Cohen lacks a discussion of how the two principles are to be weighed.[13]

There is, however, an obvious reply Cohen could give to the objection we have just outlined. Cohen can reply that if there were an egalitarian ethos in society, no one would prefer to lie on the couch. In a society where there is an operative egalitarian ethos, people would do their best, and receive according to what they need. An egalitarian ethos will in itself dampen inequalities by stopping people from lying on the couch or from demanding extra pay. Cohen's critics can reply that this ethos is completely unrealistic given what we know about human nature.

What is there to say about Cohen's position when it comes to taxation? Cohen does not provide a detailed analysis of different tax bases, and has not participated in debates specifically about tax. However, it is clear that his position will have important implications for just taxation. If people to a greater extent were motivated by an egalitarian ethos, this would have radical implications for how the state could use tax as a means to achieve a more egalitarian society. For example, Cohen points out that:

> The harder productive people bargain, within any state-imposed structure of rules, and the less willing they are to perform with industry and zeal under high marginal taxation, the worse off the worst off will, in general be. If economically productive people who accept the difference principle consequently accommodate themselves to very high redistributive taxation, then the worst off would be markedly better off than if the productive go abroad or knock off early in response to high taxation. (Cohen 2008:17)

An egalitarian ethos, in other words, will be relevant to taxation in two ways: It will make the most talented accept a much higher income tax. If this is the case, there will, as Cohen points out (Cohen 2008: 27–30), be no opportunity to justify income tax cuts by saying that this will make everyone better off. The justification for such cuts is normally that it will make talented people work harder. But if an egalitarian ethos exists, people would do their best even with very high tax rates. Furthermore, an egalitarian ethos will also entail that those who have capital will accept wealth taxes without taking their money and moving abroad. In both cases, an egalitarian ethos will, according to Cohen, contribute to a significant improvement of the situation of the worst off, and it will do so through a transformation of how the tax mechanism permits a radical kind of redistribution. We shall return to this point in Part 3.

Further reading

In *The Political Philosophy of G.A. Cohen*, Nicholas Vrousalis attempts to reconstruct a unity in Cohen's writing that is not originally present, because Cohen's ideas were shaped in a constant polemic with others. Alexander Kaufmann's (ed) *Distributive Justice and Access to Advantage: G.A. Cohen's Egalitarianism* contains a number of essays by some of the most important contributors to the debate about Cohen's political philosophy. Louis-Philippe Hodgson's *Cohen's Community: Beyond the Liberal State?* provides an interesting discussion based on the premise that the best conception of equality and justice is to be found somewhere between Rawls and Cohen. In my view, Hodgson does a good job of clarifying how one can understand Cohen's principle of community.

Philosophy bites podcast: G.A. Cohen on Inequality of Wealth.

Notes

1 Another way of putting this is to say that Cohen delivers an internal critique of Rawls; Cohen shares the fundamental ideals represented by Rawls and gives an interpretation of these. In the later chapters of *Rescuing*, however, Cohen dissociates himself more and more from the fundamental ideals in Rawls. We may therefore say that he progresses from an internal to an external critique of Rawls.
2 See Carens (2015) for a discussion of Cohen's egalitarian ethos.
3 *On the Currency* was published in 1989. In the following, I will quote the reprinted version of Cohen's book (2011) with the same title.
4 Tiny Tim is originally a figure from the Charles Dickens' *A Christmas Carol.*
5 This criticism also goes for Arneson's position in the following way: Tiny Tim, because of his disposition to be happy, has equal opportunity for welfare. However, in spite of that, egalitarians would give him a wheelchair, and Cohen points out that this cannot be explained with reference to a position that defends equality of opportunity for welfare as that which is to be equalized.
6 Compared to Arneson, then Cohen prefers advantage to welfare. Additionally, Cohen speaks of equal access while Arneson speaks of equal opportunity. Is this a relevant difference? Cohen thinks it is. The reason is that we usually do not include personal traits when evaluating which opportunities someone has. Usually, we will say that a stupid person and a smart one have the same opportunities even though there will be significant differences in how they utilize these opportunities. Egalitarians, as Cohen, will point out that personal abilities will determine which access someone has to do valuable things. And they will think that while the stupid person has the same opportunity as does the smart one, their access to advantage will be different due to factors outside their control, namely how smart they are. Therefore, we must equalize this inequality (Cohen 2011:14).
7 Advantage must not be understood as advantage *over others*. Advantage, Cohen is careful to point out, must be understood non-competitively (Cohen 2011:14, fn. 18).
8 See Ronzoni (2012), with the telling title "Life is not a Camping Trip – On the Desirability of Cohenite Socialism", for a criticism of the way Cohen uses the camping trip as a starting point for thinking about justice in general.
9 In the book *Why Not Capitalism?* – which is a parody of Cohen's *Why Not Socialism?* – Jason Brennan claims that Cohen makes an elementary mistake in comparing an idealized socialism with a realistic description of capitalism (Brennan 2014).

10 My defence of Rawls is indebted to Thomas (2017; Chapters 3 and 5).
11 For an earlier discussion of the institution vs. ethos issue, see Joshua Cohen (2001) and G.A. Cohen's reply in Cohen (2008:379–381).
12 This is giving the difference principle a different role to that normally ascribed to it, and the interpretation may therefore seem/be perceived as unreasonable. However, note that Rawls himself remarks that the basic ideal presented in *justice as fairness* makes the role of the difference principle somewhat unclear (Rawls 2003:98). In my view (therefore), Thomas' interpretation is reasonable.
13 One could also say that there is a tension between the Cohen who, in 1999, wrote *On the Currency*, and the Cohen who 20 years later wrote *Why Not Socialism?*. David Miller (2015) has argued that Cohen, who started out a socialist, made a mistake in letting himself get caught up in the debate that arose in the wake of Dworkin's *Equality* articles. According to Miller, luck egalitarianism was contrary to Cohen's most deeply held beliefs. Miller points to formulations in Cohen's later writing that indicate that Cohen found luck egalitarianism paradoxical, and Miller uses these formulations to defend a stronger thesis: Luck egalitarianism is inconsistent.

5 The capability approach

Amartya Sen and Martha Nussbaum

Dworkin's discussion of equality, and the way his central distinctions were taken up by Cohen and others, constitutes one of the most important debates in political philosophy after Rawls' *A Theory of Justice*. The contributors to this debate opened up for new theoretical and empirical work. In this chapter, we will look at a different approach that has put a different set of questions on the agenda, and which has undoubtedly also served as a springboard for other's works (Wolff 2007:125). We will discuss the capability approach, which was first developed by Amartya Sen (f. 1933) and refined by Martha Nussbaum (f. 1947).

Sen's most significant contribution to distributive justice is not a rule or principle we should use when distributing something. Rather, his contribution consists in a clarification of what this something is. In other words, he provides a novel answer to the equality of what-question. What is it that we should distribute if we care about just distribution? So far, we have seen that Rawls defends primary goods while Dworkin thinks that what should be distributed is resources, and Cohen introduces the concept of access to advantage. All three are critical of a one-sided focus on welfare. Here, we shall look closer at how Sen and Nussbaum supplement this picture by adding a new alternative: Capabilities.

The capability approach is not just relevant because it gives a new answer to the equality of what-question. In addition to this, it offers a broad normative framework that can be used to evaluate people's quality of life and to assess different policy choices. The capability approach is used in fields like development studies, welfare economics, and political philosophy, but the theoretical basis was developed in economics (by Sen) and in philosophy (by Sen and Nussbaum). Since 1990, the UN has published their Human Development Report, partly based on the capability approach. Both Sen and Nussbaum highlight Aristotle, Adam Smith, and Karl Marx as important sources of inspiration (Robeyns 2005, 2006).

In this chapter, I will start by saying something about what capabilities are, and then go on to show how the capability approach provides a new answer to the question of what it is that is to be distributed. On the basis of this understanding of the capability approach, we will proceed to contrast Sen's version with Nussbaum's. The most important difference between the two is Nussbaum's claim that the capability approach must result in an objective list identifying the most important capabilities, a claim which Sen rejects. An important feature of the capability approach is that it has formed the basis for a number of empirical studies. Because a knowledge of these studies will help us understand the approach, I will also give a brief review of some of the ways that the normative framework has been applied. I also briefly discuss what role political philosophy should have in questions of distributive justice. Here, I use Sen's criticism of Rawls as a starting point. Finally, I point out a frequent misunderstanding that sees the capabilities approach as a complete theory of justice, and I discuss what role the capability approach can have for our question of just taxation.

Functionings and capabilities

The capability approach is focused on quality of life and freedom—on the real opportunities of individuals to achieve the life they have reason to value. How can we compare the quality of life of different people? Sen claims that we must look at what people are capable of *being* and *doing*. The question of what *functionings* people achieve is therefore of fundamental importance. Functionings are things one can be or do. Some functionings are basic, such as being healthy, being able to move, or being well fed. Other functionings are more complex, such as achieving self-respect or participating in a community (Sen 1993:31, 2005:4–5). The list of functionings is long, and we shall elaborate on it later. The crucial point now is Sen's claim that functionings are necessary elements for evaluating a person's quality of life (Sen 2005:4–5).

Functionings then are what a person achieves or is able to be or do. Capabilities are a person's *opportunity* to achieve functionings. Or, put differently, functionings are realizations of capabilities; what a person actually is or does. Capabilities are opportunities to choose to be or do something (Sen 2005:5). We can use one of Sen's own examples to illustrate these notions. Imagine a person who decides to go on a fast. This person has the opportunity or capability to be well fed, but chooses to fast. Compare this with someone who does not have access to food. This person lacks the capability to be well fed (Sen 2005:8, 2009a:237). Hence, the capabilities of a given person are the set of functionings a person has access to. As the example shows, two people may realize the same functioning, while their capabilities differ widely. Both of these persons are hungry, but one of them has chosen to be hungry, and that is an important difference.

Understanding the distinction between functionings and capabilities is important. Sen writes:

> Perhaps the most primitive notion in this approach concerns "functionings" Functionings represent parts of the state of a person – in particular the various things that he or she manages to do or be in leading a life.

> The capability of a person reflects the alternative combinations of functionings the person can achieve, and from which he or she can choose one collection.
>
> (Sen 1993:31)

Capabilities are opportunities, and the capability approach is concerned with facilitating people's choice to realize (a broad range of) different functionings. The capability "religious freedom" does not tell you to be religious, but that practicing religion is one of several possibilities that you may choose to realize. Sen is interested in the individual's capacity for freedom, and capabilities can be understood as the freedom to achieve the functionings a person holds to be valuable. Like Arneson and Cohen, Sen is concerned with opportunities, not obligatory functions.

Sen prefers to talk of sets of capabilities rather than of single capabilities. Even though it may at times appear reasonable to single out particular capabilities, the capability approach is primarily concerned with the opportunity of the individual to achieve different combinations of functionings (Sen 2009a:233): "The capability of a person reflects the alternative combinations of functionings the person can achieve, and from which he or she can choose one collection" (Sen 1993:31).

The capabilities with which Sen is concerned are intentionally generic. The opportunity or capability of having a safe place to live may be realized differently in different cultures. Countries where the climate is cold need other dwellings than do countries with tropical climate. Hence, the theory is constructed so as to allow the generic capabilities identified by the approach to be differently applied or realized in different cultural contexts.

Open approach

The focus on the general aspect of the capabilities illustrates an important point in Sen's version of the approach. It is open to being used in different contexts. The name "capability approach" was chosen in favour of "capability theory" because Sen wanted to establish an open framework that can be used from different perspectives (Robeyns 2016). This openness is also expressed in how capabilities are to be distributed. Sen declines to address this question by specifying a principle of distribution. He does not say that all capabilities must be ensured equally, or that some or all capabilities must be ensured sufficiently. Sen chooses this openness to ensure that the approach is sufficiently flexible to account for differences in the democratic decision procedures in the contexts where it is to be applied (Sen 2009a:232, 2009b:514). In *The Idea of Justice*, Sen repeatedly points out that the goal should not be to arrive at a closed theory, but rather to offer tools that can be used by, for example, people who have different opinions about what principles of justice and which capabilities should be included (Sen 2009a:89, 91).

In principle, therefore, we may imagine very different applications of the capability approach, from those who think that all capabilities should be distributed equally to those who defend less demanding principles of distribution.

Sen is also open to focusing on functionings or capabilities, or a combination of these. There are good arguments for both approaches. For example, Sen frequently makes the point that a focus on capabilities tends to portray the approach as liberal. One does not address the question of what capabilities are needed to live a good life; the important thing is to allow people to choose between a range of different possibilities (Robeyns 2006:353).

However, there are also good reasons to focus on achieved functionings. Not everyone has equally good opportunities to make choices, and there are therefore those who want to focus on allowing everyone to achieve different functionings. When it comes to children, for example, we are not usually concerned with allowing children to choose whether to have an education. Here, then what is at stake is not the freedom to choose to have an education, but that a good society must ensure that everyone gets an education. Sen's point is that for each case, what matters most is an open question. Hence, the approach is neutral between applications that emphasize capabilities, functionings, or a mix of both (Robeyns 2006:353).

This also means that, even though Sen is very much concerned with the liberal aspect of the approach, facilitating people making their own choices, there are also less liberal versions of the approach which are more focused on the functionings that are achieved (the outcomes). If one is concerned with how people are actually doing, and not primarily on what they have the opportunity to be, then one should focus on functionings. That said, it is obviously true that the question of what capabilities people have is an important question for research. However, it has proved difficult to create solid datasets on people's capabilities, with the result that the most important quantitative studies that have come out of the capabilities approach have had to focus on functions.[1]

A related point, made by Robeyns, is how the capability approach emphasizes responsibility. The capabilities approach can be sensitive to responsibility in a way that would satisfy any luck egalitarian: Everyone should be given equal opportunity in the form of capabilities, and be held responsible for what they choose to do. This requires the approach to focus on capabilities rather than functionings. However, whether responsibility should be assigned weight is a matter of debate among defenders of the capability approach (Robeyns 2006:353).

Sen also does not want to specify which capabilities one should focus on. The theoretician is not the right person to write out a list of important capabilities, Sen claims; that is a job for citizens. He writes:

> What I am against is the fixing of a cemented list of capabilities, which is absolutely complete (nothing can be added to it) and totally fixed (it

> could not respond to public reasoning and to the formation of social values). I am a great believer in Theory [...]But pure theory cannot "freeze" a list of capabilities for all societies for all time to come, irrespective of what the citizens come to understand and value. That would be not only a denial of the reach of democracy, but also a misunderstanding of what pure theory can do.
>
> (Sen 2004:78)

Sen's point is that such lists must be developed for different purposes, and hence it would be counterproductive to argue for the fixation of one set of functionings and capabilities (to the exclusion of all others). As we saw above, it matters to Sen that the capability approach is also adaptable to different cultural contexts, which is yet another reason not to formulate a list. Sen agrees that in certain contexts, such as in a country with extreme poverty, one could get quite far by specifying a few capabilities. In other contexts, however, such as in developed economies, one would need longer, more comprehensive lists (Sen 1993:31).

Using the capability approach as a starting point, one can evaluate specific policy decisions based on how they affect people's capabilities (Robeyns 2005:95). One could, for example, ask whether the budget ensures people better access to education, or whether a revision of the constitution ensures (people) the opportunity for political participation. Because it offers a far more nuanced way of studying development compared to traditional methods, the approach has played an important role in development studies.

One of the basic aims of the capabilities approach is to develop an alternative measure for understanding development. Formerly, gross domestic product (GDP) per capita was used to measure the development of a country. Sen has pointed out a number of problems with this approach. The main problem, he argues, is that there is no simple correspondence between GDP per capita and quality of life. A country may have a high per capita GDP and yet poor quality of life. This may be seen by looking at, for example, life expectancy (a frequent proxy for quality of life) compared to GDP per capita. Many countries have high per capita GDP compared to other countries, while at the same time their life expectancies are lower than that of those other countries (Sen 2005:3–4).

An equally important problem is that GDP per capita does not consider the many aspects that need to be taken into consideration when evaluating quality of life. To say anything about how people in a country are doing, how they are developing, one must, according to the capability approach, take into consideration a number of factors such as health, education, political freedoms, religious freedoms, and so on. GDP per capita is one-dimensional; we need to take into consideration a number of factors. Add to this the fact that GDP per capita does not consider the distribution (of goods in society), and we end up with a measure that is badly adapted to measuring quality of life. This last point may be illustrated with the case of South Africa under apartheid, which had high per capita GDP and might therefore seem like a well-developed country, but where only a tiny part of the population had access to the goods disposed by the country (as a whole).

Criticism of primary goods and welfare

We may now turn to the question of what it is that is to be distributed.[2] The question posed by Sen in *Equality of What?* is that *if* we see equality as a distributive ideal, we need a currency that allows us to compare how different people are doing. In that way, we may decide whether they are equal or unequal (Arneson 2000:498). Sen *does not* argue that we should commit ourselves to equality as a distributive ideal. What he says is that *if* we do, then we have to ask ourselves in respect of what it is that we should be equal.

The capability approach represents an alternative to welfare, resources, and primary goods.[3] Sen tries to arrive at an answer somewhere between primary goods and welfare (Cohen 2011:47–48). If, for example, we are to find out how someone is doing with respect to food, it is not sufficient to look just at the amount of food that person has access to, as one does when emphasising primary goods. It is also not sufficient to look at the utility that the person gets from eating. Instead, we must look at that person's nutritional level (Sen 1993:43). Hence, Rawls' focus on primary goods is problematic because it overlooks the fact that different people need different amounts of food. Someone who weighs 100 kg will normally need more than someone who weighs 50 kg.

Sen thus thinks that one crucial difference between primary goods and the capability approach is that the former is insufficiently sensitive to differences between people (Moss 2014:779). We must look closer at this criticism.

Primary goods, writes Sen:

> suffers from fethishist handicap in being concerned with goods, and even though the list of goods is specified in a broad and inclusive way, encompassing rights, liberties, opportunities, income, wealth and the social basis of self-respect, it still is concerned with good things rather than what these good things *do* to human beings.
>
> (Sen 1979:218, emphasis in the original)

We cannot, Sen writes, and thereby rehashes an argument we have already discussed, simply distribute goods equally to a disabled and a normally abled person, because the former must be given more goods than the latter to be able to do the same things. Instead of fetishizing primary goods, that is, treating primary goods as if they solve all problems, we should be concerned about what someone is able to do.[4]

When we compare how people are doing, we must evaluate what they are actually able to be and do. It is not sufficient to compare what income or what things a person has access to. People have very different abilities to make use of primary goods. Put differently: People vary in their ability to *convert* a primary good into a function. Norwegians who, as we say in Norway, are "born with skis on their feet" will be able to use these skis to get from A to B much more efficiently than, say, Greek people with no experience in skiing.

Therefore, it is important to distinguish between primary goods and what a person can do with these goods; how the person can convert these resources into important functionings. In the literature, one usually distinguishes between three different conversion factors (Robeyns 2005:99). The kind discussed above is *personal conversion factors*. To people from Greece, having a pair of skis available will only marginally improve their mobility, because they do not have the personal abilities needed to make use of them. *Social conversion factors* relate to one's ability to utilize resources depending on social relations. People who live in neighbourhoods with high rates of crime will have to use more resources on security than people who live in safer neighbourhoods. *Environmental conversion factors* relate to the geographical and climatic conditions under which one lives. A pair of skis is a poor contribution to Greek people's mobility regardless of their skills in using them. If they live in Athens, climatic conditions mean that they will have less use of the skis than would someone who lived in northern Norway.

Sen is also critical of the utilitarian approaches that have dominated welfare economics. These approaches typically focus on individual utility defined as satisfaction of preference. The problem is that people adapt their preferences to the level they expect to get satisfied. People learn not to desire things the political culture does not put them in position to achieve. Women without access to education, for example, do not typically report being dissatisfied with their level of education. Instead, they adapt to the way it is (Sen 2005:5). This objection to adaptive preferences is an important objection to welfare understood as preference satisfaction, and is therefore also important to the question of what is to be equalized.

Another fundamental goal for the capability approach is to develop measures to understand inequality in a better, more nuanced way. In the introductory chapter, we looked at inequalities in income and wealth. Sen is concerned that inequalities of income and wealth only capture part of the inequality that we should be concerned about. A one-sided focus on income and wealth may, for example, make us insensitive to important gender differences. If you look at the income of a household, you risk disregarding inequalities within that household. This is important because women are often those who are worst off in terms of what they are able to be and do.

The most important strength of the capability approach is that it provides a new basis for determining individual advantages. The capabilities approach, in other words, tells us what we should look for when comparing people to discover social inequality. The approach includes information about a number of conditions that are relevant to evaluating people's quality of life. In this way, the information basis for evaluations of how people are doing is expanded, and adherents of the approach argue that such a broad basis is necessary in order to take human diversity seriously (Robeyns 2016; Moss 2015:68).

Nussbaum's list

Martha Nussbaum has developed the capability approach in the direction of a theory of justice. She has presented what she sees as an objective list of what capabilities must be secured. Nussbaum takes as her starting point the constitutions of several different countries, and claims that the capability approach can specify a set of capabilities that must be included in any constitution. Citizens should be able to use the list to make demands of their governments about including principles into their constitution that secures the capabilities specified on the list. Her approach is therefore global or universalistic, in that she argues that the constitutions of all countries should ensure the same capabilities.

Nussbaum is critical of the general way in which Sen has developed the capability approach:

> It seems to me ... that Sen needs to be more radical than he has been so far in his criticism of the utilitarian accounts of well-being, by introducing an objective normative account of human functioning and by describing a procedure of objective evaluation by which functionings can be assessed for their contribution to the good human life.
>
> (Nussbaum quoted from Alkire 2002:12)

The list defended by Nussbaum contains ten capabilities. She maintains that all these capabilities must be secured in order to give people the opportunity to live their lives in dignity:

1 *Life*. Being able to live to the end of a human life of normal length; not dying prematurely, or before one's life is so reduced as to be not worth living.

2 *Bodily Health*: Being able to have good health, including reproductive health; to be adequately nourished; to have adequate shelter.

3 *Bodily Integrity*. Being able to move freely from place to place; to be secure against violent assault, including sexual assault and domestic violence; having opportunities for sexual satisfaction and for choice in matters of reproduction.

4 *Senses, Imagination, and Thought*. Being able to use the senses, to imagine, think, and reason – and to do these things in a "truly human" way, a way informed and cultivated by an adequate education, including, but by no means limited to, literacy and basic mathematical and scientific training; being able to use imagination and thought in connection with experiencing and producing works and events of one's own choice, religious, literary, musical, and so forth; being able to use one's mind in ways protected by guarantees of freedom of expression, with respect to both political and artistic speech, and freedom of religious exercise; being able to have pleasurable experience and to avoid non-beneficial pain.

5 *Emotions.* Being able to have attachments to things and people outside ourselves; to love those who love and care for us, to grieve at their absence; in general, to love, to grieve, to experience longing, gratitude, and justified anger. Not having one's emotional development blighted by fear and anxiety. (Supporting this capability means supporting forms of human association that can be shown to be crucial in their development.)
6 *Practical Reason.* Being able to form a conception of the good and to engage in critical reflection about the planning of one's life. (This entails protection for the liberty of conscience and religious observance.)
7 *Affiliation.*
   A Being able to live with and towards others, to recognize and to show concern for other human beings, to engage in various forms of social interaction; to be able to imagine the situation of another. (Protecting this capability means protecting institutions that constitute and nourish such forms of affiliation, and also protecting the freedom of assembly and political speech.)
   B Having the social bases of self-respect and non-humiliation; being able to be treated as a dignified being whose worth is equal to that of others. This entails provisions of non-discrimination on the basis of race, sex, sexual orientation, ethnicity, caste, religion, and national origin.
8. *Other Species.* Being able to live with concern for and in relation to animals, plants, and the world of nature.
9. *Play.* Being able to laugh, to play, to enjoy recreational activities.
10. *Control over One's Environment.*
   A *Political.* Being able to participate effectively in political choices that govern one's life; having the right of political participation, protection of free speech, and association.
   B *Material.* Being able to hold property (both land and movable goods) and having property rights on an equal basis with others; having the right to seek employment on an equal basis with others; having the freedom from unwarranted search and seizure. In work, being able to work as a human being, exercising practical reason and entering into meaningful relationship of mutual recognition with other workers (Nussbaum 2006:76–78).

The list is formulated in abstract terms, with the idea that it should be adapted to specific local conditions and given specific substantive content suitable to those. All the capabilities are considered central, and there is no priority between them (Nussbaum 2006:75). This turn to an objective list brings Nussbaum closer to Arneson's defence of objective opportunity for welfare.[5] Without specifying the capabilities approach in (such) a list, Nussbaum argues, one can argue that any capability has value. This, however, does not mean that the list is set in stone. It represents a proposal that must be continually revised by being tested and made the object of debate.

A life without these basic capabilities is a life without dignity. Nussbaum thus justifies the list with reference to our intuitions about what constitutes an undignified life. The list is also elaborated on the basis of cross-cultural empirical studies, and Nussbaum shows that many of the points on the list are already enshrined in the UN declaration of human rights and the constitutions of several countries. Moreover, the list is free-standing, in the sense that it does not depend on any metaphysical or religious doctrine (Nussbaum 2006:78–79; Langvatn 2010).[6]

In contrast to Sen, Nussbaum claims that the theorist must not only specify a list, but also what principles of justice should be applied. Some of the capabilities must be ensured equally, while others must be ensured sufficiently. The right to vote and religious freedom must be ensured equally, while material rights must be ensured sufficiently (Nussbaum 2011:40–41). Nevertheless, this does not, in Nussbaum's view, constitute a complete theory of justice, but rather a minimal theory of what one rightfully has claims to. Everyone must be ensured sufficient levels of all the capabilities, up to a certain threshold. When one has ensured a minimum in the form of a guarantee for all the capabilities on the list, the minimal theory of justice is compatible with different views on how one should distribute above the threshold (Nussbaum 2006:75).

It may therefore seem like Nussbaum is defending sufficientarianism. That, however, is not the case. As Lasse Nielsen (2014) has pointed out, it is important to note that Nussbaum should not be understood as a sufficientarian. Sufficientarianism consists in two theses, a positive and a negative. The positive thesis says that everyone must be ensured a sufficient level of whatever it is that is to be distributed. The negative thesis says that when everyone is above the sufficiency level, any further distribution is morally irrelevant.[7] Nussbaum defends the positive thesis, but is adamant that she does not defend the negative thesis (Nielsen 2014:22).[8] This illustrates that the approach is only a minimal theory of justice. It abstains from taking a position on how capabilities should be distributed when the threshold is reached and everyone is ensured sufficient capabilities to live a dignified life. We shall return to this point in the final discussion.

The capability approach in practice

In part because of the openness Sen has insisted upon when it comes to the general outline of the capability approach, there are a number of different ways to apply it. Best known is perhaps the way the UN's Human Development Reports use the capability approach as a general evaluation of the development of different countries, but the approach has also been used to evaluate development projects at smaller scales (particularly in developing countries), as well as to evaluate poverty and quality of life in advanced economies.[9] Furthermore, as Robeyns has recently pointed out, the UN's Millennium Development Goals and their successor the Sustainable Development Goals are influenced by the capability approach (Robeyns 2017b:159).

Some of Sen's early applications of the capability approach later became the guide for UN development studies. These studies pointed out, among other things, how different development ratings would look depending on whether one measured development using GDP or functionalities. In a 1985 study, Sen showed that despite Brazil and Mexico having seven times per capita GDP of Sri Lanka, Sri Lanka scored better than these two in terms of life expectancy, infant mortality rates, and child mortality rates (Sen 1985, quoted in Robeyns 2006:361). The UN Human Development Reports have similarly chosen a few simple functionings to describe development. They have developed a human development index (HDI), based on the functionings of life expectancy at birth, education, and GDP per capita (the last as a proxy for resources). The most central result of this index is that for certain countries, their place in the ranking varies dramatically depending on whether one ranks them according to GDP or HDI. Robeyns shows that, for example, in 2004, the United Arab Emirates was ranked as number 23 based on GDP and number 46 based on HDI. This was largely due to the country scoring poorly on education (Robeyns 2006:361).

Sabina Alkire (2002) has adapted the capability approach to be used to evaluate development projects in developing countries. The study is interesting along several dimensions. It included a participatory procedure to identify what functionings a given society perceived as valuable. By repeatedly asking, "why am I doing what I am doing", it was possible to identify life, knowledge, play, aesthetic experiences, friendship, practical reasonableness, and religion as the set of capabilities valued in small communities in Pakistan (Alkire 2002:25–84; Robeyns 2006:356). In this way, one could construct a distinct list of capabilities adapted to delimited communities.

Using the list as a starting point, Alkire could apply the capability approach to analyse three specific projects that aimed to reduce poverty. The ambition was to be able to judge how efficient the projects had been at achieving their goal. Alkire also looked at how the projects were evaluated differently depending on whether they were measured using the capability approach or a more traditional cost-benefit analysis.

The projects studied were goat herding, literacy training for women, and the production of rose garlands. Goat herding showed the best results in a cost-benefit analysis exclusively focused on economic benefit. Literacy training for women, however, proved to have no effect on women's income because there was no labour market for literate women. However, this project had a number of other positive effects that could not easily be quantified: Women who participated learned to trust their own skill and their equality with men. The literacy training project showed the strongest results when it came to advancing knowledge and independence. The main conclusion was therefore that even though goat herding showed the best economic results, it was not necessarily the best from the perspective of functionings and capabilities. Alkire concluded that from a capability perspective, none of the three projects is clearly better than the other two. A policy choice therefore "cannot be made on technical grounds but rather is a morally significant choice" (Alkire 2002:286, quoted in Robeyns 2006:362).

In a study of life quality for children between 0 and 11 years, Shelly Phipps compared Canada, the US, and Norway. The study used ten functionings: Low birth weight, asthma, accidents, activity limitations, difficulties concentrating, disobedience at school, bullying, anxiety, lying, and hyperactivity. Phipps found that overall Canada and the US were on a par: Children in Canada were better off in some functionings, while in others they did better in the US. Compared to Norway, however, both countries fell short: Norwegian children were better off in all ten functionings. This, in spite of the fact that the average income of the families studied were comparable across all three countries (Phipps 2002; Robeyns 2006:365).

What is the goal of political philosophy?

Before discussing the capability approach, we will allow ourselves a short discussion of a more general question. We have seen that Sen thinks that it is not up to the political philosopher to provide a complete theory of justice. Instead, he wants to open up for different approaches. Sen has also levelled another criticism against Rawls, which gives us the opportunity to briefly discuss a fundamental question, namely: How should we do political philosophy? We do not need, Sen claims, a comprehensive theory about what justice is, or what principles of justice would be preferred in a well-ordered society. What we need is to identify manifest injustices, and specific solutions to how these injustices may be avoided or remedied.

The starting point of this methodological debate is Rawls' suggestion for how we should do political philosophy (Simmons 2010:5; Stemplowska and Swift 2012; Valentini 2012:655). In *Theory*, Rawls introduced a distinction between ideal and non-ideal theory. Ideal theory, according to Rawls, works on the basis of two idealizing assumptions: That all agents act according to what justice demands of them, and that natural and historic conditions are favourable so that society is sufficiently economically and socially developed to allow for the realization of justice. The first assumption is about there being full support for the principles of justice, and that nearly everyone therefore "strictly complies with, and so abides by, the principles of justice" (Rawls 2001:13). The second assumption is that society must be sufficiently developed to allow the existence of justice; Rawls talks of this as an assumption of "favourable circumstances" (Rawls 1999a:216). To illustrate, if there is an extreme scarcity of resources in society so that life is a fight of all against all, justice cannot be realized. Based on these assumptions, an ideal theory develops principles for a well-ordered society. These principles are long-term goals for the development of society.

To Rawls, the task of political philosophy is to present a set of principles that is to regulate the basic structure of society. When the basic structure is established in accordance with these principles, the institutional framework of society is perfectly just. As an idea, this is what Rawls calls a realistic utopia, which is the best thing we can realistically hope for. The goal is to investigate what one can realize given the limitations in human moral and psychological nature, but also in our social institutions, and how people can live with them (Simmons 2010:7). Ideal theory "probes the limits of the realistically practicable" (Rawls 2001:13).

Non-ideal theory is theory under conditions were one of the two idealizing assumptions of ideal theory are not in place. Non-ideal theory asks how the long-term goals can be reached, and points out that this will normally happen gradually in a stepwise process. The point is to identify opportunities that move society in the direction of the long-term goal in a way that is morally defensible and efficient. Non-ideal theory therefore has the task of establishing principles that can bring us closer to the principles established in the ideal theory.

As a contrast to Rawls' theory, Sen defends what he calls a realization-focused, comparative approach to justice. Instead of asking what is just, Sen asks how justice can be promoted (Sen 2009a:7–9). He introduces an example to illustrate the advantage of the comparative approach: When we evaluate a painting by van Gogh against one by Picasso, we do not need to know that Mona Lisa is the best painting in the world. Knowledge about what constitutes the perfect painting is not necessary to choose between a van Gogh and a Picasso. Similarly, when it comes to questions of justice, we do not need to know what constitutes ideal justice to determine that a society in which there is famine and widespread illiteracy is more unjust than one without these problems, all other things being equal (Sen 2009a:100).

Within most fields, Sen writes, we manage by comparing alternatives without having a third standard to measure them against (Sen 2009a:101). The comparativist tries to fight *manifest injustice*, and Sen thinks that one does not need to know what ideally speaking is just in order to do so. People who fought slavery in the 18th and 19th century did not do so based on the idea that a world without slavery would be just with a capital J (Sen 2009a:21). In Sen's view, ideal theory may even be negative from the perspective of justice, because it takes our attention off what we should really care about, namely fighting manifest injustice (Sen 2006:226). In other words, Sen criticizes Rawls' view that non-ideal theory is secondary to ideal theory.

In my view, Sen misunderstands Rawls. He characterizes Rawls' theory as too idealistic or too utopian to be realized. That Rawls uses the term "ideal theory" about his own position may have contributed to the misunderstanding. "Ideal" may be associated with what is perfect and therefore unrealistic, and Rawls' use of the term may therefore have been misleading. For, ideal theory means something else, namely that one must make certain assumptions when providing a sketch of what a just society is.

Rawls uses the term "unrealistically utopian" about theories that cannot be realized. This is not the same as ideal theory. That is, we must not confuse ideal theories with unrealistically utopian theories. Indeed, ideal theory should be realistically utopian in Rawls' view: "Political philosophy is realistically utopian when it extends what are ordinary thought of as the limits of practical political possibility" (Rawls 1999b:6).

Simmons has defended Rawls' view of ideal theory as primary to non-ideal theory. Simmons' point is that without long-term goals, policies that seem like an improvement in terms of justice may in fact take us away from justice. What seems like an improvement may turn out to be a hindrance to achieving long-term goals. In this way, Simmons defends Rawls' claim that without ideal theory, non-ideal theory would lack a clear goal and direction (Simmons 2010:34–36; Stemplowska and Swift 2012:379). If there is manifest injustice that can be improved without ideal theory, and without risking moving away from what is just, then we could chose Sen's approach. The problem is deciding whether one is moving towards what is just if one does not have a theory of what justice is.

Nevertheless, some of Sen's examples can be used to defend his approach. If one is faced with unnecessary famine, or people being denied access to necessary medicine, it seems reasonable to attack the question of how to solve these problems directly without support from a theory of justice. In this context, the capability approach can be an important tool. However, this approach is less useful for a discussion of just tax. Here, there is no obvious manifest injustice. For questions of just taxation, then we need theories of justice.[10]

Discussion

Let us now return to a point made in the introduction. There, I wrote that a theory of justice consists of different parts, and that a comprehensive theory must (as a minimum) answer questions of what is to be distributed and of what principle is to be used to achieve a just distribution. The capability approach is not a complete theory of justice because it does not answer what principle should be used when distributing capabilities or functions. The approach does however provide an important answer to what it is that should be distributed. Nevertheless, to give a comprehensive evaluation of a theory, one must also know what principle of justice is defended (Arneson 2010:103) Thus, if someone says that the capabilities approach is their preferred theory of justice, they must also be able to answer what principle of justice they think the theory should be equipped with. Many overlook this point (Robeyns 2018:111).

Neither Sen nor Nussbaum can be said to develop complete theories of justice. Sen does not want to specify any principle of justice, and even though Nussbaum defends something that looks like a defence of sufficientarianism, she declines to say anything about the distribution beyond the threshold. To our purpose, this is important. A complete theory of justice, such as *justice as fairness*, has more to offer on questions of what constitutes just taxation. Rawls' theory says that we must both limit the share of the richest by, among other things, taxing inheritance, but also make sure that the worst off are provided with capital. Nussbaum's theory can tell us to ensure a social minimum, but cannot provide guidelines for whether we should impose limitations on those who have the most.[11] This is an important limitation, and speaks in favour of comprehensive theories of justice that can tell us something about the need for equalization, both at the top and the bottom of the distribution.[12]

Nevertheless, the capability approach is relevant to questions of just taxation. The normative framework of the approach provides us with a different basis from which to understand inequality. This is important. Instead of looking at what resources people have, we should look at their capabilities. Briefly put, we can get a different understanding of who are the worst off by using the capability approach. This is the reason why this approach has been so influential in the understanding and measurement of poverty, and the same insight is relevant to political philosophers (interested in questions of just taxation).[13]

Further reading

Sen and Nussbaum's book *The Quality of Life* contains a number or articles by both philosophers and researchers from other fields. In my view, Sen's contribution to this book, *Capability and Well-Being*, together with the text *Development as Capability Expansion*, are the two best short texts on the capabilities approach. Nussbaum's *Creating Capabilities: The Human Development Approach* is relatively successful in its aim to present a new and more accessible presentation of the approach.

Sabine Alkire's book *Valuing Freedoms: Sen's Capability Approach and Poverty Reduction* is an important contribution to the development of the capability approach within the field of poverty research. Ingrid Robeyns' recently published book *Wellbeing, Freedom and Social Justice: The Capability Approach Re-Examined* is a good place to start to get a grasp of the capability approach. Robeyns has worked on the capability approach for 20 years, and has written a number of very good articles on the approach. Her book can be downloaded for free from Openbookpublishers.com.

For a specific discussion on the capability approach and inequality, see Burchardt and Hicks *Inequality, Advantage and the Capability Approach.*

Philosophy bites podcast: Jonathan Wolff "on Disadvantage".

Notes

1 See Robeyns (2006:354ff.) for a discussion.
2 My presentation of this debate is indepted to Moss (2014).
3 Rawls and Dworkin are normally classified as resourcists (Arneson 2010:101). This makes sense even though there are differences between them. For discussion, see Moss (2014:54ff). Sen's criticism is primarily against Rawls, and it is this criticism I focus on here.
4 As mentioned above, I will not discuss the "equality of what question" in any detail. For Rawls' answer to Sen's criticism, see Rawls (2001:168–176). For a

discussion of Sen's criticism of Rawls and a more general comparison of Rawls and the capabilities approach, see Robeyns (2018:114–118).

5 Arneson (2000) points out this similarity. The similarity consists in a defence of an objective list. While Nussbaum is concerned with ensuring everyone enough, Arneson defends priority as the principle of distribution (explained in the next chapter).

6 Nussbaum points out that her version of the capability approach should be understood as an expansion or supplement to Rawls' theory (Nussbaum 2006:69). For a more comprehensive discussion of the relationship between Rawls' and Nussbaum's theories than I am able to give here, see Langvatn (2010).

7 We will return to a more thorough discussion of sufficientarianism in Chapter 6.

8 Axelsen and Nielsen (2014) claim that capabilities are what should be distributed, and that they should be distributed based on the distributive principle of sufficientarianism. They thus defend both the positive and the negative theses.

9 I here draw on Robeyns (2006), who distinguishes between nine different applications of the capability approach. In addition to the three I mention here, the capabilities approach is also used to identify the poor in developing countries, to analyse deprivation among disabled, to evaluate inequalities between sexes, and to provide theoretical and empirical analyses of policy, to criticize social norms, practices, and discourses, and finally the notion of functionings and capabilities can also be used in purely descriptive analyses (Robeyns 2006:360–361).

10 Here, I have only given a very superficial presentation of the discussion about what the point of political philosophy is, and how we should go about doing normative political philosophy. A more comprehensive treatment would also include Cohen's understanding of political theory. To Cohen, political philosophy should identify what justice *is*, and he thinks a theory of justice should not include such facts as people only doing their best if they are paid extra (as in Rawls' incentive argument) (Cohen 2008). For a discussion, see Stemplowska and Swift (2012).

11 For a discussion of what is needed to develop the capabilities approach into a comprehensive theory of just distribution, see Robeyns (2018:124–126).

12 Note that I do not say that a comprehensive theory of justice must necessarily advocate limits on wealth accumulation. What I say is that a comprehensive theory of justice must have a *view* on distribution also above the given threshold. Frankfurt's sufficientarianism is therefore a comprehensive theory of justice (since his view is that distribution above the threshold is morally irrelevant), while Nussbaum's is not (since she declines to formulate a view of this distribution).

13 Burchardt and Hick (2018) provide a more detailed argument showing that the capability approach has so far been employed on poverty, but that it can provide important insight for the understanding of inequality.

Part 2

Controversies

6 What is the value of equality?

Introduction

Equality has been important to the normative theories we have looked at above. Excepting Nozick, all the theories have also been concerned with redistribution. But why is equality important? In the debate about equality and redistribution, one can find different answers to this question. Some point to the fact that equal societies are also societies in which people tend to be healthier and happier than in societies where inequalities are large (Wilkinson and Pickett 2009. Others emphasize that equality is good for economic growth (OECD 2014). Yet others claim quite simply that equality is a value as fundamental as freedom.

In the philosophical debate, we can distinguish between two different views on equality. Equality can be seen as something that is valuable in and of itself; that is, equality has value independently of whether it contributes to realizing other values. In this case, we say that equality has intrinsic value. The alternative is to see equality as promoting other, valuable goods. In other words, equality comes with positive effects, and we may defend egalitarian politics by appealing to our desire to see these effects. In that case, we say that equality has instrumental value (Parfit 1997:206; Moss 2015:187–188).

In this chapter, we will look at two theories that challenge the view that equality has value in and of itself. Both *sufficientarianism* and *prioritarianism* criticize the claim that equality has intrinsic value. As the most prominent proponent of sufficientarianism, Harry Frankfurt argues that if everyone is ensured enough, there is no moral problem in some having more than others. Derek Parfit defends prioritarianism which holds that in matters of distribution, it is important to give priority to those who are worse off. Parfit argues that one of the implications of ascribing intrinsic value to equality is that, in one sense, it would be good to *level down*, that is, to create equality by bringing those who are better off *down* to the level of those who are worse off. To Parfit, this implication is absurd, and reason enough to let go of the idea that equality has intrinsic value. I will discuss these views in turn and conclude with a brief introduction to Martin O'Neill's defence of egalitarianism.

Sufficientarianism

The thinker who has provided the most explicit philosophical defence for sufficientarianism is Harry Frankfurt. Frankfurt's claim is that:

> what is important from the point of view of morality is not that everyone should have *the same* but that each should have *enough*. If everyone had enough it would be of no moral consequence whether some had more than others.
>
> (Frankfurt 1987:21, 2015:7)[1]

Frankfurt illustrates his point with a joke where one person asks another: "How are your children"?, to which the other replies: "Compared to what"?. The point is that the person replying is misled by the view that one has to compare to others to know how one is doing. Instead of being concerned with how one's children are doing compared to others, one should be concerned with how they are doing in an absolute sense: What matters is that they are fed, healthy, and go to a good school, and not what they have compared to others.

There are a number of versions of sufficientarianism. I will focus mainly on Frankfurt's version. Frankfurt was the first to defend this theory, and he did so in direct opposition to egalitarian theories. Other versions of sufficientarianism are less critical of egalitarian thinking, and I will return briefly to those towards the end of this section.

Frankfurt thinks that if we see equality as intrinsically valuable, we risk alienating or losing sight of what we should really care about. In our eagerness to compare ourselves to others, we forget to look into what we really need to live a good life (Frankfurt 1987:22–23). One important reason for this, claims Frankfurt, is that it is easier to calculate what would give an equal distribution than it is to figure out how much is enough.

One of the most important arguments Frankfurt offers is that even if economic equality may have many positive effects in society, this does not mean that equality is intrinsically valuable.[2] One could, for example, argue that an egalitarian society is a society with more solidarity. Or one could claim that unequal distribution undermines the ideal that people should have equal political influence. Frankfurt recognizes that these might be good reasons to push for economic equality. But they are not arguments for the claim that equality is a good *in itself* (Frankfurt 1987:24).

To illustrate, let me elaborate on an example from the introduction: Assume that you observe a society in which the worst off really suffer under very harsh material conditions, and the elite live in abundance. The poor are at the brink of starvation, have almost no clothes on their backs, and live in shacks with very poor hygienic and sanitary conditions. The rich drink champagne and eat caviar. You decide to transfer considerable resources from the elite to the worst off. Now, it is not necessarily the case that your plan to transfer resources is motivated by a wish to reduce inequality between the groups. To see this, assume that both groups experience considerable improvements while the inequality is kept constant. The poor are now much better off than they were before. If you no longer think that there are good reasons to transfer resources, we may assume that your original motivation to do so was founded on non-egalitarian reasons. Following Thomas Scanlon, we may call this non-egalitarian reason a humanitarian justification for redistribution (Scanlon 2003:203–204). Your justification for wanting to transfer resources is then primarily to dampen the sufferings of the worst off. If, on the contrary, you had been equally concerned with transferring resources from the elite to the worst off also after both their positions improved considerably, this may indicate that your plan was motivated by a genuinely egalitarian justification.[3]

Another objection to the idea that equality is valuable in itself runs as follows: Assume that there are only enough resources in a group to allow some, but not all, to survive. Assume further that there are ten people in the group and that each person needs five of the remaining resources to survive. There are only 40 units of this resource available. An equal distribution of these resources would distribute four to each person. Given that one needs at least five to survive, an equal distribution would thus have the result that everyone dies. In situations like these, Frankfurt thinks it would be morally reprehensible to insist on equal distribution. The criticism is also directed at Rawls' difference principle: Under the conditions sketched in this example, one cannot say that the only thing justifying some being better off than others is by reference to the advantage this brings to the worst off. After all, if one arrives at the conclusion that the best one can do in a situation like this is to save the lives of eight out of the ten, one cannot justify this by reference to the advantage this brings to the two who were given no resources (Frankfurt 1987:30).

Frankfurt draws two general conclusions from this. First, distributing resources equally is wrong in those situations where many individuals find themselves below the level of resources needed for survival. In conditions of scarcity, it will be better to ensure that as many as possible have enough.

Second, and this is the most important point, Frankfurt holds that opponents of economic inequality conflate different intuitions when rejecting inequality. When many of us react negatively to inequality, we are not reacting to inequality as such, but to the fact that some do not have enough:

> What I believe they find intuitively to be morally objectionable, in the types of situations characteristically cited as instances of economic inequality, is not the fact that some of the individuals in those situations have *less* money than others but the fact that those with less have *too little*.
> (Frankfurt 1987:32)

Frankfurt wants to prod the self-conception of egalitarians. He wants to show that while many defenders of egalitarianism think they are presenting arguments in favour of equality, in reality they are arguing in favour of sufficiency (Frankfurt 1987:32). We are, for example, not particularly worried that the rich have less than the super-rich. We must therefore learn to distinguish more clearly between the things to which we react. Is it inequality we react to when we hear about mothers who cannot send their kids to sports activities because they cost too much? Or are we reacting to the fact that those who are in such a situation do not have *enough*?

What does it mean to have enough? Having enough means having sufficient resources, or being above a certain threshold. In order for a person reasonably to say that they have too little money, they must reasonably be able to say that what is "distressing about his life is due to his having too little money" (Frankfurt 1987:37). When one has enough, one does not merely scrape by. One does not live at the limit. Instead, people have enough in part when they have no reason to be dissatisfied, and in part when their reasons to be dissatisfied do not relate to money.

A person who has no reason to be dissatisfied is satisfied. However, this, Frankfurt points out, does not mean that a satisfied person might not want more. What being satisfied precludes is this person having "an active interest in getting more. A contented person regards having more money as inessential to his being satisfied with his life" (Frankfurt 1987:39). People who are satisfied know that they can improve their situation, but since they are satisfied, this is not important to them. And because they are satisfied, they do not have good reason to want to compare how they are doing to how they might be doing in an alternative situation. To Frankfurt, the threshold for what is enough is set on the basis of satisfaction. When everyone is satisfied, it does not matter what the distribution among the satisfied might be.

Objections to sufficientarianism

The debate that followed Frankfurt's article has, among other things, revolved around the question whether it is possible to define the level of the threshold in a way that is not arbitrary or ambiguous (Arneson 2005:26–31; Casal 2007:312–314; Shields 2012:101–102).[4] One version of this criticism argues that it is particularly difficult to see why justice demands distribution below the threshold, while at the same time demanding no distribution above the threshold. Furthermore, Frankfurt's version of sufficientarianism is also criticized because one of its implications is that, in some cases, one should rather lift the well off by giving them small advantages than giving large advantages to the worst off. If the goal is to ensure that as many people as possible get enough, one may sacrifice those who are far below the threshold in order to lift those close to it to a level above the threshold (Shields 2012:101). More generally, critics object that sufficientarianism seems attractive *because* it is vague when it comes to the level at which the threshold is to be set. As soon as one tries to define a specific level, the theory loses its appeal (Casal 2007:315–316).

Paula Casal distinguished between two theses of sufficientarianism. The positive thesis says that what matters is that everyone is above a certain threshold, so that no one suffers any serious deprivation. The negative thesis says that when everyone has enough, it makes no moral difference what distribution is like above the threshold (Casal 2007:297–300).

The positive thesis is supported by strong intuitions. Most people would agree that everyone should be ensured enough to meet their basic needs. The positive thesis may therefore seem like something we all agree to. That, however, is not the case: As we have seen, libertarianism contains no demand that everyone must be ensured enough, nor does utilitarianism or strong versions of luck egalitarianism (to which we will turn in the next chapter).[5] The positive thesis articulates an ideal that, in my view, any distribution should seek to satisfy.

What about the negative thesis? Is the distribution above a certain threshold morally irrelevant? Assume that everyone is above a certain threshold, and that this society is split into two groups, those who are worst off and those who are better off. Assume further that we are to formulate a tax reform, the consequence of which is that all the burdens are put on those who are worst off. Still, the worst off will be above the threshold. Can we really say that, as defenders of the negative thesis do, it does not matter in terms of justice that the reform has this consequence? Or that, in accordance with Frankfurt's specification of the theory, this result is just so long as everybody is happy? I think most people will find this kind of implication problematic, and that most people therefore have intuitions that highlight a fundamental problem of sufficientarianism. That said, I am unsure about what drives this intuition, and would like to encourage the reader to think this through. Some will perhaps claim that equality has intrinsic value, and those who hold this view can easily refute the negative thesis. Others will perhaps reject the negative thesis for instrumental reasons and then there need not be a conflict with Frankfurt. To me, the example shows that there is something problematic about the negative thesis.[6]

Casal also employs the distinction between the two theses as a basis from which to call into question the motivation behind sufficientarianism. If the defence of the theory is primarily tied to the positive thesis, this is different than if the negative thesis is the driving force of the argument. In the latter case, a defence of sufficientarianism is primarily motivated by the desire to discredit egalitarian thinking. Such a wish to discredit may hide traditional values like avoiding tax for the rich (Casal 2007:303–304). If this observation is correct, it is of course necessary to study each sufficientarian view in order to figure out what drives the position.

The outlined criticism must not be understood as a rejection of sufficientarianism as such. My claim is only that Frankfurt's version of it is problematic. Other sufficientarians have argued that the theory can be combined with egalitarianism. Shields, for example, argues that sufficientarians can drop the negative thesis and adopt what he calls a shift thesis: Instead of saying that distribution above the threshold is irrelevant from the perspective of justice, one can say that when everyone has been lifted above the threshold, our reasons for further distribution *shift*. Shields thinks redistribution above the threshold is less important, but not that it is unimportant. Given this modification, Shields claims sufficientarianism can be combined with forms of egalitarianism that do not require absolute equality. The two theories may be combined by ensuring equality when one has ensured sufficiency (Shields 2012:114).

Does this mean that sufficeintarians must follow Shields and give up the negative thesis? There is another option available. One can hold on to the negative thesis and say that we need two thresholds: One that everyone must be lifted above, and another that defines the point at which redistribution is no longer important. The idea is that there is a level of welfare that everyone should reach (the positive thesis), and a level of welfare where redistribution is no longer important (the negative thesis). This does not mean that there has to be overlap between the two thresholds. There may be a gap between them. Redistribution in favour of those below the lowest threshold is most important, but redistribution between the two thresholds is also relevant. It is only once one gets above the upper threshold that redistribution is no longer relevant. Huseby (2020) defends this form of sufficientarianism. It is, like Shields' version, also compatible with egalitarianism, in the sense that the distribution between the two thresholds must be regulated by a principle, with egalitarian principles being one option. This version is moderate compared to Frankfurt's version. One might object that the theory thereby lessens its appeal by being more complicated. However, as Hirose has pointed out, the fact that a theory is complicated is not a *theoretical* problem (Hirose 2015:133). Or to put it differently, the fact that the theory becomes more complicated is not a decisive argument against the theory.

Shields and Huseby, in my view, defend versions of sufficientarianism that are better than Frankfurt's version, among other things, because they reject Frankfurt's defence of the negative thesis. Shields' and Huseby's versions also share a resemblance to prioritarianism, to which we turn now.

Prioritarianism

Sufficientarianism holds that we should strive to ensure that everyone has enough, not that everyone has an equal share. The theory has been criticized because it is difficult to determine where the threshold should be set, and because the negative thesis is problematic. Prioritarians claim that we should strive to prioritize the worst off.

In the article "Equality and Priority" (1997), Derek Parfit provides an influential defence of prioritarianism. He does this on the background of a distinction between a principle of equality and a principle utility. I will begin by saying something about these two principles.

Parfit starts with a pure version of the principle of equality:

> *The Principle of Equality*: It is in itself bad if some people are worse off than others.
>
> (Parfit 1997:204)

This principle only states that inequality is bad. The pure principle of equality is, in other words, comparative. It focuses on comparative inequality between people and not on how much they have in an absolute sense. On its own, therefore, the principle of equality cannot tell us whether we should prefer a distribution where everyone is equally bad off to one where everyone is equally well off. To decide between these two distributions, we need to add the Principle of Utility:

> *The Principle of Utility*: It is in itself better if people are better off.
>
> (Parfit 1997:205)

The Principle of Utility focuses on total amount of utility. A condition is better than another if the total amount of utility is greater. It is frequently pointed out that utilitarianism is problematic, in that it seeks to maximize utility or welfare without taking the distribution of that utility or welfare into account. If, for example, one is to distribute welfare between two people, the Principle of Utility will be indifferent to whether one person already has high welfare and the other low welfare. All that matters is to maximize utility; and so if the aggregate utility ends up being greatest when all the increased welfare is allocated to the person whose welfare is already high, this will be the preferred choice on the Principle of Utility. Because of this, many reject utilitarianism as a theory of justice. Here, however, it is important to note that even if utilitarianism in itself is indifferent to distribution, the principle of diminishing marginal utility entails that, if, for example, money is to be distributed, there will be a redistribution from the rich to the poor. The reason is that under normal circumstances a given amount of money will create much more utility or happiness for a poor person compared to a rich person. If I find a $100 bill on the street, it will increase my happiness much more than it would that of someone like Bill Gates. Then, in practice, one implication of the Principle of Utility is that one should redistribute from those who have a lot to those who have the least. However, this is not because equality is ascribed intrinsic value, only because redistribution in this case would increase the total aggregate utility or happiness (compare Brülde and Duus-Otterström 2015:139).[7]

Prioritarianism can be understood as an attempt at uniting egalitarianism and utilitarianism. It follows utilitarianism in seeing welfare as what is to be distributed as well as seeing increases in welfare as a good. If follows egalitarianism by emphasizing the importance of the distribution of welfare, and by maintaining that the most important thing is to improve the situation of the worst off (Brülde and Duus-Otterström 2015:144). However, prioritarians agree with Frankfurt that equality is not intrinsically valuable.

Those who are pure egalitarians only care about equality, while those who are pure utilitarians only care about utility. Most people, however, would accept a pluralist view, and they may be called pluralist egalitarians: They would appeal to both principles, and say that it is good to have both equality and utility. The problem is that these principles may conflict. Following Parfit, we can imagine the following abstract situation. Assume that we are distributing something, for example, welfare, and that we can treat welfare as a sort of unit, so that it makes sense to say that someone who has ten units of welfare is better off than someone who has eight. Assume further that every unit of welfare gives the same advantage to those who have it independently of how much they already have, so that an increase from three to four gives the same advantage as an increase from 21 to 22.[8] Now, consider three different distributions:

1 Everyone has 150
2 Half have 199, the other half 200
3 Half have 101, the other half 200 (Parfit 1997:205)

This example can be used to illustrate the difference between the two principles. To pure egalitarians, (1) is the best distribution (because it is equal), while it is the worst distribution for utilitarians, because the aggregate welfare is the smallest in (1). Most people will agree that (2) is the best distribution; (2) will also be the choice of pluralist egalitarians. In many cases, however, the choice will not be so easy, because it will be unclear how one should weigh the value of equality against the value of utility. Take this example:

1 Half have 100, the other half 200
2 Everyone has 145

The utilitarian will, according to Parfit, choose (1) in this case, because the aggregate utility is greatest in this distribution (Parfit 1997:221). What Parfit wants is an approach that makes it possible to defend (2) as the better option because the worst off are better off in (2), without having to give absolute priority to the worst off (as Rawls does), and at the same time without having to say that inequality is intrinsically bad.

Parfit criticizes theories that ascribe an intrinsic value to equality. He thinks such theories force egalitarians to accept levelling the position of the better off down to the position of the worst off, even if no one is better off as a result. For example, Parfit claims that egalitarians who hold this view see it as an improvement *in one way* if a society were to blind the seeing in order to make them equal to the blind (Parfit 1997:210).[9] No one is better off by this move, but intrinsic egalitarians must still maintain that this change is an improvement in one sense.[10]

We can also find similar objections to equality in the Norwegian debate. Take, as an example, the debate about whether there should be homework in school. Adherents of homework accept that removing homework may make pupils more equal, but only through making strong pupils weaker. A representative from the Conservative party put the objection as follows: "It is typical for people on the left that they are willing to equalise by making the strong weaker, and not by making the weaker stronger" (see Bøyum 2016:10).

Parfit calls this argument the *Levelling Down Objection* (Parfit 1997:211). It is important to be clear about what this objection says. It says that there is nothing good about levelling down. The following can be used as an illustration: Assume that we have a group of well off and a group of badly off, and that the well off lose their resources as a consequence of a natural disaster. After the disaster, everyone is equal, but no one is better off in any absolute sense. The disaster has eliminated inequality, and intrinsic egalitarians will, according to Parfit, claim that this is *in one way* an improvement to a better distribution (Parfit 1997:210–211).

To Parfit, this implication means that we should abandon intrinsic egalitarianism. It is absurd, Parfit thinks, for intrinsic egalitarians to say that it is *in one way better* if we level down and no one is better off as a result. In arguing this, Parfit presupposes what he calls the person-affecting view: Something cannot be good/bad unless it is not good/bad for someone. The person-affective view leads Parfit to claim that to remove inequality can only be justified if doing so is to someone's advantage. Removing inequality cannot be defended on the grounds that equality is intrinsically valuable.

Parfit therefore defends the ideal which states that we should strive to better the absolute conditions of the worst off. Assume the following distributions:

1 Half have 100, the other half 200
2 Everyone has 145

When we are faced with this choice, we can choose (2) for two different reasons. We may choose (2) because it will lead to more equality, or we may choose (2) because it makes the worst off better off. Parfit's point is that these two justifications are often confused even though they are distinct. That they are distinct, Parfit proves with the Levelling Down Objection. This objection affects intrinsic egalitarianism because this view holds that inequality is bad in itself. Giving priority to the worst off is not affected by this objection. Inequality is not perceived as a problem *in itself* independently of whether it is *bad for someone*.

On this basis, Parfit introduces the following principle:

> The Priority View: Benefiting people matters more the worse off these people are.
>
> (Parfit 1997:213)

Benefits for the worst off should be emphasized more. This, however, is not a principle that gives absolute priority to the worst off (compare Dworkin's criticism of Rawls). Prioritarians then are not concerned with equality as such, but with improving the position of the worst off. They do not defend a relational view (Parfit 1997:214). When they give priority to the worst off, they do so because the worst off are at a lower absolute level, and it therefore does not matter that the worst off are worse off *than others*. Parfit explains:

> People at higher altitudes find it harder to breathe. Is this because they are higher up than other people? In one sense yes. But they would find it just as hard to breathe even if there were no other people who were lower down. In the same way, on the Priority View, benefits to the worse off matter more, but that is only because these people are at a lower *absolute* level. It is irrelevant that these people are worse off *than others*. Benefits to them would matter just as much even if there *were* no others who were better off.
>
> (Parfit 1997:214)

Prioritarianism is thus a theory that gives priority to the worst off. The theory is similar to utilitarianism, in that it focuses on maximizing welfare, but it adds a proviso that benefits to the worst off must be prioritized. As we have seen, this does not necessarily mean that the worst off are given absolute priority. There is room for variation in this. One can give *absolute* priority to the worst off. Rawls' defence of maximin (see Chapter 1) is an example of giving absolute priority to the worst off. However, one can also reject absolute priority, and argue for a morally weighted sum of utility. In that case, one thinks that utility is morally more important the lower the level of utility of the recipient. However, according to this version of prioritarianism, one might give benefits to the better off, given that their gains are sufficiently large. Richard Arneson has defended this version of prioritarianism (Moss 2014:33).

Objections to Parfit and defence of equality

Parfit's objection about levelling down has been widely debated. Larry Temkin has defended egalitarianism by pointing out that egalitarians normally do not defend levelling down. Temkin argues that equality is only one among several important values, also to egalitarians. He uses the example of blinding the seeing to illustrate his point:

> The anti-egalitarian will incredulously ask, do I *really* think there is some respect in which a world where only some are blind is worse than one where all are? Yes. Does this mean I think that it would be better if we blinded everyone? No. Equality is not all that matters. But it matters some.
>
> (Temkin 2002:155)

Temkin here develops what is called a pluralistic reply to the Levelling Down Objection: Equality must be weighed against other values when considering what is just. If one takes all factors into consideration, no egalitarian would advocate for blinding the seeing to achieve equality.

Martin O'Neill has questioned Parfit's presuppositions. O'Neill claims that Parfit employs an abstract, numbers-focused approach that reduces everything to a question of individual welfare. O'Neill thinks this approach comes up short compared to an approach that values the quality of social relations. O'Neill introduces the following examples to illustrate his point:

Take the following distributions:

1 Half at 100, the other half at 150
2 Everyone at 99

Faced with this distribution, the Levelling Down Objection says that it would be absurd to think (2) is in any way better than (1). This is wrong according to O'Neill. For example, (1) can represent a society that is rich, but plagued by class differences where those in power repress the rest. This may in turn manifest in social relations characterized by servility on the part of the worst off. It may therefore be rational, not absurd, to go from (1) to (2), even if this move would not better people's welfare. The value of equality can, O'Neill claims, sometimes trump the value of welfare. Egalitarians may therefore reject the Levelling Down Objection (O'Neill 2008:141–142).[11]

In addition to providing a convincing answer to the Levelling Down Objection, O'Neill's argument can also help us to understand the question of an intrinsic instrumental value in a better way. This also gives us a deeper understanding of the arguments introduced by Rawls, as seen in Chapter 1.

Let us first look at Scanlon and Rawls, who have developed justifications for equality in close dialogue (Rawls 2001:130, 2007:244–248). Scanlon mentions five reasons to be concerned with equality: We should fight inequality to avoid poverty and suffering, avoid stigmatization and status differences, ensure everyone equal opportunity for political influence, provide everyone with a more or less equal starting point in life, and ensure everyone a fair share of what we collectively produce.

Scanlon elaborates on this by analysing which of these reasons are egalitarian, and which are non-egalitarian reasons to be against inequality. The first and fourth of these reasons are not egalitarian justifications. Avoiding suffering and poverty is compatible with there being large inequalities, provided that everyone has enough. Ensuring roughly equal opportunity is compatible with large inequality of outcomes. The most egalitarian justifications are thus to avoid stigmatization and status differences, to ensure everyone equal opportunity for political influence, and to ensure everyone a share of what we collectively produce (Scanlon 2003:207–208).

On the topic of inequalities of status, Rawls writes that this reason:

> brings us closer to what is wrong with inequality in itself. Significant political and economic inequalities are often associated with inequalities of social status that encourage those of lower status to be viewed both by themselves and by others as inferior. This may arouse widespread attitudes of deference and servility on one side and a will to dominate and arrogance on the other. These effects of social and economic inequalities can be serious evils and the attitudes they engender great vices. But is inequality wrong or unjust in itself? It is close to being wrong in itself that in a status system, not everyone can have the highest rank.
>
> (Rawls 2001:131)

Rawls then thinks that large inequality of status can be damaging, both for those who have the most and for those who have the least. In a just society, we should avoid both servility and arrogance, and the danger that these attitudes will infect relations between people increase with large inequality.

Then, to the argument that what we collectively produce should be distributed equally. Within a business, we would think it reasonable to distribute equally if Peer, Paal, and Espen jointly establish the venture by injecting equal amounts of capital, and each puts in the same number of work hours. An unequal distribution of the surplus from business would then be a deviation from equality, and something in need of special justification. This line of thinking can also be transferred to society as a whole. In Rawls, society is seen as a kind of cooperation to achieve collective benefits. The fruits of this cooperation should, in Rawls' view, be distributed equally, unless an unequal distribution is to the advantage of the worst off.

Rawls argues for this view through the device of the original position. The veil of ignorance deprives parties of any information about their place in society. In such a situation, no party will have any reason to accept that anyone would get more than others, unless this inequality improved the outcome of the worst off. Equality would be the norm, or basis, and it is this equality-oriented justification that I am concerned with here, not the differences allowed by the difference principle. As members of a society, understood as a cooperation to achieve common benefits, everyone is entitled to an equal share of the goods that follow from this cooperation. Scanlon claims that this argument is genuinely egalitarian because it states that inequalities are unacceptable independently of how much people have, and hence also independently of whether they are above a certain threshold (Scanlon 2003).

Rawls and Scanlon thus argue that there are kinds of inequality that are *unjust in themselves*. I am unsure whether these arguments succeed in showing that equality is intrinsically valuable, and will allow myself to stay agnostic about this question. O'Neill, however, has elaborated on the Rawls/Scanlon argument, and in my view clarified what follows about the question of whether equality is intrinsically valuable. Drawing on Rawls and Scanlon, he gives the following list of egalitarian reasons against economic inequality:

1 Inequality might lead some to dominate and control others
2 Inequality can create stigma and differences in social status
3 Inequality might be bad for the self-respect of the worst off
4 Inequality can create servility and deferential behavior
5 Inequality can undermine social relations.

(O'Neill 2008:121–123)[12]

Inequality can lead to domination, if society is so arranged that economic power translates into political power. We will look at specific examples of this in the next chapter. Inequality can lead to stigmatization and status differences, if society is so arranged that economic power translates into social status. If some have nearly unlimited means to purchase status-conferring material goods like expensive houses, cars, and clothes, while others have no such means, the result can be large differences in status and stigma. Such differences in status and the corresponding stigma may also negatively impact the self-respect of those who are badly off. This, in turn, can lead to servile and submissive attitudes towards the well off, while the well off may become arrogant and self-righteous. Good relations between members of society may thus become difficult if there are large inequalities between people. Cohen's bus example, as discussed in Chapter 4, is an example of this. If two people, due to economic inequalities, inhabit different worlds, this may weaken their chances of establishing or maintaining good relations with one another.

The point is that these reasons are related. Inequalities in status can lead to servile and submissive citizens. This, then, is the connection between (2) and (4). Similarly, the fact that some control and dominate others (1) will impair the quality of social relations (5). Put together, this gives us strong reasons to defend equality and oppose inequality. O'Neill claims that the absence of 1–5 provides fertile ground for egalitarian social relations, which can be seen as a good in itself (O'Neill 2008:130).

Just what this implies remains, in my view, unclear in O'Neill. He seems to think that a society characterized by equality may give rise to symmetrical relations between individuals, and that symmetrical relations are intrinsically valuable. However, this point is not developed into what we might call a positive ideal. Whether this is a problem is a topic for discussion in the next chapter.[13]

Conclusion

The debates that followed in the aftermath of Frankfurt and Parfit's articles have contributed to an improved understanding of the ideal of equality. It is, for example, important to distinguish between humanitarian and egalitarian reasons for helping the worst off. It is also important to ask oneself why, if at all, we should support the goal of improving the position of the worst off. One reason may be that equality is intrinsically valuable, another that it is important to better the absolute condition of the worst off. The first justification is comparative, while the latter is not.

I will end by trying to clarify what the above discussion implies for *justice as fairness*. The Levelling Down Objection is a possible criticism of Rawls' claim that we must put constraints on how much the best off should be allowed to make or own. One could say that with Parfit, it would be absurd to tax the wealthy more if it does not make anybody better off. The Rawlsian answer to such an objection is that this kind of taxation may still be appropriate because it reduces the chances of some citizens controlling and dominating others, which may, in turn, be connected to the other problems on O'Neill's list. This can be tied to O'Neill's point that Parfit's approach is too abstract and too focused on individual welfare. If one taxes the best off, this can be defended regardless of whether it improves the welfare of the worst off. It can be defended because it reduces the danger that the worst off are dominated and repressed by the better off. The Levelling Down Objection thus does not affect Rawls.

O'Neill's list also contributes to clarifying the justifications for *justice as fairness*. The list shows how avoiding dominance and status differences is important to the self-respect of citizens. A society where the social relations are egalitarian is a prerequisite for a well-functioning democracy. Rawls points out that *justice as fairness* requires "equal citizenship" that ascribes to all the status of being "free and equal persons" (Rawls 2001:132). In my view, O'Neill's list provides a robust defence of equality. The list shows that one can defend the ideal of equality without having to commit to equality being intrinsically valuable. In the next chapter, we will, among other things, look more closely at how large inequalities can be problematic for a democratic practice.[14]

Further reading

Three important articles about sufficientarianism are Harry Frankfurt's *Equality as a Moral Ideal*, Roger Crisp's *Equality, Priority and Compassion*, and Robert Huseby's *Sufficiency: Restated and Defended*. Casal's *Why Sufficiency Is Not Enough?* puts forward the most important criticism of sufficientarianism. The most important text of prioritarianism is Parfit's "Equality and Priority". Holtug's *Prioritarianism* provides a more recent defence of the doctrine by taking on important objections that have been raised after the publication of Parfit's original defence. In the article "Why It Matters That Some Are Worse Off Than Others: An Argument against the Priority View", Otsuka and Verhoove deliver a much-debated criticism of prioritarianism. In 2012, the journal *Utilitas* published a special issue discussing prioritarianism. This issue also contains a reply by Parfit, where he, among other things, addresses the criticism by Otsuka and Verhoove.

Notes

1 Frankfurt's defence of sufficientarianism was originally published in two articles: "Equality as a Moral Ideal" (1987) and "Equality and Respect" (1997). The articles were published as a book in 2015 with a short introduction (Frankfurt 2015). In the following, I will refer to the original articles and not the book.
2 What is it that people must be ensured sufficient amounts of according to sufficientarianism? Frankfurt is concerned that everyone be secured sufficient amounts of *money*. However, as we shall see, he also suggests *satisfaction* as a measure or currency for sufficientarianism, and it has been pointed out that Frankfurt is not consistent on this question (Kanschik 2015:97). Others have suggested welfare (Crisp 2003; Huseby 2010), capabilities (Axelsen and Nielsen 2014), or that one must be ensured sufficient to cover one's basic needs (Page 2007) as an answer to the sufficiency of what-question.
3 The example is inspired by Scanlon (2003).
4 I appreciate conversations with Robert Huseby on this topic; see Huseby (2020) for details.
5 I owe this point to Robert Huseby.
6 For a similar example, see Shields (2012:104). Shields also rejects the idea that one can counter this objection by setting a very high threshold, because the theory would then have no practical relevance. In a Norwegian context, a threshold defined, for example, as everyone earning over kr3 million (€300,000) per year would be of very little help in solving questions of distribution below the threshold (the average yearly income in Norway pre-tax is about €50000). For a critical discussion of Shields' tax argument, see Kanschik (2015). Kanschik deals with what we might call the indifference objection to sufficientarianism. This objection states that sufficientarianism is indifferent to distribution above the threshold, and that this is wrong. Critics of sufficientarianism have pointed out that this implies that the theory is also indifferent with regards to whether one should have a progressive or regressive tax regime. Kanschik argues that this does not follow, because it is possible for defenders of sufficientarianism to place the greatest burdens on the richest also above the threshold because those who have least, and hence are closest to the threshold, have the greatest *risk* of falling below it.
7 It should be added that even if utilitarianism has egalitarian implications in many situations, this will not always be the case. Assume that everyone is in a situation where basic needs are met, and there are a few very rich people who gain tremendous utility from consuming luxury goods. In such a situation, there is no reason for the utilitarian to redistribute (compare Hirose 2015:22).
8 Parfit includes this assumption so that the advantages in question are not treated in the utilitarian manner of diminishing marginal utility.
9 Parfit develops Nozicks eye lottery, discussed in Chapter 2.
10 Parfit distinguishes between telic and deontic egalitarianism. This distinction has been much discussed. However, in order not to complicate things, I will not discuss that distinction here.
11 O'Neill develops this argument using Rawlsian thinking, and with the help of Thomas Scanlon.
12 The list is somewhat changed from O'Neill's original.
13 Drawing on O'Neill (among others), Moss has suggested that, in addition to talking of equality as something that is either an instrumental or an intrinsic good, we can also understand equality as a *constitutive* good. Equality can be seen as a constitutive good because it contributes to the realization of other goods that are intrinsic goods. Without equality, these intrinsic goods would not have the value they have. Equality can, for example, be said to play a constitutive role for

the realization of self-respect. Equality takes part in an intrinsic good, and one can therefore say that equality is a kind of intrinsic good because it allows for the realization of something that is an intrinsic good. One cannot remove equality without the intrinsic good of self-respect losing something of itself. Equality (co-)constitutes self-respect (Moss 2014:38–39). Equality thus becomes something that has value beyond its instrumental value (Moss 2015:187). Moss claims that this is important because an understanding of equality that sees equality as constitutive of other goods can provide a stronger defence of equality compared to those that see equality purely as an instrumental good. If we see equality purely as an instrumental good, it is easier to put it aside if this value conflicts with other values, like freedom (Moss 2015:188). If we see equality as a constitutive good, however, this highlights how important equality is to the realization of other goods. In other words, we get a more solid egalitarian basis by understanding equality as constitutive of other goods.

14 An interesting newcomer to the field that might supplement sufficientarianism, prioritarianism, utilitarianism, and egalitarianism is limitarianism. Limitarianism is defended by the Belgian philosopher Ingrid Robeyns (2017). The core of the theory is that it is wrong to have more resources than those one needs to live a rich life.

7 Equality—a distributive ideal or an ideal of social relations?

Equality may be understood to be an important ideal, whether one perceives it is valuable in and of itself or as something with instrumental value. Furthermore, equality can be understood as an ideal for distribution (that everyone should have the same) or an ideal for social relations (that everyone should be on the same footing). In this chapter, we will distinguish between equality as a distributive ideal and equality as a relational idea. Equality can be seen as something that is directly tied to distribution. If so, the goal is an equal distribution, and the crucial question to be answered is *what* it is that citizens should be equal in terms of. This is the topic at the centre of the equality of what-debate. The participants in this debate have, as we have seen, argued over whether welfare, resources, or something else is to be distributed. Cohen, for example, assumes that this is the right way of answering questions of distributive justice when he writes that he "takes for granted that there is something which justice requires people to have equal amounts of" (Cohen 2011:3; Scheffler 2015:21). Cohen, Arneson, Frankfurt, and Parfit all understand the ideal of equality in this way.

The alternative way of understanding equality is to understand it as a relational ideal. If we understand equality as a relational ideal, what becomes important is to arrange society in such a way that we can relate to each other as equals rather than achieving an equal distribution of *something*. Relations between individuals are what matter. Equality is then understood more broadly. Understanding equality relationally does have consequences for distribution, but what matters is the egalitarian social relations that result from such distribution rather than the distribution itself. To the relational egalitarian, the question is what kinds of distribution are compatible with a society in which citizens are equals, not what it is that should be distributed (Scheffler 2015:22). Rawls and O'Neill understand equality relationally, and together with Elizabeth Anderson and Samuel Scheffler, they are the most important representatives of this view.[1]

The relational view has long roots in political philosophy. However, only recently has it been established as a criticism of the dominant view of equality as a distributive ideal. The luck egalitarian position has been one of the main targets of this criticism, and in what follows we will look closer at luck egalitarianism, which is an important version of equality understood as a distributive ideal. In the 1990s and 2000s, luck egalitarianism was one of the leading theories of distributive justice. As we saw in Chapter 3, luck egalitarianism builds on Dworkin's framework.[2] Elizabeth Anderson's influential article, "What is the Point of Equality?" (1999), represents the starting point of the debate between luck egalitarianism and the relational understanding of equality. Additionally, Anderson's article also raised a number of fundamental questions about the luck egalitarian framework: What follows from incorporating a sensitivity to responsibility into an egalitarian theory? What happens to the traditional focus on the politically oppressed in the luck egalitarian framework?

I will approach these questions by first presenting Anderson's understanding and criticism of luck egalitarianism. Using that as a starting point, we will look at what answers central luck egalitarians have provided to these criticisms, and then turn to the relational understanding of equality and compare that to equality understood as a distributive ideal. Finally, I show that the relational ideal of equality thematizes power more convincingly than competing understandings, and discuss whether economic power can be converted into political power in a comparatively egalitarian society such as Norway.

Anderson's criticism of luck egalitarianism

The term luck egalitarianism was introduced by Anderson in *What is the Point of Equality?*. Anderson defined luck egalitarianism as a position that sees the goal of an egalitarian theory to "compensate people for undeserved bad luck", where "undeserved bad luck" is, among other things understood, as "being born with poor native endowments, bad parents, and disagreeable personalities, suffering from accidents and illness" (Anderson 1999:288). The goal of luck egalitarians is, according to Anderson, to "eliminate the impact of brute luck" (Anderson 1999:288). Luck egalitarianism is also called responsibility-sensitive egalitarianism because the opposite of luck is something for which one can be held responsible. Luck egalitarian thinkers may therefore be said to defend versions of what Parfit calls the egalitarian principle: It is wrong for some people to be worse off than others as a result of conditions outside of their control (Parfit 1997:204; Cohen 2011:13; Knight 2013:924). To Anderson, the most important luck egalitarians are Dworkin, Cohen, Arneson, Philippe Van Parijs, Eric Rakowski, John Roemer, and Thomas Nagel.[3]

On Anderson's reading, luck egalitarianism rests on two moral premises: That people must be compensated for undeserved disadvantages, and that the compensation must come from that part of other people's advantageous circumstances that they have not deserved (Anderson 1999:290). If Peer through no fault of his own gets hit on the head by a falling brick, it is just that Paal—who, due to his naturally razor-sharp brain, enjoys a high income—contributes to covering the cost of Peer's healthcare.

With the exception of Cohen, luck egalitarians, according to Anderson, have a common starting point: They claim that a mix of capitalism and welfare state provides the institutional structure best suited to realize the ideals they espouse. The welfare state is understood (by luck egalitarians) as a kind of insurance scheme, the task of which is to provide citizens with a safety net to dampen the negative effects of brute bad luck. The role of the state, in other words, is first and foremost tied to providing citizens with such insurance schemes in those cases where there are no private schemes available. The most responsibility-oriented versions of luck egalitarianism (Rakowski) claim that if there are private insurance schemes and citizens do not take out insurance, there is no justification for claiming that the state should cover the costs of a non-insured citizen who is unlucky. Most luck egalitarians, however, are in favour of mandatory insurance schemes (Anderson 1999:292).

Anderson divides luck egalitarians into two camps based on where they stand on the equality of what-question. Dworkin, Rakowski, and Van Parijs argue for resource equality, while Arneson, Cohen, Roemer, and probably also Nagel may be classified as welfare egalitarians (Anderson 1999:290).

The most important reason why luck egalitarians have gained support from people with an egalitarian bent is, according to Anderson, the care they show for people who have been unlucky in life. This group includes people with congenital disabilities, and those with low levels of talent or talent that is not valued in the market. These people should, according to this doctrine, be compensated. Anderson, however, thinks that the luck egalitarian position has significant weaknesses, also in its views on unlucky people. This is evident in the fact that luck egalitarian thinking fails one fundamental test: That the principles on which it builds express equal respect and care for all citizens (Anderson 1999:289). There are three reasons for this, and in the following these three reasons are presented as objections to the luck egalitarian framework.

To see the first of these objections, imagine a driver who is not insured, and who, in a momentary inattention, makes a wrong turn and crashes into another car. When the ambulance arrives, they discover that the driver is uninsured. They refrain from providing help, and the driver dies. The driver is responsible for the wrong turn, and hence the crash, but also for not being insured. Hence, the community has no obligation to help (Anderson 1999:295–296). This seems overly harsh, and the objection is therefore often referred to as "the harshness objection".

The second objection points out that, according to luck egalitarianism, there is no good reason to compensate someone who quits the workforce to take care of people in need, such as children or elderly people. Anderson argues that it is unclear whether luck egalitarians can offer, for example, (wo) men who stay at home with children—and because of this end up being dependent on their spouse—any compensation for their unpaid labour (Anderson 1999:298). This objection is referred to as "the vulnerability of dependent caretaker's objection".

The third objection is that luck egalitarians treat people condescendingly. Call this "the condescension objection". Anderson is concerned with who the typical recipient of luck egalitarian benefits are. Luck egalitarians will compensate people for congenital differences. According to this way of thinking, the smart should compensate the stupid, the talented the talentless, and the pretty should compensate the ugly to the extent that appearance is tied to potential earnings. Anderson imagines that the state's equality department would send out the following messages along with any compensation paid to the worst off:

> To the disabled: Your defective native endowments or current disabilities, alas, make your life less worth living than the lives of normal people. To compensate for this misfortune, we the able ones, will give you extra resources, enough to make the worth of living your life good enough that at least one person out there thinks it is comparable to someone else's life.
>
> To the stupid and untalented: Unfortunately, other people don't value what little you have to offer in the system of production. Your talents are too meager to command much market value. Because of the misfortune that you were born so poorly endowed with talents, we productive ones will make it up to you: we'll let you share in the bounty of what we have produced with our vastly superior and highly valued abilities.
>
> To the ugly and socially awkward: How sad that you are so repulsive to people around you that no one wants to be your friend or lifetime companion. We won't make it up to you by being your friend or your marriage partner – we have our own freedom of association to exercise – but you can console yourself in your miserable loneliness by consuming these material goods that we, the beautiful and charming ones, will provide. And who knows? Maybe you won't be such a looser in love once potential dates see how rich you are.
>
> (Anderson 1999:305)

The way Anderson sees it, people, according to the luck egalitarian ideal, may only claim compensation based on their inferiority compared to others. The worst off do not have what it takes to succeed, and hence need compensation. The problem with this is that an egalitarian theory, according to the egalitarian thesis of equal respect and care, should allow people to raise claims based on equality. People should be able to claim compensation because they are entitled to be treated with respect as free and equal citizens. But instead of fostering mutual respect, the luck egalitarian thinking ties redistribution to pity for those who are badly off. And pity is diametrically opposed to respect. Luck egalitarians, according to Anderson, therefore undermine the most fundamental feature of the ideal of equality, that is, equal respect for all persons.[4]

A related problem (which is not an independent objection to luck egalitarianism) is how we are to justify a welfare state on this position. This problem comes to the fore in what Anderson calls the "problem of paternalism". The basis of this problem is that luck egalitarians claim that people must be equal when they enter adulthood. After this, a number of inequalities will result from differences in the risks voluntarily chosen by each individual. For some, these choices will have very bad outcomes. The luck egalitarian solution to this problem is to introduce mandatory insurance schemes to protect the worst off from the worst consequences. The problem with this, according to Anderson, is that luck egalitarians can *only* justify this kind of arrangement by way of paternalism. A mandatory insurance scheme cannot, in Anderson's view, be justified by reference to the need to ensure equal respect, but only as an arrangement necessary to protect irresponsible or unwise people from the consequences of their own choices (Anderson 1999:300–301). If we understand the welfare state as a mandatory insurance scheme, it is hard to see how this can be legitimized if the only justification we can provide is that it protects irresponsible people from the consequences of their bad choices. Here too, then, luck egalitarian thinking violates the basic egalitarian ideal, which states that citizens should be treated with equal respect.

How have leading luck egalitarians responded to this criticism? Dworkin has rejected the label luck egalitarianism for his own theory, arguing that the goal of his theory is not to compensate for undeserved (bad) luck, but "to make circumstances equal under some appropriate version of the envy test" (Dworkin 2003:191, see also Arneson 2018:44–45). Dworkin's claim is probably that the difference between his view and the luck egalitarian view has to do with what we identify with, as discussed in the photographer debate with Cohen (Chapter 3). Dworkin holds that there are some aspects of our personality that are brute luck, but which it is not just to compensate for. This distinguishes him from luck egalitarianism.[5] Cohen has largely accepted the luck egalitarian label, replied to parts of the criticism, and also tried to change his own position to accommodate some of the objections. His reply to the criticism has, among other things, appealed to the distinction between theory and practice: His goal is to discuss what justice *is*, not what the consequences would be if one were to *implement* a specific ideal of justice.

Arneson has noted that what matters is neither patterns of distribution nor the quality of social relations, but the *quality of life* that people can achieve. "The aspect of social life that Anderson takes to matter intrinsically, the quality of relationship, is itself reasonably regarded as instrumental to well-being, not morally important in itself" (Arneson 2000 a:342). Hence, criticism (of luck egalitarianism) only affects those who hold on to resource equality (as the right answer to the equality of what-question), because they cannot point to any more fundamental ideal that justifies their concern with the distribution of goods.

Relational equality

If luck egalitarianism does not provide an attractive answer to how we should understand the ideal of equality, what are the alternatives? Here, there are two possible routes. We can, as Anderson and Samuel Scheffler do, try to establish a theory about relational equality by providing a positive answer to the question of what relational theory is *for*. If we are to follow this route, we must provide a positive theory of what relational egalitarians are in favour of. Alternatively, we may follow Jonathan Wolff in abandoning this strategy in favour of providing an answer to what it is that adherents of the relational ideal of equality are *against*.

Anderson defends what she calls democratic equality. She points to three central differences between democratic and luck egalitarian equality. First, adherents of democratic equality are concerned with removing social repression rather than the congenital inequalities with which luck egalitarians are concerned. Second, Anderson thinks equality must primarily be understood as a relational ideal: Equality is first and foremost about social relations, not about an equal distribution of something. How goods are distributed may of course affect social relations, but "democratic egalitarians are fundamentally concerned with the relationship with which goods are distributed, not only with the distribution of goods themselves" (Anderson 1999:314). Third, and finally, democratic equality is concerned that demands for equal recognition must be integrated alongside demands for equal distribution in any egalitarian theory.[6] "The basis for people's claims to distributed goods" she writes, "is that they are equals, not inferior to others" (Anderson 1999:314).

Anderson wants to remind us of the egalitarian political movements and what they have fought for. A fight against repression and dominance has been central to the LGBT movement and the movement for equal rights for the disabled. The egalitarian demand has not primarily been a demand for distribution of economic goods, but rather a fight against repressive stereotypes and lack of recognition. Anderson argues that egalitarians should tie themselves more closely to such social movements and fight against hierarchical relations, status differences, and exploitation. This includes fighting racism, sexism, cast, and class, and ties in with historic egalitarian movements that Anderson thinks we have lost sight of in the abstract discussions of *what* it is that should be distributed (Anderson 1999:312).[7]

Scheffler thinks equality must be understood as a social and political ideal that governs relations between people. The core of the ideal, writes Scheffler, is "a normative conception of human relations" and the relevant question when we are to interpret this ideal is "what social political and economic arrangements are compatible with that conception" (Scheffler 2003:31). Scheffler argues that this ideal is present in the writings of Rawls, and that it is the role of the citizen as free and equal that forms the basis for the ideal of equality. People cannot, for example, participate on a par with others—in political life or in civil society—if their basic needs for food, clothes, or education are not met (Scheffler 2003:23).

To relational egalitarians like Scheffler, equality is a moral ideal that pertains to how people relate to each other. This ideal does not emphasize the difference between people that are emphasized by luck egalitarians, that is, the difference between people's abilities and talent. Thus, in contrast to luck egalitarians, who emphasize the *differences* between people—their different abilities and skills—relational egalitarians bracket these differences and start with the assumption that everyone is basically *alike*.

Therefore, the ideal of equality is not a matter of eliminating the influence of luck, but of fighting repression, inherited status hierarchies, and class privilege, and to ensure a democratic distribution of power. Adherents of the relational ideal of equality take pains to note that there are a number of differences between people, but that these differences must not be allowed to play any role when it comes to the status of all as free and equal. The point of equality is not to eliminate differences, but to ensure that our institutions facilitate the exercise of our freedom and equality, for example, by ensuring all citizens equal opportunity to influence elections and achieve political positions. Everyone is equally morally valuable, and this moral equality must be safeguarded by the political institutions.

Jonathan Wolff has pointed out that for those who defend the relational interpretation of the ideal of equality, it is easier to say what they are against than what they are for. This is also true for Anderson's attempt at specifying what the relational ideal of equality implies. It is clear that defenders of the relational ideal of equality are against repression and for a society in which everyone is equal. However, as soon as one tries to specify what it means that everyone is equal, things get complicated. In other words, it is difficult to give substantive, positive content to the relational ideal of equality (Wolff 2015a:213).

This is also evident in O'Neill's list expressing a relational ideal of equality. In the last chapter, I argued that this ideal constitutes a robust defence of equality, but the list only really tells us to fight inequality and does not really say why relational equality is good. O'Neill's list of reasons to fight economic inequality runs as follows:

1 Inequality might lead some to dominate and control others
2 Inequality can create stigma and differences in social status
3 Inequality might be bad for the self-respect of the worst off
4 Inequality can create servility and deferential behaviour
5 Inequality can undermine social relations (O'Neill 2008:121–123).

The attempt at restating this list in the form of a positive defence of equality ended—also in O'Neill's case—in a half-hearted defence of egalitarian social relations.

Some will see the failure of relational egalitarians to provide a positive defence of their theory as a problem. Those who defend equality as a distributive ideal have been able to discuss what it is that is to be distributed (the equality of what-question) as well as which principles of justice the distribution should be governed by. Distributive egalitarians have been able to develop detailed theories through deep discussions of central terms, tying these to practical examples. The different understandings of luck that have been discussed in the luck egalitarian tradition is one example of this. Compared to distributive egalitarians, defenders of relational equality have been unable to articulate a similarly positive project (Wolff 2015a:214).

However, in my view, Wolff has successfully argued that this lack of a positive project is not a serious problem. Relational egalitarians may simply state that they are *against* asymmetric social relations, which is another way of expressing the core of O'Neill's list. They can do so without formulating a positive ideal. In other words, relational egalitarians do not need a "currency" in the same way that defenders of equality as a distributive ideal need one. It is enough to be against stigmatization and status differences, social relations in which one part dominates and controls others in a way that threatens their self-respect as well as creates servility and submissiveness. Social equality is the absence of social inequality (Wolff 2015a:220).

In my view, Wolff's argument clarifies the relation between equality as a distributive and as a relational ideal. Adherents of the relational conception of equality do not necessarily need a detailed theory of what they are for. It may suffice for a relational egalitarian to know what one is against.

The discussion of equality as a distributive and as a relational ideal is important to the debate about just distribution. In the luck egalitarian version of equality understood as a distributive ideal, for example, responsibility plays a central role. Speaking of responsibility, we should take care to avoid a possible misunderstanding: The debate between luck egalitarians and relational egalitarians is not about whether our ideal of equality should be sensitive to responsibility (Moss 2014:104). Both sides are concerned with responsibility, but in different ways. Luck egalitarians are concerned with the distinction between choice and circumstance, and want to equalize inequalities that are due to circumstance (or matters outside of our control). Relational egalitarians are concerned with reciprocity, meaning, for example, a willingness to work if one is able. If you choose to stay on the couch, this will have consequences for which goods you may lay claim to. However, relational egalitarians will not accept every difference due to free choice: The point of departure of this ideal of equality is the view of all citizens as free and equal; hence one cannot allow inequalities that undermine this ideal of citizenship.

I have discussed luck egalitarians using Anderson's criticism of this position. In my view, the Harshness Objection and the objection that luck egalitarians treat people condescendingly are apt criticisms of at least some forms of luck egalitarianism. It should however be noted that there are a large number of luck egalitarian theories today, and that some of these have been adapted to meet Anderson's objections. This is, for example, true of Kasper Lippert-Rasmussen's (2015) defence of pluralist egalitarianism and Tan's institutional luck egalitarianism (2012). The fronts in the debate between the two theories of equality have therefore shifted, and one important discussion in the last few years has turned on the question whether the two theories are sufficiently similar to be reconciled (Lippert-Rasmussen 2015), or are fundamentally different and irreconcilable (Anderson 2010).[8]

Does Norway's wealthiest people have too much power?

The first point on O'Neill's list is that too much inequality may lead to some people being able to control and dominate others. This must be understood on the background of the basic democratic ideal which posits citizens as free and equal, with equal opportunity to influence the political process (see Chapter 1). This is, as we have seen, a key claim by relational egalitarians. In this final part of the chapter, we shall look at *how* the wealthy may convert economic resources into political power, and thereby come to dominate and control others by in effect having better opportunity to influence the political process.[9] As we saw in the last chapter, the different ideals on O'Neill's list are interconnected. If some are allowed to dominate and control others, this may negatively impact social relations, and lead to some citizens becoming servile and submissive. In order to tie this theoretical discussion to a specific example, I will end this chapter by investigating whether the economic inequalities in Norway—usually perceived to be a very egalitarian country—are sufficiently large to allow some people to dominate and control others with the aid of economic resources.

In 2015, Donald Trump was asked why he donated so much money not only to Republican candidates, but also to Democratic candidates. He answered that "I give to everybody. When they call I give. And you know what, when I need something from them two years later, three years later, I call them. They are there for me" (Ornitz and Struyk 2015).

Trump's answer indicates that power can be bought. If power can be bought, this constitutes a violation of the fundamental democratic ideal which states that all citizens are free and equal with equal opportunity to influence the political process. Are there similar opportunities for rich citizens to buy political power in Norway?

We know that Norwegian political parties use more money on elections now compared to previously, and that an increasing share of the financing of political campaigns comes from individuals and organizations (NTB 2017).[10] We also know that wealth is more unequally distributed than income, and that compared to other countries, Norway has a higher proportion of rich and super-rich citizens (Moene 2015). But how can wealth be turned into power? One of the best discussions of this comes courtesy of Thomas Christiano. Using his work as point of departure, I will highlight five mechanisms of how money may be converted into political power.[11]

First of all, rich people can finance political parties, candidates, or electoral campaigns. In the US, we know that the probability of a given presidential candidate to be elected is often judged on the basis of how much money the candidate can raise. The well off people who finance electoral campaigns may expect to get something in return, since the candidates who receive money are in one sense indebted to their donors. This may vary from the recipient politicians feeling themselves particularly obliged to come through on a campaign pledge, in which the donor is especially interested, to allowing donors easier access to important politicians (Christiano 2012:242).

Moreover, economic capital can also be converted into political capital by using money to influence what gets on the agenda. In this way, individuals may influence collective decisions. Financing think tanks that help shape public opinion is one example of this mechanism. In contrast to the previous mechanism, donors do not expect to get anything specific in return for their donation. Instead, they simply donate to people or organizations that have the same values and goals as themselves (Christiano 2012:244–246).

A third and similar mechanisms is to control the media. Silvio Berlusconi, who owned a large share of Italian (mass) media while he was prime minister, is a clear example. Those who control the media also control what political information is available. This contributes to shaping public opinion, and is therefore a possible source of influence (Christiano 2012:249).

Another mechanism for influence is to affect those who make decisions. Those who lobby tend to provide politicians with crucial information, thus contributing to shaping politicians' impressions of which issues are important. Lobbyist may, for example, provide politicians with arguments that they can use to convince others. Lobbyists play an important part in all modern democracies. Those who pay the lobbyist thus have one important source of political power (Christiano 2012:247–248).[12]

A final and more direct mechanism for converting money into political power can be exercised by capital owners against the authorities. If you have significant economic capital, you may threaten to withdraw your investments unless you get the conditions you want.[13] This kind of power can also be exercised in a less explicit way. To some extent, the authorities have to think about how rich people will react to proposed policies that are made, which may result in a kind of self-censure or limit on the freedom of politicians to make autonomous decisions (Christiano 2012:250).

What significance does economic resources have for the opportunity for political influence in Norway? Even though the role of money in politics is likely to be smaller in Norway than in the US, it would be naïve to think that money cannot be converted into power in the Norwegian system. Still, we must be careful not to claim too much in comparing Norway to the US. In Norway, parties, not individual politicians, accept gifts, and this seems to be a relevant difference. Furthermore, political advertising on television is prohibited. Thus, Trump's *description* of a corrupt system would probably not fit the Norwegian context.

Nevertheless, this does not imply that donations to political parties cannot buy political power in Norway. Take the example of the businessman Trond Mohn, whom the newspaper *Bergens Tidende* crowned the most powerful man in Bergen (the second largest city in Norway). Mohn donated kr2.5 million (€250,000 Euro) to the Labour Party (Arbeiderpartiet) electoral campaign in 2017. It does not seem entirely unreasonable to assume that Mohn by so doing achieved greater influence over the Labour Party and thus greater political power than others, and that this power is tied to his economic resources. However, it is difficult to say what exactly Mohn achieves by giving. On the one hand, one might think that the politics of parties are not influenced by who their donors are. On the other hand, it seems unlikely that Mohn's influence over the Labour Party is equal to that of every other person associated with the party. It is, for example, reasonable to assume that Mohn has easier access to central politicians compared to other people, and possibly also that, consciously or not, his views are accorded greater weight.

Mohn's opportunity to influence does not stop there. Since the founding of the centre/left think tank *Agenda*, Mohn has donated a total of kr24 million (approximately €2.4 million).[14] By helping to finance a group of people who help set the agenda and affect how voters think about core political questions, Mohn achieves political power as a result of his economic muscles. Therefore, we have reason to conclude that, even in Norway, economic resources can be converted into political power.

Money is converted into power also on the political right. In 2017, billionaire Stein Erik Hagen donated kr5 million (€500,000) to the electoral campaign of the Conservative Party (Høyre) (Spence 2017). In the 2015 election, the amount was kr1 million (approximately €100,000), and Hagen explained the donations by saying that he and his family "did not want the Labour party and property tax" (Haugan and Tjersland 2015). The right-wing think tank Civita is also financed through considerable donations from a number of rich individuals, including Hagen.[15]

I cannot here enter into a detailed explanation of how think tanks exert political power, and as far as I know, no study has looked at the influence of Norwegian think tanks (on politics in Norway). However, in a discussion of Civita and their role in Norwegian politics, sociologist Halvor Fosli writes the following:

> On the homepage of Civita, they present 49 books, 39 reports and 197 notes (working papers)... How these publications – together with a vast number of blogposts and newspaper articles – influence the development of Norway is not easy to measure. And the same goes for the breakfast meetings that Civita regularly hosts and which have 5000–6000 participants each year. It is not clear how each participant is influenced through these meeting. It is influence through *soft power*, influence through power of definition, agendasetting, establishing of trust from some influencers, and distrust by others.
>
> (Fosli 2017:14–15)

The point is that big think tanks like Agenda and Civita play an important role in the Norwegian public debate. Civita is, for example, good at rebutting its opponents. This is legitimate, and a natural part of what a think tank does. It is nevertheless important to garnering support for Civita's view of how society should be organized. The role the think tanks plays is, in part, made possible by a number of rich donors (Civita) or one dominating owner (Agenda). Power is, among other things, a matter of being able to influence what people think. In that sense, it is evident that those who can contribute to financing organizations like Agenda and Civita have a source of power, and this is an opportunity not available for most people.

Does this mean that we should ensure a more equal distribution of income and wealth to avoid the situation where some may convert their economic capital into political capital? Many deny this. The solution, according to these, is not to redistribute. Instead, society should introduce mechanisms to hinder the conversion of economic into political power. We touched upon this argument in Chapter 1. One could, for example, put a limit on how much individuals can contribute to electoral campaigns or simply make it illegal to donate, ban political advertising, and ensure all political parties equal access to the media.[16] These are measures to prevent the influence of money in politics. In my view, these are necessary but not sufficient conditions for hindering that those who are better off also have the most opportunity for influence. To avoid economic resources being used to achieve political power, it is necessary *both* to redistribute *and* to put in place the kinds of special measures mentioned here.

The reason for this is that one can deny individuals the right to donate money to political parties, but if the wealthiest want to achieve influence, they will find other ways of doing so. They can, for example, fund think tanks. In this way, those with the largest fortunes can gain influence, and it is likely the case that society cannot limit how much an individual can donate to a think tank without conflicts arising with other liberties, like liberty of conscience and freedom of association (Volacu and Dumitru 2018:footnote 15). Moreover, rich people may threaten to withdraw their investments if they do not get what they want.[17] If one takes seriously the ideal of free and equal citizens who must be ensured equal opportunity for political influence, this implies limiting the wealth of the super-rich.

The problem is, of course, not that Mohn donates money to the Labour Party and Agenda. The problem is that Norway has an economic system which allows some people to become so rich that they are able to dominate and control others. The problem is that the basic structure allows some to become extremely rich.

To elaborate, we could add that the problem is not solved by pointing out that only a few super-rich will use their money to achieve power. The problem lies in an economic structure that provides some people with the *opportunity* to dominate and control others, not in the *likelihood* that they will use this opportunity.[18]

Let me also substantiate this point with a personal story which involves the think tank Agenda (owned by the billionaire Trond Mohn). In the run-up to the 2017 national election in Norway, I published the opinion piece "Can power be bought?" ("*Kan makt kjøpes?*") in the newspaper *Bergens Tidende*. The piece is fairly similar to what you have just read about the conversion of economic into political power in the previous paragraphs and similarly drew on Christiano's framework. However, the piece was originally slated to be published in Agenda Magasin, the official publication of the think tank Agenda, where I had been invited to contribute a text. Right after sending them the text, I was called by a representative of the think tank. They wanted to discuss whether I might consider revising it. The most explicit reason given for why they could not print the text was that they might risk Trond Mohn withdrawing his support to Agenda. The representative made the point that they could not know how Mohn would react if they published such a text and emphasized that "without his contribution, we are finished" (personal conversation, August 25, 2017). I found this unacceptable, and decided to publish the text elsewhere.

What does this illustrate? First, it is evident that the representatives from Agenda had very good reasons to act as they did. After all, much of the think tank's financing comes courtesy of Mohn. Ultimately, it could be a matter of people losing their jobs, and Agenda therefore seems to have acted prudently by choosing not to print the text. At the same time, this of course shows something deeply problematic about how money can be converted into power. Agenda finds it necessary to censure itself in order not to step on the toes of a rich donor. One of the most important agenda setters in the Norwegian public debate is not free to do as they see fit, but are subject to the will of a rich person.

In my view, there is also nothing wrong with the generosity of Trond Mohn. He donates money to causes he finds worthy, and mostly without strings attached. Hence, the actions of an individual are not primarily what this problem is about. The problem is structural. Norway has an economic structure that allows some people to become extremely rich, and this can have negative consequences. Again, this also illustrates the need to limit the opportunity of individuals to amass wealth, because there is a conflict between democracy and a form of capitalism that allows very large inequalities.

The deeper point in all this is that actors may have the best intentions and yet the outcome may still be bad. A servile and submissive attitude may result from skewed economic circumstances, even though Mohn does not want anyone to be servile and submissive. If people are servile and submissive towards those who have a lot of money, this is a violation of the ideal of relational equality.[19]

It is important to point out the limitations of what I argue for here. I am not saying that all or most of the extremely rich convert money into power. As far as I know, we do not know how many of Norway's super-rich have the kind of political ambition displayed by Mohn and Hagen. We know something about how much the richest donate,[20] but we know little about the influence one can achieve by giving gifts, or about how gifts affect those who receive them. My point is that Norway's economic structure provides the extremely rich with *opportunity* for extraordinary political influence, and that this is a problem. We need more research on the role money plays in Norwegian politics.

In spite of these limitations, I think the example shows that money *can* buy political influence even in an egalitarian country like Norway, and that the wealthiest therefore have an opportunity to convert their economic resources into political power. This argument against inequality can be supplemented by an argument to the effect that if inequalities continue to rise, there is reason to fear that it only becomes easier to buy politicians. In a discussion of Piketty, Martin Sandbu points out that:

> One consequence of Piketty's logic is that, if he is right, the integrity of Norwegian politics will be under ever greater pressure. More inequality worsens the temptation of a penniless politician. More capital lowers the price of influence for the richest, compared to the means they possess. And greater wealth gives them more reasons to invest in political influence since they have more to lose on policies that do not suit them.
>
> (Sandbu 2014:482)

There are many indications that, in the short term, economic inequalities will continue to rise. And one does not need to be particularly conspiratorial to see that these inequalities can also lead to inequalities in power, whether in terms of corruption or other ways of gaining influence with money. A recent study found that "one to three in ten local government unit managers have been subject to pressure for undue advantages" (Oslo Economics 2017:4). Local government employees are thus subject to pressure to favour the interests of certain individuals. This is in part due to the fact that for businesses in the Norwegian private sector, much rides on decisions made at the local government level. With more money in private hands, it would not be surprising if some of these would be used in unethical ways.

Rawls adds another dimension to this debate by pointing out the danger that those who are best off may join forces to promote their common interests:

> As Mill said, the bases of political power are (educated) intelligence, property, and the power of combination, by which he meant the ability to cooperate in pursuing one's political interests. This power allows a few, in virtue of their control over the machinery of the state, to enact a system of law and property that ensures their dominant position in the economy as a whole.
>
> (Rawls 2001:131)

I do not think that we need to go so far as to say that the wealthiest people control the apparatus of the Norwegian state. But Norway's wealthiest do have common interests tied to their desire to keep the privileges they enjoy, and there is no reason to be naïve about the existence of such a shared interest.[21]

Conclusion

The way I see it, the criticism levelled against the luck egalitarian distributive ideal for being too abstract and not adapted to a specific practice is at least partly right. The relational ideal of equality, as developed by Rawls, can criticize the distribution in society for allowing too much inequality for a democratic society. If citizens are to be free and equal, they must have a fairly equal chance to influence the political process, and this requires the inequalities not to grow too large. The luck egalitarian ideal is not situated in a practice in the same way. It simply claims that differences are unjust if they are due to circumstances outside of control. Luck egalitarianism can therefore allow large inequalities that may be problematic in a democratic context. The luck egalitarian ideal can allow outcomes where relations between people are characterized by dominance, status hierarchies, and servile citizens, who lack self-respect and who cannot therefore play the role of free and equal citizens. In my view, Rawls' distributive ideal has a clear advantage by tying democracy to distribution in a theory the basis of which is that we are free and equal citizens within the frame of a constitutional democracy.

I thereby conclude the presentation of the most important theories and debates in political theory within the framework of the nation state. I have presented *justice as fairness* and confronted this theory with different objections. I have shown that *justice as fairness* has good answers to objections from Nozick, Dworkin, Cohen, and Sen. I have also emphasized that the Levelling-Down Objection does not affect Rawls' position. In this chapter, I have defended a relational ideal of equality and shown that this ideal can be applied to criticize the distribution of goods in Norway. In the next section, we will use this relational ideal to discuss just tax.

Further reading

For luck egalitarianism, there are three articles that can be said to be classics: Ronald Dworkin's *What Is Equality? Part 2: Equality of Resources*, G.A Cohen's *On the Currency of Egalitarian Justice*, and Richard J Arneson's *Equality and Equal Opportunity for Welfare*. The article that sets the premises of the debate between relational egalitarians and those who defend equality as a distributive ideal is Anderson's *What Is the Point of Equality?*. Scheffler's *What Is Egalitarianism?* has also played an important role. The book *Social Equality: On What It Means to Be Equals*, edited by Fourie (et al.), contains a number of interesting contributions. Gideon Elford's *Survey Article: Relational Equality and Distribution* provides a nice overview over the literature. For an interesting attempt to bridge the two egalitarianisms in a discussion of inheritance tax, see Daniel Halliday's *The Inheritance of Wealth: Justice, Equality and the Right to Bequeath*.

Notes

1 Two other important early contributions to the understanding of relational equality are Miller (1998) and Norman (1998).
2 For example, Knight (2013:925) claims that luck egalitarianism is the most discussed post-Rawlsian theory of justice.
3 Note that the criticism against luck egalitarians that we will look at later is directed at what we might call first-generation luck egalitarians. In the last decade, a number of (second-generation) luck egalitarian theories have been established (in response to these criticisms?). One example is Kok-Chor Tan's institutional luck egalitarianism (see Halliday 2018:86–90).
4 Two objections against the luck egalitarian hardliner Eric Rakowski also deserve a brief mention. Rakowski has claimed that a responsibility-sensitive theory has the consequence that people must bear the responsibility of any consequence that follows from settling in a high-risk area. If, for example, one were to choose to settle in an area where there are frequent avalanches, one must (also) bear the consequences if an avalanche tears down a person's house and the person is uninsured. According to Anderson, this also implies that only those who settle in safe parts of a country can expect state-financed emergency responses (Anderson 1999:296). A related objection makes the point that people who *choose* dangerous professions—firefighters, fishers, or military personnel—expose themselves to significantly higher risk than the average person. According to Rakowski, choice of profession is a perfect example of option luck, and hence it is only just that the risk-taker must themselves bear the consequence of their choice. Consequently, if one chooses to become a firefighter, one cannot expect the state to offer any help in the case of a work-related accident (Anderson 1999:298).
5 Thanks to an anonymous reviewer for helping me clarify this point.
6 Anderson refers to Nancy Fraser and Axel Honneth as important representatives for the claim that justice is not just about distribution, but also about recognition. Fraser and Honneth (and Charles Taylor) have made important contributions to what is often called the turn towards recognition theory in political philosophy. This thinking has roots in Hegel's master-slave dialectic from *The Phenomenology of Spirit*, and highlights the need for symmetrical relations between people as a necessary precondition for a good society. Fraser, for example, has used the following example: A black stock broker who, upon leaving the Wall Street stock exchange, cannot get a cab due to the colour of his skin is not the victim of injustice along the axis of distribution. The injustice from which he suffers is lack of recognition (Fraser and Honneth 2003).
7 Anderson (2010a) expands upon this. As one anonymous reviewer notes, it is important to see that relational egalitarianism is essentially about difference between groups, whereas luck egalitarianism is (allegedly) more atomistic and asocial.
8 For a recent attempt to include resources from both forms of egalitarianism that is connected to taxation, see Halliday (2018).
9 There is a certain overlap between "power" and "influence", and in the following I shall use these terms as synonyms. However, note that the overlap is not complete. Influence normally refers to control that is not formal and open, whereas power does not have this limitation (see Morris 2002:11–12).
10 Election researcher Anders Todal Jensen was quoted in the Norwegian newspaper VG 08.08.2017 saying that "Norwegian political parties follow an international trend. They spend more on campaigns, and more of the money comes from rich individuals and from organizations" (NTB 2017). This need not be a problem, of course. One may, for example, think that political parties should not be financed by the state, given that it is politicians themselves who grant such funding, thus creating a fox and geese type situation; for a discussion, see Svåsand (2001). I will

put this question aside, given that I am interested in how rich individuals can achieve extraordinary political influence.

11 The mechanisms I discuss are somewhat changed from Christiano's terminology.

12 A recent Norwegian example connects lobbyism to tax policy. In 2019, an NOU was released on the issue of land value taxation for the aquaculture industry. The report recommended that Norway should adopt such a taxation, and that the revenue would amount to almost kr7 billion (more than €700 million). However, even before the publication of the report, the conservative government had announced that they would not consider such a tax. The leader of the committee, economic professor Karen Helene Ulltveit-Moe, commented on the process in the aftermath of the publication of the report, and said that the industry had conducted an intense form of lobbyism (Kristiansen and Wiederstrøm 2019).

13 One example from Norway is businessman Oddvar Røysi, who built a large wharf for tourist boats in the small municipality of Luster, and then threatened to tear it down unless he was allowed to use helicopters to fly tourists to a nearby mountaintop (see Aarre 2016).

14 Mohn owns 60% of Agenda, while 40% are owned by the labour union LO (Agenda 2018). What about the media? Is it fair to say that Mohn controls the media? No, but it is interesting to note that Mohn supposedly saved the regional newspaper *Bergensavisen* (*BA*) from bankruptcy in 1998. Bergens Tidende writes that:

> Within BA, one does not speak ill of Trond Mohn. Those with knowledge of the economy of the newspaper know that Mohn saved BA from bankrupcy in the fall of 1998. —I can confirm that we were mere weeks away from bankrupcy. If Trond Mohn had not injected money into the paper, we would have been bankrupt, says CEO Olav Terje Bergo.
>
> (BT 2004)

15 The financial model (of Civita) is, however, not tied to large donations from any single person, as is the case with Agenda; see Grihamar (2013).

16 For a nice overview of how campaign finance systems differ in different countries, see Waldman (2014). For an argument that the US should look to Norway in order to improve its campaign finance system, see Rensin (2014).

17 For further discussion about whether this strategy can succeed, see Robeyns (2017:9–10).

18 This point draws on Pettit and the republican tradition, which holds that a free society is a society without arbitrary power.

19 The general issue of money in politics connects with discussions of philanthropy. Recently, Rob Reich has developed a "political theory of philanthropy" discussing, among other things, whether "philanthropy in its different forms is compatible with liberal democratic ideals" (Reich 2019:13).

20 When it comes to the financing of political parties, we know that Norwegian political parties receive 67.7% of their income from public funding and that 13.3% comes from other contributors (SSB 2018). When it comes to think tanks, the picture is as we have seen somewhat different, and the most extreme here is that one person can be main owner and contributor.

21 Economist Kalle Moene has similarly expressed worry about the rising number of super-rich people in Norway. Moene holds that an increased number of super-rich people:

> is problematic in the sense that, in most political systems, rich people have more political influence than other people. If this group grows too large, their weight increases even more. This means that they would be able to influence the economic policies so that it becomes even easier to be rich.
>
> (Halvorsen and Moene 2015)

Part 3

Intervention

Just taxation

8 Foundational philosophical issues

Thomas Piketty once claimed in a televised interview that "the history of tax is the history of realized utopias". Tax may, in other words, be understood as one of if not *the* most central tool to realize a just society. Nevertheless, political philosophy has not properly involved itself in discussions of just tax. There have been less sophisticated discussions among professional philosophers about tax than about other moral questions. The general theories of just distribution have also rarely been applied to the ideologically fraught questions surrounding tax (Murphy and Nagel 2002:3–4). Recently, this has started to change, and we can now observe an increased attention to the question of just tax among political philosophers (Dietsch 2015; Gaisbauer et al. 2015; Halliday 2018; O'Neill and Orr: 2018).

That tax has not been a subject for political philosophers is regrettable, but understandable. Taxation is a complex matter. It requires, as mentioned in the introduction, insight into what effects a particular tax will have, and clarity when it comes to the normative values or principles one should apply when evaluating a given tax. It further demands a holistic picture of the economy in which the proposed tax would operate. If, for example, the country under consideration is a comprehensive welfare state, where those who have the most contribute the most, but everyone gets the same services, this will ensure some redistribution. If there is also a compressed wage structure as a result of strong unions, the argument can be made that additional measures like redistributive taxes are less necessary than they would have been had these arrangements not existed.

Holding a particular theory of justice to be true is therefore not sufficient to evaluate whether a specific tax policy, for example, a tax cut, should be recommended or not. To do this, we must know whether the tax cut in question will contribute to increase investments, create more jobs, and other questions typically the domain of economists. There is—as we shall see in Chapters 10 and 11—a large degree of uncertainty among economists about such questions. Hence, an economist will frequently be unable to provide clear answers to which effects a given tax or tax cut will have. Nor can economists tell us what is just. As the authors of one of the most well-known economic text books about taxation put it: "fairness is not in the end a question of economics" (Slemrod and Bakija 2017:89; see also Halliday 2018:185).

Theories of justice have traditionally been the purview of political philosophers. Philosophers cannot provide an accurate and detailed defence on how a tax should be designed in order to best realize a particular ideal of justice. However, philosophers can challenge our everyday understanding of central ideas such as property rights. We will see an example of this in the present chapter. Moreover, political philosophers can contribute to clarifying and applying ideals of justice so that these ideals can be used to inform a discussion of just tax. We will see examples of this in Chapters 10 and 11. Such application of theories of justice should be undertaken in dialogue with economic insight, but should not be reduced to economics.

The discussion of just taxation must involve different disciplines and rest on a public debate that is as broad and informed as possible. In Parts 1 and 2, I have discussed some of the normative ideals that is important to be knowledgeable about. In this part of the book, I will apply *justice as fairness* to questions of just taxation.

To that end, I will first, in this chapter, discuss some foundational questions of just taxation, using the book *The Myth of Ownership* by Liam Murphy and Thomas Nagel as point of departure. This book is the most important published work on just tax, and the authors' approach shares much in common with Rawls' theory of justice (O'Neill and Williamson 2015:827). Using a statement from the leader of the Progress Party (Fremskrittspartiet [FrP]; and then Norway's minister of finance) Siv Jensen as an example, I will discuss what it means to have just claims to income and how we should think about property rights in a theory of just tax. Towards the end, I will briefly weigh the strengths and weaknesses in Murphy and Nagel's approach to just tax.

Pre-tax income and everyday libertarianism

In the so-called ideology lectures that were held in Oslo prior to the 2013 national election, the leader of the right-wing populist party Siv Jensen wrote the following: "Lower taxes are a matter of allowing people to hold on to more of their rightfully earned money. If people are allowed to keep more of their income, they also have more latitude to act as they choose" (Jensen 2013). How are we to understand the expression "rightfully earned money" in Jensen's statement?[1] I suggest three readings:

1 "Rightfully earned money" means that people must be allowed to keep everything they earn.
2 "Rightfully earned money" means that pre-tax income provides the basis for evaluating what is rightfully yours. People do not have the right to keep everything they earn, but what is rightfully theirs is calculated using pre-tax income as a basis.

3 "Rightfully earned money" is not tied to pre-tax income at all. The expression loosely refers to the claim that we are entitled to somewhat more than what we are currently left with after taxes. "Rightfully" basically means "earned legally".

There may be other interpretations. However, of the three mentioned, 2 seems most reasonable. The Progress Party are in favour of a state, even if they may think that it should be considerably smaller than it is today. This state must be financed, which means that taxes must be collected. Because of this, 1 is excluded from consideration. Point 3 simply says that we should have a lower income tax level, without saying anything about what would count as benchmark. As far as I can tell, Jensen's statement indicates that "rightfully earned money" points to something more concrete than that. Therefore, I read Jensen as claiming that we should use pre-tax income as our basis when judging what would be just. How can we proceed to evaluate this statement? I think we will better understand the statement and be better able to evaluate it if we tie it to everyday libertarianism.

Everyday libertarianism is a light version of the theory of justice from which it derives. It is a view that has significant political influence, in spite of the fact that the philosophical thinking on which it draws does not stand up to scrutiny (see the discussion in Chapter 2).

The core of everyday libertarianism can be reconstructed through five steps:

1 We have a tendency to think that what we have earned belongs to us. Our net income is ours, in an original sense (even though value added tax is a limitation on this).
2 Therefore, politicians can trick people into thinking that increased taxes involve taking something that is rightfully theirs.
3 From this, it is but a short jump to the corresponding idea that tax cuts return to us "our own money".
4 Thus, the idea that the taxes we pay really belong to us.
5 Finally, this leads to the thought that we have a rightful claim to our pre-tax income (Murphy and Nagel 2002:35).

Even though few, if any, think that all taxation is bad because it takes away "my money", many think that the state, through taxation, take something that actually belongs to them. Here, the idea of pre-tax income plays an important role.

What, then, is pre-tax income, and what role does pre-tax income play in a theory of just distribution? Your pay check states how much you earn before taxes. Does that mean that pre tax income is an actual thing? Murphy and Nagel deny that it is. They think pre-tax income is a myth. How can they claim that, given that pre-tax income is listed on everyone's pay check?[2]

The basic claim is as follows: Pre-tax income may exist as a concept in accounting, but that does not mean that it should be ascribed normative value (Murphy and Nagel 2002:36). Or, to put it differently: The concept of pre-tax income should not be given a significant role in determining what constitutes just taxation. We could perhaps say that pre-tax income does not arise in social isolation, and that the idea of one's own income is therefore not something with which to begin a discussion of justice.

Let me try to clarify. Discussing justice in taxation is a complex matter. People work and produce stuff and then the state comes in and demands a part of it. If people do not comply, the state will use its machinery to force them to comply. From this perspective, it is no surprise that many people are hostile to taxation. What Murphy and Nagel's discussion asks us to consider is whether this picture is correct. If people instead were to consider how much of what they do in their daily life that has been possible because of taxation, the hostility might change: When I go to work, the roads and pavements I walk on, the fact that the colleagues I work with are healthy and able to work, and the fact that they are educated is all made possible through taxation (Barry and Halliday podcast). Without all of this, I would not be able to produce much, and my own and my fellow citizens' well-being would be reduced. What this shows is that the idea of the solitary individual with absolute property right to the fruit of her labour is misconceived. Reflections like these are an encouragement to follow the abstract Rawlsian idea of society as cooperation and to see what we produce as part of a social product.

Now, let us return to Siv Jensen's statement. Interpreted as I suggested above, this means the following: "rightfully earned money" points to pre-tax income and Jensen's statement represents a kind of everyday libertarianism.

Murphy and Nagel hold that pre-tax income is a myth and that everyday libertarianism is fundamentally confused. Pre-tax income is income in the absence of any tax. But in the absence of tax, there is no state, and in the absence of a state, there is no market (in the modern sense).[3] In the absence of a market, there is no income. Therefore, pre-tax income is a myth (Murphy and Nagel 2002:32). However, pre-tax income is not an innocent myth. It perverts many people's understanding of what is just, and is tied, in particular, to everyday libertarianism.

The problem with everyday libertarianism is that, in part, it rests on a logical fallacy and that, in part, the assumption about the justness of market outcomes is wrong. First to the logical fallacy: Libertarianism states that people have rights to their pre-tax income. However, since there can be no market (in the modern sense) without a state, and since there can be no state without taxes, it is "logically impossible that people should have any kind of entitlement to all their pretax income" (Murphy and Nagel 2002:32). Without a legal/judicial system—which must be financed by taxes—it is hard to imagine a well-functioning market economy.

Specifically, without a legal/judicial system, it is hard to imagine the existence of the kinds of institutions that are indispensable for a modern market economy: Money, banks, corporations, stock exchanges, and so on. Without a legal/judicial system, meaning in practice a state, it is, put briefly, impossible to have an income. From this it follows that one cannot evaluate the justness of a given tax on the basis of pre-tax income.

Second, consider the claim that market outcomes are just. By market outcomes, we here mean the outcomes of an unregulated market. There are mainly two arguments that are used to justify the claim that the outcomes of an unregulated market are just. The first is that market outcomes are just because they give people what they deserve. In Chapter 1, we looked at Rawls' arguments against desert. I will not repeat them here, but only note that market outcomes are affected by arbitrary factors such as genetic and social luck, and hence cannot be deserved. The second argument—which is the argument of the libertarian—is that market outcomes are just because they give people what they are entitled to. This argument builds in particular on the view that voluntary transactions are just. In Chapter 2, we questioned this view by showing how voluntary transactions also affect third parties who have no say in the transaction. Voluntariness is not a sufficient condition for justice, and this is an important argument against the view that the outcomes of an unregulated market are just.[4]

These theoretical considerations about market outcomes can also be supported by common sense. Just think about how arbitrary the distribution provided by the market may be. If a real estate broker earns ten times more than a medical doctor trying to cure Alzheimer, one may point to supply and demand as a justification. However, there are no good reasons to assume that what follows from supply and demand is just. Or, to use an example that frequently crops up in the Norwegian debate, one may think it unjust that certain business executives earn more than the prime minister (the "executive" of the whole country). It is difficult to see what good reasons there are for saying that people have a rightful claim to whatever the market gives them. Market outcomes rest on a whole range of arbitrary factors, and hence are not just. Therefore, discussion of just taxation must be freed from everyday libertarianism, which implicitly presupposes that the distribution created by the market is just, and hence that all departures from this distribution must be justified (Murphy and Nagel 2002:36).

To Murphy and Nagel, the state is a precondition for any market in the modern sense. There are no markets, and there can be no markets (again, in the modern sense), which are not framed and regulated by a state-sanctioned set of rules. Therefore, the "logical order of priority between taxes and property rights is the reverse of what assumed by libertarianism" (Murphy and Nagel 2002:33). Pre-tax income is, as we have already seen, a fictitious entity that is morally irrelevant (Murphy and Nagel 2002:99). The way I see it, this argument shows that Jensen's claim about allowing people to keep their rightfully earned money is nothing more than a rhetorical move, and not something that has any normative value.

To complicate matters, consider how discussions of tax justice are often myopic: It is often the case that taxes are discussed without mentioning how the proceeds are used. In contrast to this, Murphy and Nagel hold that one cannot discuss just taxation without taking into consideration the distribution of the services of the state. The question of whether a given tax is just or not cannot be separated from how the state uses the income generated by this tax. "It seems clear", write Murphy and Nagel, "that a tax burden that is matched by an equivalent transfer is not, in the relevant sense, a burden at all" (Murphy and Nagel 2002:14). Taxes therefore cannot be evaluated in isolation—that is, without taking into consideration the services provided in return by the state—when we are concerned with evaluating whether they are just. What matters from the perspective of justice is whether the services of the state and the state's collection of taxes are just when seen under one. This point is similarly put by Piketty: "Taxation is neither good nor bad in itself. Everything depends on how taxes are collected and what they are used for" (Piketty 2014:481).

If "rightfully earned money" cannot be understood the way Jensen does, what is the alternative? The Rawlsian answer is that a just basic structure determines what we can call "rightfully earned money". People do have a claim to their income, but the moral force of this right depends on the background of procedures and institutions that have made this income possible—procedures that are just only if they include taxation in order to enable some version of equality of opportunity, public goods, distributive justice, and so on. Since income only results in rightful claims if the system is just, rightful claims to income cannot be used as an assumption to evaluate the justness of the tax system (Murphy and Nagel 2002:74).[5]

Put briefly, just institutions and procedures define what we may rightfully lay claim to, and not, as libertarians think the other way around: Property rights are prior to justice. Because of this, the idea of rights to pre-tax income must be replaced by a conception of property rights that is partly defined by the frames established by the tax system. The tax system does not intervene in an antecedently just distribution of goods. Instead, the tax system is one of several "conditions that create a set of property holdings" (Murphy and Nagel 2002:37). Another condition closely linked to the tax system is the system of property rights. To bring this line of reasoning to completion, we must look closer at different conceptions of property rights.

Property rights and taxes

Property includes things like land and material resources. To avoid conflicts about these things, we need a set of rules. Generally speaking, one can have private or collective ownership. Persons may have private property rights, which imply that the person who owns the thing has the right to decide over that thing. If something is owned collectively, the collective decides. How property rights are to be justified and delimited are important questions to answer when deciding how goods are to be distributed in society.[6]

What is the relationship between property rights and tax?[7] This question has not been sufficiently illuminated by political philosophers (Biron

2018:81–82). Murphy and Nagel's book represents an exception. They show that there have traditionally been two ways to answering this question in political philosophy. Deontological theories with roots in John Locke have claimed that individuals own themselves and have strong demands on what they modify through their own labour. In Chapter 2, we saw how Nozick grounds his entitlement theory in Lockean natural law thinking. Deontologists claim that fundamental rights are pre-political, and that the legitimacy of the political system depends on whether the system honours these rights. Deontological theories often support the belief that individuals have rightful claims to something that can be said to be their own, and that the state must provide special justification if it is to levy taxes.

Consequentialist theories trace their roots to David Hume. Those who defend consequentialism think that rights in general and property rights in particular have normative force because they contribute to the general welfare of society. Rights are justified to the extent that they are useful or necessary mechanisms, not because they are natural, of given prior to the political order. Consequentialist theories deny that there are any pre-political rights, and claims that the tax system is part of the system that establishes property rights (Murphy and Nagel 2002:44).

Taxes can be understood as a modification of the property right. The state takes control over parts of the goods that follow from social cooperation and/or the economic activities of individuals. Murphy and Nagel's point is that how one evaluates this intervention largely depends on whether one chooses the one or the other understanding of private property rights (Murphy and Nagel 2002:44). This distinction between two different perceptions of what tax most fundamentally is, is useful. I think this distinction captures two different, fundamental intuitions about how people think, and it is therefore important to investigate these.

Murphy and Nagel are especially critical of the libertarian way of understanding property rights:

> Private property is a legal convention, defined in part by the tax system; therefore, the tax system cannot be evaluated by its impact on private property, conceived as something that has independent existence and validity. Taxes must be evaluated as part of the overall system of property rights that they help to create.
>
> (Murphy and Nagel 2002:8)

The tax system helps create property rights, in the sense that it contributes to financing the apparatus that is necessary to enforce property rights. To repeat a point of the previous discussion: The question is not how the state should distribute something already owned by individuals. Instead, it is a matter of how one should determine the content of or the definition of ownership.

What can we say about the claim that property rights are a legal convention? One important point for Murphy and Nagel is to discredit the libertarian view of property rights as a concept with independent normative value. In libertarian thinking and political practice, the concept of property rights is used as justification for the claim that individuals have rights to the fruit of their labour. If, however, property rights are understood as a legal convention, then this is something that is established and defined in human practices, and not a natural right inscribed in the order of nature. The question is whether it is reasonable to define property rights exclusively as a legal convention, thereby excluding it as a morally founded right.

In my view, the answer is that this is not entirely reasonable. To point out a problem with the consequentialist view, assume that I arrive at an area not owned by anyone, establish a farm there, and start to grow potatoes. Do I not then have a natural right to the income of my sale of these potatoes? Can the state decide to confiscate all my potatoes if they find that doing so would benefit society as a whole? Is it not reasonable to say that, if the state does so, it violates my natural rights to own what I have created with my own hands? The consequentialist acknowledges that individuals have rights, but not that these are natural or pre-political and ascribed with a fundamental moral status. Instead, rights must be justified based on the use they have in creating good outcomes or consequences. Rights are then understood, not as something that trumps other considerations, but something that can be set aside if setting them aside results in better consequences.

The problem with the consequentialist model is that it lacks guarantees for individual rights. If the state can confiscate goods by pointing to what causes the overall best consequences, it can be argued that the protection of rights defended by consequentialists is too weak. At the same time, there are problems in the deontological understanding of property, because it builds on the view that I can have legitimate demands to something prior to it being taxed. I cannot fully discuss this problem here. Instead, I will suggest that Rawls' concept of private property overcomes some of the problems of these other two theories of property rights. My purpose of doing so is not to give a full defence of Rawls' understanding of private property rights, but only to sketch how it may provide a solution to the problems in the alternative theories.

To Rawls, it is crucial that everybody has a "right to hold personal property" (Rawls 1999:53). This right is essential because it guarantees "a sufficient material basis for personal independence and a sense of self-respect, both of which are essential for the adequate development and exercise of the moral powers" (Rawls 2001:114). The two moral powers include a capacity for thinking in terms of justice, and an understanding of the good. That everyone has a capacity for thinking in terms of justice implies that they are able to consider what is reasonable: Provided that everyone else sticks to the rules on which a cooperative society rests, reasonable citizens will also uphold these rules even if they are not directly advantageous to themselves. That citizens are rational means that they have the ability to pursue and adapt their views on what counts as a conception of a good life (Rawls 1996:48–54). The right to private property is therefore of fundamental import to the idea that citizens are free and equal, and to the idea of social cooperation, and this, as we have seen, are two of the most fundamental ideas in *justice as fairness*.

However, as Rawls points out, we should not treat a right as fundamental unless it is necessary to exercise the two moral powers. The possibility of having the opportunity to own one's own home may be seen as a fundamental right. However, the right to own or control the means of production and natural resources cannot be accorded a fundamental status. In Rawls' view, property rights also do not imply the right to bequeath one's assets (Rawls 1996:298). The justification for these restrictions on property rights is that it is not crucial to the two moral powers that a person can own the means of production and natural resources, nor is it crucial that one is able to freely transfer assets in the form of an inheritance. Roughly put, we may perhaps say that citizens must be able to hold *some* personal property in order to be able to live in accordance with their principles of justice and understanding of the good. Some private property allows individuals to act without always having to be concerned with survival, and may therefore be seen as a precondition for being able to act on one's own convictions about what is right and good.

On this basis, we may distinguish between a thick and a thin theory of property rights (Persky 2010; see also Brennan and Tomasi 2012). A thick theory of property rights provides a strong defence of the institution of private property. It does not give full freedom to do as one may please with one's property, for, as Nozick points out, I am not free to place my knife in your chest (Nozick 1974:171). What the strong defence of property rights does establish is that the state cannot put limits on property. Concentration of capital is not seen as something bad. The thin theory of property rights is in line with Rawls' general view of distributive justice, and in my view provides sufficient protection of private property. The thin theory maintains that individuals have an inviolable right to private property, but not to owning natural resources and the means of production. Rawls therefore provides a limited defence of property rights, something that is in line with his view on the negative consequences of a high degree of capital concentration.

Rawls' theory may be said to overcome the problems in consequentialist theories by giving an unconditional defence of the right to private property. The right to private property is unconditional because it ensures the self-respect of the individual. A consideration for the common good cannot overrule the right of individuals, for example, to have the opportunity to own their own homes. At the same time, Rawls' way of understanding property rights avoids the negative consequences of the thick theory, according to which the state should not meddle with private property at all. The thin theory does not give an unconditional defence of the right to own means of production and natural resources, and cannot therefore be used to argue for the protection against state intervention into such ownership.[8]

Rawls and Murphy/Nagel share the view that property rights play no determining role as an argument against taxation. For Murphy and Nagel, this follows from seeing property rights as a legal convention. It is up to society to decide how the tax system is to be designed, and there are no pre-political limitations that must be accorded weight in this decision. To Rawls, what matters is (as we have seen in this chapter) that everyone is ensured the right to own personal property as a precondition for the self-respect of free and equal citizens. As we saw in Chapter 1, one important role for the tax system is that it should hinder large concentration of capital. As long as this is done in a predictable manner, it does not represent a problematic intervention into the freedom of the individual.

Purpose: change the debate

If we are not to discuss tax based on pre-tax income, and also cannot discuss tax without including the services provided by the state, what then should we discuss? What we should discuss is what people are left with after taxation, including state transfers and services, and whether this is just. Murphy and Nagel therefore think that we must leave behind the narrow discussion of what constitutes just tax, and replace this with a comprehensive perspective on justice: "Our main message throughout this book has been that societal fairness, rather than tax fairness, should be the value that guides tax policy" (Murphy and Nagel 2002:173). If we discuss what people should be left with after tax, we have entered the general debate about justice, and it is more important to tackle this debate than to continue the debate on false premises. According to Murphy and Nagel, this is exactly the consequence if one continues to debate what the state is to be allowed to "take of what is mine".[9]

We can therefore distinguish between the following ways of discussing these questions: The libertarian asks: "How much of what is mine should be taken from me to support public services or to be given to others"? The egalitarian asks: "How should the tax system divide the social product between the private control of individuals and government control, and what factors should it cause or permit to determine who ends up with what"? (Murphy and Nagel 2002:175–176).

Murphy and Nagel want to show that the libertarian way of approaching this question is fundamentally flawed. We must therefore shift from a way of thinking where tax is a matter of the state taking something that individuals own to one where the question is how the state is to regulate ownership. Therefore, the core of Murphy and Nagel's perspective is the following: We must first disrobe or deconstruct the everyday libertarianism that influences thinking about just taxation, and then turn the attention towards questions that theories of justice can answer.

Hence, it is a matter of changing the debate, or about what the authors call a gestalt shift (Murphy and Nagel 2002:175): Away from the question of how much of what is mine the state may take, and over to how we are to design basic institutions like property rights and the tax system in a just way. Such a shift will not end all disagreement, but one will thereby have gotten rid of a way of thinking that is fundamentally flawed, and have turned one's attention towards things that are truly worth discussing:

> The question would become what values we want to uphold and reflect in our collectively enacted system of property rights – how much weight should be given to the alleviation of poverty and the provision of equal chances; how much to ensuring that people reap the rewards and penalties for their efforts or lack thereof; how much to leaving people free of interference in their voluntary interactions.
>
> (Murphy and Nagel 2002:177)

This brings us back to Rawls' insistence that what is to be distributed is a social product. How are we to distribute the social product? This is the right way of posing the question, not how the tax burden can be defined using pre-tax income as a basis. If people are convinced that we deserve what we earn and that the state afterwards comes to take money away from us, this will naturally lead people to be hostile, both towards the state and towards taxes. If we instead see the state as something that makes having an income possible in the first place, and thus a necessity for being able to create something together, one can avoid this hostile attitude and turn towards truly important questions.

Conclusion

An important reason to use so much space on an exposition of *The Myth of Ownership* is that several of the fundamental claims in that book are also relevant to the Norwegian debate. Siv Jensen's claim that people must be allowed to keep more of their rightfully earned money is one example of this. Another is Bent Høie (health minister) from the Conservative Party, who was quoted in a national newspaper saying that if the Labour Party were to enforce their policies towards pensioners, then the result would be that "the Labour Party would take their money through higher taxes" (Høie quoted in Haugan 2018). There are many such examples of politicians and others claiming that higher taxes means taking from people what they have a right to. This kind of claim deserves to be questioned. Equally important is showing that one need not give carte blanche to large inequalities by maintaining an absolute, but thin defence of private property rights.

A possible objection to my reasoning here is that, in the Norwegian context, this amounts to knocking down open doors. In egalitarian Norway, we accept that what we distribute is a social product, and there are but few elements of libertarian thinking. I think this objection is partly right. There is a clear distinction between Norway and the US, which is the country to which Murphy and Nagel's book is primarily addressed. At the same time, everyday libertarianism is not absent in Norway, and it is therefore important to take this kind of thinking seriously.

This, of course, does not mean that everything claimed by Murphy and Nagel is correct. The title of their book is particularly problematic. The authors do not claim that property or property rights are myths. What they really mean is that pre-tax income is a myth. Perhaps the book would have communicated better if this had been the title. Previous reviews indicate that the title contributed to misunderstandings (Zelenak 2003:2268–2269; Brennan 2005b:207–208).[10]

A more serious problem is that the justification for the central thesis that pre-tax income is a myth should be better unpacked and more thoroughly discussed. I think Murphy and Nagel's claim that pre-tax income has no normative value is open to the following objection: The libertarian can say that she has a rightful claim to her pre-tax income, if this income has been made without *in any way* relying on the state. Theoretically speaking, libertarians may therefore maintain that they have a right to pre-tax income and that the state takes something that belongs to the individual. We can *imagine* a state where there is no compulsory levying of taxes. The state must then be financed using voluntary contracts, and it also does not perform any of the other tasks we are used to being performed by the state: All education would then be privately funded, all roads paid with the aid of tolls, and so on.[11] In this extreme version of libertarianism, it is not inconsistent to claim that one has a right to one's pre-tax income. One would then have paid for all the services one is used to being performed by the state, including—even if this is hard to imagine—a legal system and the enforcement of law and order.

In the real world, there are no true minimal states, and all income depends on a state apparatus that creates and maintains infrastructure, ensures the enforcement of contracts, and ensures the education of people that are needed in the private sector. In the real world, therefore, it is wrong to claim that one has any right at all to pre-tax income. The criticism here is not that Murphy and Nagel are wrong, but that their argument at this point is a little too fast.

Finally, notice that the argument here would not convince the hard-core libertarian who would respond to my argument about there being no minimal states in the real world by saying that the real world is unjust *because* the state has forced people to use roads and other infrastructure put up by the state. The extreme libertarian will maintain that one cannot say that it is fair that one has to pay taxes after having been forced to use the infrastructure. The argument for why one should not be convinced by libertarianism was given in Chapter 2. The argument here is directed at all those who accept that there is a state apparatus and still maintain that they have a right to pre-tax income.

Further reading

Questions of just taxation are interdisciplinary, involving disciplines such as tax law, public finance, and microeconomics. Here, I must limit myself to say something about the most important works on taxation in political philosophy that deal with *The Myth of Ownership*. In 2005, the *Australian Journal of Legal Philosophy* arranged a symposium on the book, with an introduction by Liam Murphy, as well as critical articles by Geoffrey Brennan, Miranda Stewart, and Robert Young. This was followed by a reply by Murphy. Brennan's contribution was later developed into "The Myth of Ownership. Liam Murphy and Thomas Nagel. A Review Essay".

In the course of the last few years, others have added to the discussion. Martin O'Neill and Shepley Orr's *Taxation: Philosophical Perspectives* contains a number of important essays that discuss Murphy and Nagel. This includes Geoffrey Brennan's most recent engagement with *The Myth of Ownership*.

Podcast: Barry, Christian and Halliday, Dan: Dialogues 06: Equality.

Notes

1 If we permit ourselves a simplification, we may perhaps distinguish between two main arguments made against a high tax level: The pragmatic argument states that we must lower taxes to stimulate investments and create jobs, and the moral argument that is concerned with allowing people to keep "their own money". Here, I will discuss the moral argument, returning to the pragmatic one in the next chapter.

2 This way of framing the question is inspired by Zelenak (2003).

3 Murphy and Nagel do not themselves employ the distinction between simple and modern markets. However, because it is likely that there may have existed forms of barter between individuals independently of any state, I think this clarification is necessary. That said, the fact that there may historically have been state-independent markets does not affect the normative question with which we are here concerned. It does not justify Jensen's statement that we have a right to our pre-tax income.

4 I cannot provide a full discussion of these two arguments here; for a fuller discussion, see Olsaretti (2004).

5 This way of putting it suggests something to which we will return in the conclusion, namely that what we must evaluate is what people are left with after taxes (have been paid), and whether this is just.

6 For various ways to think about property and its limits in historical context, see Piketty (2020:486–577).

7 For a discussion of how difficult it is to define the term property rights, see Waldron (1988:26ff).

8 The thin theory of property rights has some commonalities with a third theory, briefly discussed by Murphy and Nagel, which was originally developed by Hegel. This is the view that *all* individuals have the right to own a minimum of property. Everyone must be ensured such a right because this is necessary to allow them to realize their freedom by imposing their will on external objects. This understanding of property rights shares a certain likeness with Rawls' in its focus on the demand that *everyone* must be ensured the right to own *something*. It focuses primarily on the positive right to personal property, and emphasizes that this right is crucial for individual freedom. At the same time, this view does not support the general objection against state intervention in private property that is central in the Lockean tradition (Murphy and Nagel 2002:45). For Rawls' take on Hegel's concept of private property rights, see Rawls (2000:340–344).

9 For an illustration of the importance of this point, see Liam Murphy's recent essay *How Not to Argue for Tax Justice* (2019). Murphy argues that in the book *The*

Triumph of Injustice, Emmanuel Saez and Gabriel Zucman falsely focus on the distribution of tax burdens and not on overall justice. As Murphy puts it:

> Justice in taxation is not a matter of some fair distribution of tax burdens as measured against pretax income. It is about how well or badly the tax system, together with the other elements of the economic and welfare system secures just *results*... The distribution of tax burdens is important only insofar as it is informative for policy makers thinking about how taxes can play their part in overall social policy aimed at making our society more just.
>
> (Murphy 2019:4)

10 In the preface, the authors emphasize that it was the editor who persuaded them to choose the title.

11 Murphy and Nagel suggest that one can interpret libertarianism in this way, and they ascribe it, wrongfully in my opinion, to Nozick (Murphy and Nagel 2002:31).

9 The Norwegian tax system

The purpose of this chapter is to provide preliminaries to the discussion of whether the Norwegian tax system sufficiently takes care of justice. Recall that the Norwegian case serves as an illustration of how it is possible to proceed in order to discuss issues of justice in taxation. In Parts 1 and 2, I have defended *justice as fairness*. I also showed—in Chapter 1—that an understanding of this ideal requires understanding it within the frame of a property owning democracy. Rawls claims that the most serious problem with capitalist welfare states is that they allow too much concentration of capital. States that allow concentration of capital open up the possibility of some individuals controlling and dominating others, in a way that conflict with the ideal of free and equal citizens. In Chapter 7, I have given an example of how rich people in Norway can achieve political power through their economic resources.

In the last chapter, I argued that in discussing the tax system, one must also be aware of the rest of the economy of the country. The fact that there is a compressed pay structure and a comprehensive welfare state in Norway contributes to reduce capital concentration. A tax system that ensures a progressive taxation of income, wealth, and inheritance could, in combination with the compressed pay structure and the comprehensive welfare state, further reduce the concentration of capital and bring Norway closer to the ideal defended in *justice as fairness*. The purpose of the following chapters is to investigate whether this potential is realized.

The following is divided into two sections. I start with a review of some central terms and distinctions from the literature on just taxation. Here, I will briefly show what purposes a tax system typically has as well as what it is that is to be taxed, and discuss whether a tax or a tax system should be proportional or progressive. I proceed to introduce the distinction between an instrumental and a constitutional approach to taxation. This distinction is important because the constitutional approach justifies absolute limits to how much the government can be allowed to tax, whereas the instrumental approach does not. Rawls defends the instrumentalist view, and I shall conclude this section with some brief discussions of what Rawls demands from tax systems.[1]

Next, I outline important aspects of the Norwegian tax system. Here, I use the Scheel committee report (NOU 2014:13) as my basis, which is the most recent comprehensive Official Norwegian Report (NOU) to discuss the Norwegian tax system. The goal here is first and foremost to demonstrate what role different taxes play in the tax system. This review shows that the Norwegian tax system is not particularly progressive. When Norway, in many measurements of inequality, is among the countries with the least inequality, this is in part due to the fact that the welfare state and the pay structure take care of much of the distribution. However, it is also in part due to the fact that inequality measures are often focused on income rather than wealth. If one looks at wealth inequality, Norway drops down the lists, and it is this kind of inequality that is most relevant from a Rawlsian perspective.

The following review focuses mainly on four different kinds of taxation. The purpose is to provide an overview over some important features of the Norwegian tax system, in order to evaluate this system in the light of *justice as fairness*.[2] First, we will look at corporate taxes, which form the bases of the discussions in the Scheel report. Next, I will describe the most important features of the Norwegian income tax, followed by some brief remarks about taxation of capital stock. Inheritance and wealth taxes belong to taxation of capital stock. However, as these two types of taxes are of particular importance to my argument, I have reserved single chapters to them. In the two final sections, I look briefly at indirect taxes such as VAT, and close with some remarks about the importance of replacing the distributive effect lost by reducing the corporate tax and the income tax.

Preliminaries on taxation and tax systems

Traditionally speaking, a tax system is expected to serve three purposes:

- Finance public expenditure
- Contribute to just distribution
- Promote an effective use of resources (NOU 2000, Nr. 8:46, 2014, Nr. 13:53; Dietsch 2015:13).[3]

That is, the tax system should provide the necessary revenue to offer public services. The chosen tax level will be crucial in determining what services can be offered. As we have seen, there is considerable disagreement in the political philosophy literature on how comprehensive the state should be in terms of the services it offers. In the Norwegian political debate, there is also disagreement, but not of this fundamental character. There is, for example, no disagreement about whether Norway should have publicly financed education and a universal health care system financed by the state.

Most tax systems have redistribution as one of their main aims. Which mechanisms matter most for redistribution is another question that is frequently debated and frequently misunderstood. While the following chapter will not settle these debates, I hope to help remove some of the misunderstandings.

For reasons of efficiency, the tax system should be as simple as possible, so that (a) the costs of administering it are as low as possible; (b) it facilitates economic growth; and (c) offers services to the population at the lowest prices possible (Bamford 2015:135). However, even succeeding in this goal, it is important to emphasize—as does the Scheel report—that "one disadvantage of most taxes is that they negatively impact the value creation" (NOU 2014, Nr. 13:15). For example, an increased income tax will make work less profitable, and if the consequence is that many people work less, this will contribute to making the economy less efficient.[4]

Thus, one frequently sees the claim made that there is a conflict between efficiency and distribution. Taxes have what economists call distortional effects; they influence economic behaviour. It is also commonly assumed that the higher the taxes, the greater the distortional effects. However, as one of the most important official reports (*Fordelingsutvalget*) note "[H]ow high the tax rate can be before such unfortunate effects become too great" is an empirical question (NOU 2009, Nr. 10:194).

It should be added that what effects follow from taxation also depends on the preferences and ideals of individuals. To simplify: If everyone only thinks in terms of their own interest, it is more likely that they will work less after a tax hike than if they are also motivated by a concern for justice of one egalitarian kind or another. Moreover, the effect of diminishing marginal utility also plays a role. If people have diminishing utility from increased income, one may tax those who earn the most without this having the same negative effect on efficiency as taxing those with lower income would have.

It is also clear that different taxes have different distortional effects: "The loss of efficiency will vary considerably depending on the tax or fee studied" (NOU 2009, Nr. 10:194; see also NOU 2014, Nr. 13:75). One part of the argument in this and the following chapter will therefore turn on what empirical research reveals about the effects of different taxes.

Another central discussion within the current tax debate concerns how one can prevent tax avoidance through companies moving profits across borders. In this discussion, there is an important distinction between mobile and immobile tax bases. Capital is the most important mobile tax base. Capital can be moved across borders, and is therefore more mobile than tax bases that are primarily immobile, such as work, consumption, or land (Dietsch 2015:13). The difficulty of taxing mobile tax bases has increased with increased globalization and internationalization. Exposure to tax avoidance is a big problem for any tax system; the fact that some avoid taxes means that others have to pay more, provided that the state is to uphold the same level of service.

Thus, tax avoidance and tax competition constitute a significant challenge for most tax systems today, and is likely to continue to do so in the future.[5] Here, I shall briefly mention two other trends that might be understood as challenges with implications for inequality and taxation in the future. It is, of course, risky to try to predict how things will develop. Nevertheless, there are, in my view, two broad tendencies that deserve a mention. The first has many names: Digitization, robotization, automation. In certain sectors, such as the banking sector, this development has already come a long way: From going to a physical bank to talk to a bank teller, most things are now sorted in web-based banking solutions. Many believe that this tendency will spread to more sectors, and some predict that self-driving cars will take over the jobs of drivers and that automated tellers will take over the jobs of store clerks. If this development removes more jobs than it creates, it will have distributive consequences. The fear is that it will both lead to higher unemployment and increase capital concentration, because the profit produced from robots will accrue to a few, rich owners (Moene 2018).

The second tendency is tied to reduced degree of unionization. In 1990, approximately 57% of workers in Norway were organized, while in 2016 the number was 49% (Nergaard 2017). Unions are an important explanation for the compressed pay structure in Norway. Centralized negotiations over income, led by strong unions, have ensured that the differences in income are small in Norway compared to other countries. This is a result of strong unions pushing the income of workers up, while the income of CEOs (and the profit of capital owners) is reduced (Ahlquist 2017:414–416). When the degree of unionization goes down, unions are weakened. If this is accompanied by an ever larger share of negotiations taking place locally, this will probably lead to greater income inequality (Wangberg and Moene 2015). I shall not discuss these trends in depth here, but will return to these issues in conclusion.

Two crucial questions for every tax system are *what* it is that should be taxed, and what should the tax level be? First, the question of what it is that should be taxed. This is a question of what tax base one should have. Should we tax income, consumption, inheritance, or wealth, or other things such as use of natural resources? How are we to tax corporations, or behaviour that has negative consequences such as driving? Moreover, what should the relationship between these different tax bases be? These are contentious questions. Generally, the convention in most jurisdictions is to treat income as the central and largest tax base. However, this might change in the future, given the growing wealth inequality witnessed in many countries recently.

Despite disagreement on tax base, most economists agree that having a broad tax base is an advantage.[6] This means spreading the tax on different things like income, wealth, and inheritance. By doing this, one can avoid the negative consequences of taxing one thing very harshly (NOU 2014, Nr. 13:55). If, for example, one were to cut the tax on inheritance and wealth and compensate for the lost revenue by increasing tax on income, the resulting income tax might cause people to work less. Moreover, having a broad tax base reduces the incentives for evasion (Dietsch 2015:14).

I will briefly run through the most important of these taxes, putting particular emphasis on their distributive consequences. Discussions of tax rates (how much should be taxed) differ with different taxes. Here, we will use the income tax as an example. In principle, a tax on income can have two distinct effects. It may lead people to work more to compensate the income loss they get through their net income being reduced. This is called the *income effect*. However, income tax may also have a *substitution effect*, which means that people work less because they get less income from each hour worked. In that case, the tax has the consequence of causing people to substitute time off for income, hence the name. Income tax may thus have two separate effects pulling in different directions (Murphy and Nagel 2002:22; NOU 2009, Nr. 10:213–214).

The three traditional ways of taxing income is the so-called poll tax, proportional tax, and progressive tax. Poll tax (or head tax or capitation) is simply a tax where everyone pays the same amount, regardless of income level and regardless of other conditions. Proportional tax (which is the same as a flat tax) involves everyone paying the same proportion of his or her income (the same percentage rate). Progressive taxation means that the proportion that one pays in tax increases with increased income. If one has an income of kr1 million, one will typically pay a higher percentage rate than if one earns kr500,000. The opposite of a progressive tax is a regressive tax, where the proportion one pays sinks as income rises.

There are few defences of poll tax today, and most discussions are therefore about the relationship between proportional and progressive taxation.[7] Austrian economist Friedrich Hayek, often portrayed as a representative of the libertarian tradition, defends proportional taxation.[8] Proportionate taxation is just, he claims, because it treats everyone equally. Progressive taxation, however, is unjust because it departs from equality by assigning different rates to different people. Hayek quotes McCullochs classical formulation of this criticism:

> The moment you abandon the cardinal principle of exacting from all individuals the same proportion of their income or of their property, you are at sea without rudder or compass, and there is no amount of injustice or folly you may not commit.
>
> (McMulloch quoted in Hayek 1976:308)

A number of commentators agree with Hayek.[9] Some even claim that a flat tax-rate is “the fairest tax of all” (Hall and Rabushka quoted in Fried 1999:157). I am not going into this debate here. In my view, Fried is right to say that “no sensible theory of distributive justice would fix on rate structure themselves as fair or unfair” (Fried 1999:159). This connects to a more general point. Taxes are instruments to achieve justice. No tax or no rate structure is necessary as such. It all depends on the other mechanisms that are operative in a given context. Therefore, a highly progressive wealth tax can be necessary, given a high level of wealth inequality. Alternatively, there might be no justification for a wealth tax at all in a context where there are other mechanisms in place to ensure the appropriate level of wealth distribution.

Another concern raised by Hayek is that tax policy must be regulated by some restrictions on the political process in order to make sure that a majority cannot impose harsh taxes on a minority:

> That a majority, merely because it is a majority, should be entitled to apply to a minority a rule which does not apply to itself is an infringement of a principle much more fundamental than democracy itself, a principle on which democracy rests.
>
> (Hayek 1976:314)

The principle Hayek refers to is that laws must be general to ensure that, in principle, they can be supported by those who enact them and those who are affected by them. A similar point has been developed and given the term tax and/or fiscal constitutionalism.[10] A fiscal constitution implies restrictions on the government's ability to borrow and spend, and is therefore broader than a tax constitution (TC) which is simply about restricting the government's ability to tax. In the following, I shall discuss tax constitutionalism in the narrow sense.

The TC approach challenges the view that governments are benignly motivated and oriented towards the common good. Instead, governments must be assumed to follow its own interests, and a crucial interest is of course to be re-elected. From this premise, it is argued that it is necessary with a TC that sets limits to government's discretion.

The TC approach worries that given the self-interested motivation of governments, there will always be a danger of the government exploiting the taxpayers. Therefore, it is necessary to restrict the power of government through mechanisms such as limits on the tax revenue. Thus, the TC approach challenges the standard economist view that a broad tax base is preferable:

> The TC points out that, in the absence of a well-motivated government, broader tax bases clearly provide greater opportunities for tax exploitation, so that constitutional restrictions on allowable tax bases might be motivated despite their narrowly economic inefficiency.
>
> (Hamlin 2018:29)

Another important issue where the TC approach challenges orthodox economics is on levels of government. Standard economics normally assume that a unitary government structure is an advantage due to efficiency. The TC approach argues in favour of separated tax raising powers within a federal structure. This, in order to reduce the danger of monopoly power on the level of the federal state and to allow tax competition between different states (Hamlin 2018:29).[11]

Tax constitutionalism challenges the instrumental view of taxation defended by Rawls and Murphy/Nagel. According to the instrumental view, outcomes are the only thing that matters, and rate structure is not important in itself. According to the TC approach, rates are of fundamental importance in order to reduce the potential for tax exploitation of the citizens. I shall not explore this here. More work needs to be done on this issue.[12]

I shall close this section with some brief remarks about Rawls and taxation. Despite the 50 years since the publication of *Theory*, and despite the enormous amount of literature on Rawls and distributive justice, there is much work to be done when it comes to the implications Rawls will have on issues of taxation (O'Neill and Williamson 2015:827). The following should be understood as an attempt to reconstruct what a Rawlsian position on these issues could be.

Rawls' take on taxation has been described as puzzling (Fried 1999; Sugin 2004:1994; O'Neill and Williamson 2015:826). To a large extent, this has to do with Rawls' comment that taxing consumption proportionally might sufficiently take care of justice. In *Justice as Fairness: A Restatement*, Rawls notes that "income taxation might be avoided altogether and a proportional expenditure tax adopted instead" (Rawls 2001:161). Similar formulations can be found in *Theory*. Commentators find this puzzling because Rawls seems to support proportional over progressive taxation and tax on consumption over income tax. Both measures are normally considered deficient if the ambition is to employ the tax system to achieve a more equal society. As Fried puts it:

> In the context of the overall Rawlsian scheme, the right not to have one's income taxed at a higher marginal rate than one's neighbor's stands as an island of deontological rights swamped by a sea of redistribution.
>
> (Fried 1999:185)

What can explain Rawls' comment here? The first thing to note is that we must distinguish between two different levels of theorizing (O'Neill and Williamson 2015:826). Ideally, in a property owning democracy, Rawls assumes that there are mechanisms in place that secures procedural justice. To simplify, this means that there are mechanisms to safeguard the political liberties and to ensure fair equality of opportunity. In other words, if there are measures of predistribution to protect the conditions necessary, additional taxation might be proportionate and on consumption. With such a system in place, we can understand what Rawls has in mind when he suggests that we might even avoid the income tax altogether. People will instead be taxed based on how much they consume of what has been produced (Rawls 2001:161).

Under less ideal circumstances or, to be more precise, under conditions in most countries in our present time, Rawls must be understood to be in favour of strongly progressive taxation of income, wealth, and inheritance. The predistributive mechanisms in Norway exist, but they cannot guarantee pure procedural justice. In contexts where there is a level of capital concentration threatening the political liberties and fair equality of opportunity, it is necessary to employ tax measures suitable to address these problems. The political liberties and fair equality of opportunity has absolute priority in the Rawlsian system.

However, this does not mean that a Rawlsian can claim that a specific tax is necessary to guarantee pure procedural justice. If inheritance taxation alone would deconcentrate capital, no wealth taxation would be necessary. However, some of the richest people have created their own wealth, and the inheritance tax will therefore not be suited to reduce their wealth until they pass away. If there are other mechanisms available, they must be considered. It is, to repeat an important point, not essential what mechanisms one employs in order to safeguard the political liberties and fair equality of opportunity. What is essential is that they are secured, one way or the other. Sugin has put this point accurately:

> Rawls uses the tax system as a means of achieving distributive justice, rather than as a requirement of justice itself – the features of the tax system are not constitutional essentials.
>
> (Sugin 2004:1997)

Constitutional essentials, for Rawls, are those rights and liberties that it is essential that the constitution must safeguard. Securing the two principles of justice is thus a constitutional essential, whereas what mechanisms employed to guarantee them is not.

I will now move from these general tax issues to a discussion of the Norwegian tax system.

A sketch of the Norwegian tax system

On March 15, 2013, the second Stoltenberg government (named after Prime Minister Jens Stoltenberg of the Labour Party) initiated what has later come to be known as the Scheel committee, named after the head of the committee, Hans Henrik Scheel. The committee's mandate was to evaluate the Norwegian corporate tax in light of the international development in corporate taxation. In the mandate of the committee, the international trend towards lower corporate taxes is emphasized. Because of this trend, it was important to harmonize Norwegian tax rules with the rules of other countries. This need was reinforced by the fact that multinational corporations move money between countries in order to achieve the lowest taxes possible (NOU 2014, Nr. 13:12).

In 2014, the Norwegian state had a total income of taxes and tolls of kr1,261 billion, or approximately €125 billion. The largest share of this state income was due to four sources: Income tax, VAT, employer tax, and petroleum tax. Figure 9.1 shows how the income is distributed across all sources (NOU 2014, Nr. 13:33).

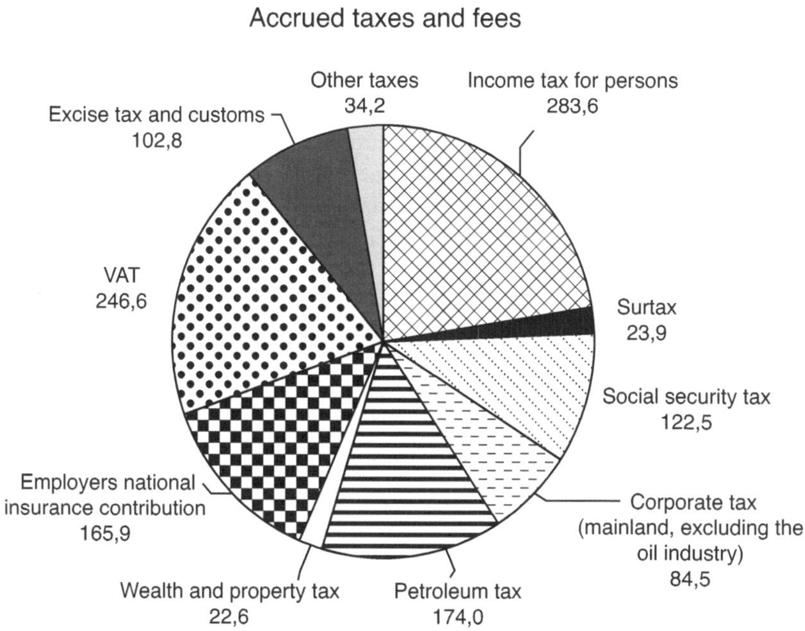

Figure 9.1 Norway's income from taxes.
Source: NOU (2014, Nr. 13:33).

If one disregards the petroleum tax, the composition of the Norwegian tax system is similar to that of its neighbour countries. As for the general tax level, Norway is not exceptional:

> Measured as a share of GDP, the Norwegian tax level in 2012 was 42.2 percent. This is lower than the nearest neighbours (Sweden [44.4), Finland [44.1], and Denmark [48.0]), but considerably above the average in OECD countries, which was at 34.1 percent in 2011.
>
> (NOU 2014, Nr. 13:36)

Before describing the four taxes mentioned above and discussing these more in depth, I want to head off a possible objection to this approach. The objection is that individual taxes must always be seen in light of the tax system as a whole. One can, for example, object that one cannot discuss whether inheritance taxation is just without looking at the other distributive taxes in the tax system. Kristin Clemet (a prominent right-wing ideologue in Norway), for example, has argued for a holistic perspective when discussing inequality in Norway; a perspective that does not look at the tax system, not to mention individual taxes, in isolation, but which takes into consideration the entirety of the budget or the politics that are being advanced (Clemet 2017).

In my view, Clemet is partly right. She is right that we must have a holistic perspective when debating inequality and taxes in Norway. As we have seen, such a broad perspective is in line with Rawls' take. However, this should not get in the way of approaching the issue analytically, discussing the consequences of changing or removing individual taxes. Different taxes have different justifications and different consequences. The holistic perspective must not stop us from discussing individual taxes, or from giving explicit justifications for why we find these particular taxes necessary. Here, we must mobilize normative theory and ask which taxes best realize the ideals we support.

Corporate tax

Corporate tax is a tax levied on the profit of corporations. The basis of the Scheel committee was the context of international competition in a day when many countries have gradually lowered their corporate taxes. Figure 9.2 shows an overview of the corporate taxes in a number of OECD countries.

In Norway, the corporate tax was 27% in 2014, and thus higher than in its closest neighbouring countries (Sweden, Denmark, Finland). The neighbouring countries are the countries to which it makes the most sense to compare Norway, because it is with these countries that Norway mainly competes for investments. Furthermore, these countries had made announcements about further reductions in the corporate tax. While the Norwegian corporate tax had been the same from 1992 to 2014, the average corporate tax in EU countries had fallen from 35.3% to 23.5% from 1995 to 2012 (NOU 2014, Nr. 13:12). The Scheel report therefore points out that the Norwegian corporate tax is high, seen in an international context. However, the report

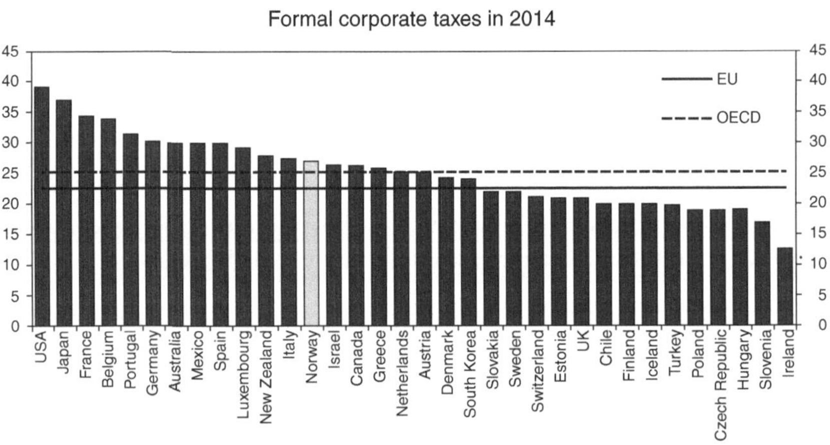

Figure 9.2 Corporate taxes in OECD countries.
Source: NOU (2014, Nr. 13:17).

warns that if Norway were to lower its corporate tax too much, then it would contribute to increased competition among countries to lower their taxes, creating a race to the bottom (NOU 2014, Nr. 13:18).

The Scheel report suggested lowering the corporate tax rate to 20%. The committee also argued that a lowered corporate tax requires a lowered tax on ordinary income in order to avoid tax adaptations (NOU 2014, Nr. 13:263). Let me explain: Ordinary income comprises all forms of income, including share dividends. Income from share dividends is also called owner earnings, and the tax system must avoid people being motivated to shift their income, meaning that one takes out earnings from labour in the form of owner earnings in order to be taxed less. For, as the committee writes, "a separate, lower tax rate for corporations will provide incentives to transfer capital from person to corporation" (NOU 2014, Nr. 13:281). The committee therefore recommends a continuation of the close coupling between personal and corporate taxes, which has been a feature of the Norwegian tax system since 1992.

In the tax settlement agreed upon by six political parties in 2016, corporate taxes were to be lowered to 23% by 2018, with corresponding lowering of tax on ordinary income.[13]

Income tax

The Norwegian income tax for individuals has two parts, in the sense that it is calculated using two different bases. First, there is a flat tax on ordinary income. Ordinary income is not just earnings from labour, but also income from business and capital/investment. Second, private taxpayers in Norway pay a national insurance, and if one's personal income is above a certain level, one also pays surtax. In 2014, the flat tax rate was 27%, while the national insurance contribution was 8.2%.[14]

The income tax is progressive due to the standard deduction and the surtax on higher incomes. In 2014, the standard deduction was kr48,800, or about €4,900. The surtax on higher income had two steps. Step 1 was for personal incomes above kr527,400 (approximately €53,000), which was levied with a 9% surtax. Step 2 was for personal income above kr875,300 (€864,000), which was levied with a 12% surtax. The standard deduction makes income tax progressive by making a large share of a low income tax-free compared to a higher income. If I make kr50,000 a year, I will be taxed on anything above kr48,800; kr1,200 will be taxed, while the rest is tax-free. Someone who makes kr500,000 will also be taxed on anything above kr48,800; but in that case, the share of income that is taxed is kr451,200, and thus much larger.

The surtax on higher income adds further progressiveness by taxing high incomes extra. The highest marginal tax rate in 2014 was 47.2% (27 + 8.2 + 12%); marginal tax means the tax you pay on the last euro you earn. The standard deduction and the surtax for higher income means that tax on labour earnings has a "clearly progressive structure" (NOU 2009, Nr. 10:197–198).

Income tax thus makes up an important share of state income. At the same time, taxation of income in Norway has become less progressive since the middle of the 1980s (NOU 2009, Nr. 10:197–198). The Scheel committee concludes that income tax has a negative effect on economic growth (NOU 2014, Nr. 13:79), and this insight has probably contributed to a reduced emphasis on income tax in the Norwegian tax system. Seen in isolation, this development has contributed to making the tax system less progressive.[15]

However, there is no guarantee that a lowered income tax results in a more efficient economy. In 2015, the International Monetary Fund (IMF) conducted a study showing the correlation between changes in the top marginal tax rate and the share of the total income that accrues to the richest 1% in the period from 1960 to 2009. The conclusion is that Norway, along with most other European countries, has lowered the marginal tax on the highest incomes considerably, and that this has contributed to the top 1% getting a larger share of the total income (Dabla-Norris et al. 2015:22).[16] In another report, IMF pointed out that equality is good for economic growth, and that progressive taxation has little effect on growth (Ostry et al. 2014).

OECD has also recently looked at the effect of income inequality on economic growth in Norway. The resulting report is clear: The increased income inequality that has taken place in Norway from 1985 to 2005 has reduced economic growth by nearly nine percentage points. The reason is that income inequality reduces educational opportunities for the worst off, which reduces social mobility and the ability of many to develop their skills in the best way possible. This lowers GDP, and the pie that is to be distributed among all members of society becomes smaller (OECD 2014). There is then a limit to how far one should go in following the logic of the claim that income tax is bad for growth. The OECD report suggests that Norway has followed this logic too far in recent years—and this is true even in the absence of any consideration of justice.

These reports do not offer any final proof that Norway should have more progressive income taxation. Still, they are representative of a shift in central global institutions, which in recent years have become more and more convinced that equality is good for economic growth. Growth may then be reduced by allowing the kind of income inequality we see in Norway today.

Tax on capital stock

Wealth tax, property tax, and taxes on inheritance and gifts together constitute tax on capital stock. Inheritance tax will be the topic of the next chapter, whereas the wealth tax is discussed in Chapter 11. Figure 9.3 provides an overview over tax on capital (stock) in countries that are comparable to Norway:

In Norway, the municipalities levy the property tax. The municipalities are to set the rate between 2,000th and 7,000th of the estimated value. The valuation of the real estate is however low at 25–30% of market value.

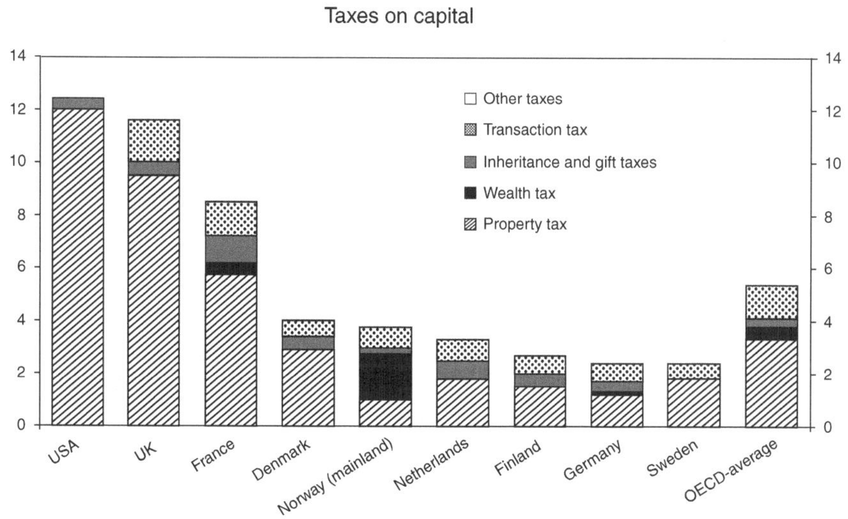

Figure 9.3 Income from different taxes on capital stocks as a share of total tax and toll income in a selection of countries. Percent numbers from 2011.
Source: NOU (2014, Nr. 13:284).

Gains from sale of real estates are in principle liable to taxation in the same way as income.[17] However, if you sell your house and have lived in it for at least one of the last two years, you will be exempt from taxation. Similar rules apply for a holiday home, but you must have owned it for at least five years and used it for five of the last eight years. Thus, in practice, most gains from transactions of real estate is exempt from taxation (NOU 2014, Nr. 13:43).

This means that Norway has very favourable arrangements for homeowners, allowing, for example, owners to rent out parts of their homes tax-free and by offering considerable tax rebates on interest payments for mortgages. Partly as a result of this, 77% Norwegians own homes (SSB 2017b), whereas the same figures for the UK is 63% and (GOV.UK 2018), and 65% in the US (Statista 2020).[18] Thus, compared to other countries, Norway comes closer to the ambition in a property owning democracy that everyone should be able to own some property (see Chapter 1).

However, possible negative effects of this policy are that people invest in property rather than job-creating businesses. Thus, the Scheel committee suggests that real estate should be taxed harder. They argue in favour of a much stricter tax on income from residential property (NOU 2014, Nr. 13:294), combined with a valuation which is more in line with market value. The proposal is to increase the assessed value to 80% of market value (NOU 2014, Nr. 13:297).

Indirect taxes

Income tax, corporate tax, and wealth tax are called direct taxes. These taxes are drawn directly from those on whom the tax is levied, for example, individuals or corporations. Indirect taxes, by contrast, are typically levied on those who sell a good, and these may then pass the cost on to the customer by adding to the price of the good. The VAT is an important form of indirect tax that is collected by the seller, but paid by the buyer of an item. In Norway, the general VAT is 25%, but there are also reduced taxes for certain goods and services. Foodstuff such as food and drink is charged a 15% tax, while a number of services such as transport, cinema, and sports events are charged a fee of 8% (NOU 2014, Nr. 13:52).[19]

Indirect taxes, then, are taxes on consumption, even though not all consumption, such as health care services, is taxed. Tax on consumption is an important source of revenue for the state, while at the same time such taxes have less of an impact on economic growth than do other direct taxes (NOU 2014, Nr. 13:79). Tax on consumption therefore has an important role to play in the economy. However, there is wide agreement that it does not work as a distributive mechanism. This, because a person who is poor and a rich person pay the same tax on consumption for any given item, and the smaller someone's income, the larger the share of their income will go to pay for that item (Halliday 2013:1116).[20] The Scheel committee therefore concludes that the VAT should only be aimed at obtaining revenue for the state (NOU 2014, Nr. 13:29).

The tax system also contains various special taxes. Special taxes are taxes on consumption that are added to particular goods. Tobacco and alcohol are examples of goods that are not subject to VAT. Instead, you pay a special fee. Such fees can be justified by their role in generating revenue for the state, but they can also be justified by their role in influencing people to buy less of products that have harmful effects. In addition to fees on tobacco and alcohol, there are also debates in a number of countries about whether one should tax actions that harm the environment.[21]

Conclusion

In Norway, the income tax has become less progressive since the 1980s, and the corporate tax has been reduced substantially.

The question then becomes how to organize the tax system so that it can contribute to a fair distribution. The corporate tax and the income tax are, in my view, the most complicated taxes to evaluate. A reduction in corporate tax may be necessary to uphold competitiveness when other countries lower their corporate taxes. The danger of income shifting is an argument in favour of lowering the income tax. At the same time, there are considerations that pull in the opposite direction. The OECD report, mentioned above, concludes that increasing inequality in Norway has caused lower growth because the worst off cannot fully develop their abilities. This is an argument to the effect that even egalitarian countries like Norway are not, in fact, ensuring equal opportunities.[22] That is both unjust and bad for growth. This speaks in favour of limiting the cuts in the income tax and perhaps even increasing the rate for those with the highest income.[23] Note also that *if* the corporate tax and the income tax are reduced, it is necessary to replace them with other taxes to ensure redistribution. The discussion in the two following chapters must be seen in light of this trend towards a less progressive tax system.

Further reading

Barbera Fried's *The Puzzling Case for Proportionate Taxation* is an important intervention into the debate on proportionate vs. progressive taxation. Linda Sugin's *Theories of Distibutive Justice and Limitations on Taxation: What Rawls Demands from Tax Systems* provides a discussion of Rawls and taxation. For a short, but good discussion of the same topic, see O'Neill and Williamson's *Taxation*.

In the *Philosophical Explorations of Justice and Taxation* (edited by Gaisbauer, Schweiger, and Sedmak), there are important articles on different kinds of tax. Peter Dietsch's *Catching Capital: On the Ethics of Tax Competition* is first and foremost about how one can deal with the increasing tax competition between countries, but the book also contains general insights into taxation. Slemrod and Bakija's *Taxing Ourselves* provides an introduction to key issues on the tax system in the US, whereas the Institute of Fiscal studies' *A Survey of the UK Tax System* provides an overview for the UK. For two shorter texts that provide introductions into tax and theory of justice, see Daniel Halliday's *Justice and Taxation* and Colin Farrelly's *Taxation and Distributive Justice*.

On the Norwegian context: In this chapter, I have drawn on two relatively new NOUs. The Scheel committee (NOU 2014, Nr. 13) and the Distribution committee (NOU 2009, Nr. 10) are good sources of questions about tax in the Norwegian context. The Distribution committee report is broader than that of the Scheel committee, with the former considering distribution in general, while the latter looks at taxes, primarily the corporate tax. Three other important NOUs are the Commission on Tax (NOU 1984, Nr. 22), the Aarbakke committee (NOU 1991, Nr. 17), and the Skauge committee (NOU 2003, Nr. 9). Einar Øverbye's *Likhet and ulikhet under Erna Solbergs regjering* provides a brief and pointed discussion of the developing inequality in recent years. Clemet and Doksheim's *Underlige konklusjoner om ulikhet* criticizes some of Øverbye's conclusions.

Notes

1 I borrow this phrase from the title of Linda Sugin's paper "Theories of Distributive justice and Limitations on Taxation. What Rawls demands from tax systems" (Sugin 2004).

2 In order to provide the reader a possibility of comparison, I have tried to complement the picture by introducing data from the US and the UK.
3 In addition, tax systems are commonly employed to *influence individual behaviour*, for example, to dissuade people from buying stuff that is harmful (tobacco, alcohol, gasoline); see Halliday (2013:section 4).
4 This, however, is not given, and I will discuss this assumption later on.
5 I will return to this in the second part of this chapter and in Chapter 11. For an important discussion on tax avoidance and tax competition, see Dietsch (2015).
6 I shall return to a different view shortly.
7 For a defence of the head tax, see Schoenblum (1995). For a discussion of such a tax in a Rawlsian scheme, see Sugin (2004:2000).
8 For further discussion of Hayek's theory of distributive justice, see von Platz (2020:22–52).
9 This is particularly true for writers in the libertarian tradition where Hayek and Friedman must be considered the most important representatives. For Friedman's take, see Friedman (2002:Chapter X. The classical essay on proportional taxation is Walter J. Blum and Harry Kalven's "The Uneasy Case for Progressive Taxation" (1952). The essay is briefly discussed (and its argument refuted) in Murphy and Nagel (2002:130–132). See Fried (1999, 2003) for an overview of the literature.
10 My presentation of these issues draws on Hamlin (2018).
11 The Norwegian tax system includes, as we shall see, a wealth tax of 0.85% where 0.15% goes to the state and the rest goes to the municipality who is entitled to set the rate. In 2019, Bø, a municipality in the north of Norway, reduced the wealth tax that goes to the municipality to 0.2% in order to attract capital and stop people from moving to other parts of the country (Alsberg 2019). Thus, it is not only in a federal system that the tax system can encourage tax competition.
12 An important point of departure for this discussion is Brennan (2018).
13 Similar rates by 2018 in the UK were 19% and 25.8% in the US (OECD Stat 2020).
14 In 2018, the total tax on income in Norway was 35.8, whereas similar figures for the UK were 30.9 and 29.6 for the US (OECD 2019).
15 This will contribute to increased income inequality. Note however that the development of inequality in income is also affected by other factors such as immigration, housing prices, and unemployment. See Øverbye (2017) for an elaboration of this.
16 The report shows that Norway has reduced its top marginal tax rate by almost 30% in this period, and that this has given the top 1% a 4% higher share of the total income.
17 In addition, Norway has a special tax on dividend (*utbytteskatt*) which resembles capital gains tax. Capital gains taxes can be seen as an indirect wealth tax because the tax is typically levied on the stock of wealth, such as houses and how much their value has increased. Capital gains are treated very differently by different countries (Piketty 2014:283). In 2019, the Norwegian tax was 22%. The tax is calculated according to the "shareholder model". "The dividend must be reduced by a tax-free amount (deduction for risk-free return), and multiplied by a factor of 1.44", according to the 2019 rules (Altinn 2019).
18 Note that there can be differences in how these figures are established.
19 In 2018, the VAT in the UK was 20% (OECD 2018a). The US does not have a federal consumption tax, but on state level, there is a retail sales tax. As the recent OECD tax report notes on the US, the country has the lowest proportion of revenue from general consumption in its total tax revenue (7.3%), far below the OECD average (21.2%) (OECD 2018b). Saez and Zucman claim that the US has

a "poor man's VAT" (Saez and Zucman 2019a:16) in taxing regular consumption, but exempting services that the affluent consume more of, like going to the opera.

20 This means that ordinary tax on consumption is actually regressive, and therefore unfair in the eyes of an egalitarian who thinks that fair taxes should tax people more the better their ability to pay. There are, however, a number of attempts at making taxes on consumption progressive. One can, for example, make the tax one pays depend on one's income and/or raise the tax for luxury goods. For a much-discussed American suggestion, see McCaffery (2002). See also Piketty (2020:1001), who argues in favour of abolishing indirect taxes, except for cases where these taxes are necessary to correct externalities.

21 For a discussion of whether this kind of tax is regressive, and whether one can reform such taxes so that they do not have a regressive effect, see Halliday (2015). For a general discussion of environmental taxes, see Casal (2012). Interestingly, Casal thinks that environmental taxes can be made progressive. If one flies a lot, one must pay more the more one flies, and if one does not fly at all, one could get money back from the state (Casal 2012:426). For a similar suggestion about taxing business class tickets to finance poor countries' adaptation to climate change, see Chancel and Piketty (2015).

22 Redistributive taxes and offers of job training programmes that increase the skill level of those with little formal education are suggestions for specific measures.

23 I must add a proviso here. So-called optimal tax theory suggests that those who are extremely rich have lower tax morale than those who belong to the upper reaches of the middle class (doctors and lawyers). If there is a very high income tax for those with the highest income, one will therefore increase the chances that they retire (early) or start extensive tax planning. According to this theory, one therefore should not tax the highest incomes the hardest (Gruber and Saez 2002:3).

10 Inheritance tax

A number of economic studies show that inheritance will play an increasingly important role in the years to come (Piketty and Saez 2013; Piketty 2014; Atkinson 2015). In Norway, three-fourth of the 100 richest have inherited their wealth (Nicolajsen 2016), and those who inherit most also have the highest incomes (NOU 2009, Nr. 10:201).

The inheritance tax was first introduced in Norway in 1792, and has existed in different forms until being abolished in 2014. Before 2014, the following rules applied: All inheritance below kr470,000 (approximately €47,000) was tax free. On the next kr330,000 (€33,000), a 6% tax was levied, while everything above kr800,000 (€80,000) was levied a 10% tax.[1] If, for example, one were to inherit kr2.5 million (€250,000), one's total tax rate would be 5.2%, or an inheritance tax of kr129,000 (€12,900).[2]

In 2013, the newspaper *Aftenposten* gave an interesting illustration of how the Norwegian inheritance tax worked and the normative intuitions it gave rise to. Øystein (19 years old) had inherited from his mother, who had died after a long struggle against cancer, an apartment worth kr3.9 million (approximately €390,000), a fourth of a cabin owned by his mother together with her siblings worth kr725,000 (€72,500), and received her life insurance of kr615,000 (€61,500). After a while, he got a tax bill from the tax authorities for the sum of kr425,000 (€42,500). *Aftenposten* cites Øystein's maternal grandfather:

> The rules are shaped so that what was supposed to be limited resources to a young boy, who has just finished high school, instead have to go to pay an inheritance tax of almost half a million kroner. And this only because he has also become the owner of a perfectly ordinary apartment built in 1957, where, in addition, he has lived most of his life.
>
> (Johansen and Haug 2013)

Øystein's story captures many of the intuitions that people tend to have about inheritance tax. On the one hand, there is the view that the state should not interfere in the transfer of assets within families. This intuition can be given different justifications, and in the following, we will look closer at some of these. On the other hand, many will react to the fact that tax regulations allowed Øystein to receive assets totalling almost kr5 million, with relatively little being claimed in taxes. People who receive these kinds of sums when entering adulthood are given a completely different start in life compared to those who do not inherit. This conflicts with many people's intuitions about justice.

The inheritance tax was an unpopular tax before it was abolished.[3] Was that because it was unfair? I will argue that the tax is in fact fair, and moreover that considerations of economic efficiency speak in favour of reintroducing it.[4] To show this, I will first present the most important arguments for and against inheritance tax. This review of the main arguments shows that there are good reasons to tax inheritance, but also that there are arguments to limit the tax. Next, I will present what I see as the most attractive proposal for how and why one ought to tax inheritance. This proposal was first put forth by John Stuart Mill, and later advanced by Rawls and Anthony Atkinson. Finally, I show how this proposal is a viable compromise with the potential to unite adherents and opponents of inheritance tax.[5]

Arguments for tax on inheritance

In the Official Norwegian Reports (NOUs) on the topic, inheritance tax is mostly justified in the same way that the wealth tax is justified: It provides revenue for the government, and ensures a broader tax base while also ensuring redistribution (NOU 2009, Nr. 10:211). But what are the most important justifications for inheritance tax in the philosophical literature? We will start with the most important justifications for taxing inheritance.[6]

One important argument in favour of inheritance tax is that it is necessary to realize the ideal of equality of opportunity. In brief, this argument states that it is unjust if some people get a better start in life than others, just because they are born to rich parents (compare Scanlon 2018:40). Because inheriting wealth is something that gives people better opportunities, it seem reasonable to tax inheritance to realize the ideal of equality of opportunity.

There are different ways to apply the principle of equality of opportunity to questions of inheritance tax. One approach is to say that equality of opportunity is the only or the most important ideal to be realized in society; if so, we should institute a 100% (or confiscatory) inheritance tax (Alstott 2007).[7] Another approach is to say that equality of opportunity is just one ideal among other important ideals that must be given weight. If so, the recommended tax rate will be lower than 100%. This is the view that Rawls defends. The ideal of equality of opportunity is, in my view, an important part of the justification for taxing inheritance.

A second argument is that inheritance tax is important due to the sinking marginal utility of wealth (see Chapter 7). This argument is utilitarian, and states that we should make sure to spread wealth around, because this will increase the total amount of happiness in society. So long as there is considerable inequality in society, we should ensure redistribution. This is an example of a general argument in favour of redistribution here being recruited to justify inheritance tax (Mill 1848/1976:228; Nagel 2009–2010:114).

A third argument holds that inequality due to inheritance is unjust compared to inequalities due to success in the market. So, inequalities are objectionable if they are produced by arbitrary factors such as whether your parents are rich or poor, hard working or lazy. But they are not objectionable if they follow from your own effort. This argument holds that inheritance taxes are justified because inherited wealth is not due to the recipients' own efforts (Mill 1848/1976:808; Piketty 2014).

A fourth argument, and the last argument we will consider here, is that tax on inheritance is necessary to ensure democratic equality. This argument, which is Rawls' most important argument in favour of inheritance tax, states, as we have seen, that we must make sure to limit the concentration of capital in a country so that it does not impact the important principle that everyone must be ensured equal opportunity to affect the political process. This, yet again, is an example of a general argument in favour of redistribution being recruited to justify taxing inheritance. Because the most important of these arguments have already been discussed, I will primarily focus on the most important arguments against inheritance tax.

Arguments against inheritance tax

A general argument against inheritance tax states that if a person owns something, it must be up to that person to decide for themselves how these means are to be disposed. This argument is often backed by pointing to the fundamental value of individual liberty, and that individuals must themselves be allowed to choose between different conceptions of the good life (Vallentyne 1997:333; Alstott 2007:476). If my perception of the good life entails that I must be able to transfer assets to my best friend, tax on inheritance and gifts will undermine my opportunity to live out my conception of the good life. If this freedom is absolute, it follows that people must be free to bequeath. The result will be large inequalities. Therefore, one cannot see this as an absolute right, but as a right that must be balanced against other concerns.

A more specific version of this argument states that parents have a right to promote the good of their children. To act partially to one's children is perceived by many as a duty or a virtue. Giving children material means through inheritance is therefore something with which the state should not interfere (Nagel 2009–2010:120). However, it is often unclear *why* parents ought to be able to transfer wealth to their children. Or, in other words, why it is acceptable to be partial to one's descendants when general considerations of justice suggest that we should think impartially (compare Chapter 1). In my view, Nozick provides an interesting answer to this question.

Nozick claims that it is crucial that those who create assets are able to transfer these assets to their children. The ties between parents and children are among the strongest ties that exist between humans. When the child grows up, these ties are weakened, and it is legitimate to look for something that can function as a symbolic replacement for them. Because giving in the form of inheritance can be understood as an act of love for the child, giving money can contribute to strengthening these bonds, and create a feeling of identity and continuity between parents and children. Nozick, however, also thinks that the right to give without being taxed must be limited to assets created by those who have themselves created the assets:

> Many philosophers – Hegel, for one – have commented on the ways in which property earned or created is an expression of the self and a component of it, so that one's identity or personality can become imbued or extended in such a creation. When the original creator or earner passes something on, a considerable portion of his self participates in and constitutes this act, far more than when a non-earner passes something he has received but not created.
>
> (Nozick 1989/2000:293)

Nozick therefore thinks that the person who has created the assets must have an unlimited right to transfer these to others. If one's assets have not been created by oneself, but are something one has got through inheritance, then these assets can be taxed. In this way, one can reduce the danger of the kind of dynastic inequalities that are established in some rich families. At the same time, this solution provides incentives to increase the value of one's wealth, if one has the desire to pass assets along in the form of inheritance.[8] I will argue that Nozick here articulates an important family value that should be accorded a certain weight in evaluating the how and why of just inheritance taxation.

The core of this argument—which we can call Nozick's argument for identity and continuity—is that inheritance can be justified because it strengthens the ties between donor and donee. When the donor dies, the fact that she is able to transfer assets ensures a kind of continuity in the family. If I take over a cabin that my father has built, this is important because it creates a feeling of identity and continuity between my father and myself. Inheriting the cabin gives me a connection to the past and to the family, and a connection to the past and the family is valuable (compare Brighouse and Swift 2009:53). Being able to transfer can therefore be seen as important to the family, and it should therefore be accorded a certain worth. I consciously emphasize *a certain worth* because, in my view, this value should not be given absolute priority. It is not the case that it supersedes the significance of democratic equality and fair equality of opportunity. However, the need to strengthen bonds between giver and donor should be ascribed a certain worth.[9]

One can also argue that the family has a kind of collective ownership over property. Even if, legally speaking, only individuals are property owners, one may think that, *normatively* speaking, the family owns things collectively, and hence that there is no real transaction involved when funds are transferred within the family, for example, from a mother to a daughter (Hegel 1991:§171, quoted in Beckert 2008:53). I think this way of thinking is one important reason why inheritance tax is so unpopular, and it is possible that it may explain why the tax seemed unfair to Øystein (in the example above). Children feel that they already own the property of their parents, and therefore perceive it as unreasonable that "their" assets are taxed.[10] It is, however, unclear what justifies this idea of collective property ownership within the family. When it is a question of two spouses, one can justify their collective ownership based on there often being a kind of division of labour between them. In the western nuclear family of the 1950s and 1960s, it was fairly typical for one spouse to be responsible for earning money, while the other took care of house and children. In that case, it is reasonable to say that they own the family wealth together. In modern families, it is not the case that children participate as equal partners in a division of labour, and it is therefore unclear how collective ownership might justify the right of children to their parent's wealth.

One possibility is that they have a right, say, to the wealth represented by a house, because they have grown up in it. The maternal grandfather of Øystein, from the example in the introduction, may have had something like this in mind. However, it is not the case that one automatically gains ownership over something by using it. If I play football every day for ten years on my neighbour's property, I cannot protest if she one day decides to sell the grounds. If the argument from use is to be valid, it will probably only be convincing when connected to other supporting arguments (e.g., family bonds).

Many are also critical of taxing inheritance because, they claim, it will have a detrimental effect on the economy. This argument comes in two different versions. The first version is a variation of the trickle-down argument, which will be considered in the next chapter. This argument states that we should not avoid capital concentration, because those who are rich are also the best at saving money. To allow concentration of capital will, in the end, be to the advantage of all (McCaffery 1994:309). Representatives of neoclassical economics have often advocated this view (Chester 1982:21). As we shall see in the next chapter, however, economists disagree about the strength of this argument, and I will not ascribe any worth to it here.

The second version states that tax on inheritance is detrimental to the economy because it will create negative incentives. The argument claims that the tax will negatively impact people's motivation to work and save. If saving up and transferring funds to others is an important motivation for one's work effort, limiting such transactions by taxing inheritance will have a negative effect (McCaffery 1994:287; Bracewell-Milnes 1997). This is an important argument of efficiency. To evaluate it properly, we have to look at what empirical research has to say about the effect of inheritance tax on people's behaviour.

Three American studies indicate that tax on inheritance will not have any significant effect. Murphy and Nagel point to different studies and argue that there is agreement that "a tax burden on gifts and bequests has little or no proven impact on donors' decisions whether to work or save" (Murphy and Nagel 2002:152). In a more recent review of the literature, Alstott concludes that "existing empirical studies, limited as they are, suggest that inheritance taxation would have modest negative effects on work, saving and capital accumulation, but there is still significant uncertainty" (Alstott 2007). Finally, in a much-quoted study, Gale and Slemrod claim that there is little evidence to indicate that inheritance tax will have any significant negative effect on peoples motivation to work and save (Gale and Slemrod 2001:3–4).

These studies thus show that there is considerable uncertainty. They agree that one can exclude tax on inheritance having significant effect, but also that it will have no effect at all. If the tax had been 100%, it is therefore likely that it would have a significant negative effect. How can we explain these findings?

To understand what lies behind these results, the literature distinguishes between accidental and planned inheritance (see NOU 2009, Nr. 10:211–212). If the testator's saving is first and foremost motivated by the desire to have a secure economy at the end of life, there is little reason to think that the inheritance tax will affect the testator's motivation to work and save. The tax then minimally effects the incentives of the testator, and this is therefore called accidental inheritance. The beneficiary gets whatever inheritance remains without this having been planned by the giver.

However, testators may also have a strong wish to leave behind wealth, for example, to their children. This, then, is planned inheritance. If this is the dominant motivation to work and save, it is probable that the inheritance tax will affect the incentives of the testator. A high tax could result in a reduced effort to work and save. Which motives are dominant in the Norwegian context is unclear. One study points out that there is no "empirical basis for drawing clear conclusions when it comes to the question of which motive for inheritance is dominant in Norway, and thus which effects the inheritance tax has on economic behaviour" (NOU 2009, Nr. 10:212).

International research, however, indicates that inheritance is rarely planned. In 2009, Batchelder published a study based on a detailed review of the literature. She concluded that 50% of the transfer of wealth from one generation to the next was unplanned, 30% could be tied to other motives that would not be affected by the inheritance tax, while only 20% of the transfers were planned with the view to promote the welfare of the recipient (2009:38).[11] This indicates that there is little reason to think that tax on inheritance will have any large negative effects on people's incentives to work and save.

In extension, it is also important to say something about the negative effects inheritance tax may have compared to other taxes. I will not fully review the debate about which tax base is best, but simply notice that there is much to indicate that tax on income has larger negative effects than tax on inheritance. Income tax reduces what people are left with in terms of payment for the effort they put in, and is therefore assumed to have negative effects, even though it is unclear how large this negative effect really is (Caron and Repetti 2013:1280). This is confirmed by OECD's "tax and growth ranking" which concludes that "corporate income tax is the most harmful type of tax for economic growth, followed by personal income tax" (OECD 2010:3). Tax on inheritance is significantly less damaging in part because "a large part of inheritances is unplanned" (OECD 2010:119).

To sum up, we can say that the incentive argument suggests that one should not tax inheritance 100%. However, the incentive argument does not say that we should not have a moderate or high tax on inheritance. In fact, the argument from incentives indicates that, if we think purely in terms of economic efficiency, inheritance should be taxed more than income.

Certain arguments are also prominent in the public debate, but almost absent in the academic discussions of inheritance tax. The most important example of this is the argument about double taxation. In an opinion poll we conducted in 2013, a large majority gave this argument as the most important reason to be against the inheritance tax.[12] This argument therefore deserves a closer look.

The argument about double taxation says that taxing inheritance is unjust because hard-working people must first pay income tax, and then a new tax on their wealth when they die. This, however, is a weak argument. If it were right, it would also be wrong to tax consumption. Given that we accept taxes on consumption, it seems unreasonable to single out inheritance tax as unjust (O'Neill 2007:64). It is not the number of times wealth is taxed that matters, but the total effects of the different taxes that together make up the tax system (Murphy and Nagel 2002:143). Most of those who have discussed the double tax argument therefore agree that it is mistaken, and that it is strange that so many people still find it convincing.[13]

One reason why this argument remains popular may be because it is frequently tied to other arguments. For example, it is common in debates, both in Norway and the US, for opponents of inheritance tax to call it a death tax. It comes into people's lives at a time when things are particularly difficult, and perhaps also when the family has lost an important provider.[14] When these two arguments are then coupled to the argument that the inheritance tax contributes little to state revenue, you get a powerful mix of bad arguments that can explain why inheritance tax is so unpopular, and why the argument from double taxation has such strong appeal. None of the argument can withstand scrutiny. Taxing inheritance is no more double taxation than are other taxes. In practice, it is not the dead person who is taxed, but the recipient of the inheritance, and the goal of the tax is not primarily to ensure revenue for the state, but to ensure redistribution.

One final argument that often crops up in public debates is the argument that taxing inheritance will make it hard (or impossible) to transfer farms and family businesses from one generation to the next. This is an important argument that is also taken seriously by advocates of inheritance tax (Haslett 1986:151; Brighouse and Swift 2014:140). Nevertheless, it is not necessarily the case that the solution is to remove the tax completely or reduce the rates. One can also solve this by saying that if the farm or the business stays in the family for a long time, the tax is reduced year by year. This would allow people to keep businesses they want to carry forward, but the tax would come into play if one sells the business or farm. The Christian Democratic Party (KrF) at one point suggested such a modification of the Norwegian inheritance tax (Halvorsen 2012).

Mill's suggestion: a lifetime-based recipient tax

John Stuart Mill (1806–1873) belongs to the same liberal-egalitarian tradition as Rawls. However, where Rawls defends a contract theory approach to justice, Mill is a utilitarian. Ultimately, the question of whether we should tax inheritance must be settled based on the total utility or happiness that follows from having such an arrangement. If inheritance tax increases the total societal utility, we should have it; if it reduces the total utility, we should not tax inheritance.

Mill starts with private property rights.[15] What follows from private property rights in terms of inheritance and the right to bequeath? The way Mill sees it, a person who has produced assets has the right to transfer these to others. To limit this right will entail an illegitimate limitation on property rights (Mill 1848/1976:218–221). The right to bequeath thus follows from private property rights. However, Mill thinks that the right to receive an inheritance is less strong. This sharp distinction between the right to give and the right to receive is central to Mill's proposal. As Mill sees it, taxing inheritance will have the positive consequence that one reduces the concentration of capital, spreading capital to more people, who in that way will have greater use of it (Mill 1848/1976:229). Tax on inheritance, in other words, will increase the total amount of utility or happiness in society.

Mill therefore suggests taxing the recipient of inheritance, and to put an upper limit on how much a person can receive in inheritance in the course of one's life:

> Were I framing a code of laws according to what seems to me best in itself, without regard to existing opinions and sentiments, I should prefer to restrict, not what any one might bequeath, but what any one should be permitted to acquire, by bequest or inheritance. Each person should have power to dispose by will of her whole property; but not to lavish it in enriching some one individual, beyond a certain minimum, which should be fixed sufficiently high to afford the means of comfortable independence.
>
> (Mill 1848/1976:227–228)

To Mill, it is reasonable to define an upper limit of what people should be able to receive, and he argues that if one wants additional means beyond what one receives, one has to work for it. As Mill sees it, we have to accept inequalities that result from talent and hard work, but not inequalities due to inheritance.

How the tax will pan out depends on how much the beneficiary has already received in terms of inheritance throughout life. If we assume that the upper limit is set at kr10 million (approximately €1 million), and you inherit kr5 million from your father, you will pay no tax. However, if you then go on to inherit kr15 million from an uncle a year later, you will be taxed for everything above the kr10 million. How much tax is levied above the standard deduction may vary, but Mill, who is critical of progressive income tax, is an advocate of a progressive tax on inheritance (Mill 1848/1976:809).

With such a proposal, the testator will be free to give as much as she wants without being taxed, provided that she spreads the assets on several people. If the assets are spread, the goal of the tax is achieved without imposing any actual tax. In other words, the arrangement of inheritance tax proposed by Mill provides incentives to spreading inheritance across several people, and can therefore contribute to avoiding concentration of capital as a consequence of inheritance. To Mill, this arrangement has the distinct advantage of not interfering with private property rights, since the giver remains free to give as much as she wants.

In this way, one can achieve what we may call an egalitarian goal without having to let go of its liberal foundation in private property rights. The proposal can therefore be said to realize a kind of balance between the right to give and the need to limit capital concentration. Another way of putting this is to say that the proposal ascribes worth both to the perspectives of the giver and recipient: The giver remains free to give as much as she wants without tax.

Mill provides three principled justifications for the proposal. First, it will advance the ideal of equality of opportunity while also ensuring an equalization of inequalities that are not deserved. Mill distinguishes between deserved and undeserved wealth. Wealth that is the result of hard work and innate skills is deserved while assets gained without being linked to any effort is undeserved:

> It is not the fortunes which are earned, but those which are unearned that it is for the public good to put under limitation… if all were done which it would be in the power of a good government to do, by instruction and legislation, to diminish this inequality of opportunities, the differences of fortune arising from people's own earnings could not justly give umbrage.
>
> (Mill 1848/1976:808)

Mill thus justifies his proposal for inheritance tax by recourse to desert and equality of opportunity. Nevertheless, note that total utility is the most ultimate justification for his proposal. Mill distinguishes between primary and secondary principles (Crisp 1997:9–11). The primary or most fundamental principle is the principle which states that we should choose actions or institutional arrangements that provide the largest total sum of utility or happiness. Secondary principles are such as the principle "you should not lie". Mill's point is that in specific situations, we will not think in terms of how we can maximize total utility, but if the secondary principles are followed, they will ensure the promotion of the total sum of utility/happiness. In questions of tax on inheritance, it is reasonable to understand desert and equality of opportunity as secondary principles that are important because they contribute to realizing the first principle of morality (Mill 1970:257). Ultimately, then, tax on inheritance is just *because* it promotes total utility or happiness.

However, there is an ambiguity in Mill's suggestion that needs to be addressed. Mill proposes to put an upper limit to how much one is to be allowed to receive. This sum is meant to allow the recipient a "moderate independence" (Mill 1848/1965:887).[16] As pointed out by Bain, Mill realized that this was an extremely radical proposal, and that if it were put into practice, it would "pull down all large fortunes in two generations" (Bain 1882:89; Hollander 1985:879). The ambiguity consists in the fact that it is unclear whether Mill argued that we should confiscate all assets above the upper limit, or that we should tax everything above the limit harshly and based on progressive rates.

To progressively tax everything above the upper limit is, of course, the less radical proposal (even though it seems radical to us today, which is interesting in itself), and Mill does not seem to have decided what he thought would be best. To see the distinction, let us first consider the most radical proposal. If the upper limit is defined as €1 million, a person who receives an inheritance of €10 million will be allowed to keep 1 million euro, while the remaining €9 million will go to the state. This is if the person in question has not previously received any inheritance. With the moderate proposal, the result depends on what the tax rates are. Let us say that we operate with progressive rates up to a top marginal tax rate of 65%. This corresponds to Anthony Atkinson's Mill-inspired proposal (Atkinson 2015:195). We would then tax the first €1 million above the limit 30%, the next €2 million 50%, and the last €6 million with 65%. Based on this tax structure, the recipient will receive €4.8 million.

Rawls' connects his own proposal to that of Mill, but justifies it slightly differently:

> We borrow from Mill (and others) the idea of regulating bequests and restricting inheritance. To do this an estate itself need not be subject to tax nor need the total given by bequest be limited. Rather the principle of progressive taxation is applied at the receiver's end. Those inheriting and receiving gifts and endowments pay a tax according to the value received and the nature of the receiver. Individuals and corporate bodies

> of certain kinds (educational institutions and museums say) may be taxed at different rates. The aim is to encourage a wide and far more equal dispersion of real property and productive assets.
>
> (Rawls 2001:160–161)

Rawls' thus supports Mill's proposal to how we can design a just tax on inheritance, but justifies the need for such taxation by pointing to this being necessary to ensure everyone fair value of political liberties and fair equality of opportunity.[17]

From the kind of a liberal egalitarian point of view that both Mill and Rawls defend, inheritance tax is a very important tax.

A compromise

In my view, the attraction of the Mill/Rawls/Atkinson proposal is that it represents a way of balancing different concerns.[18] There are good arguments, both for and against tax on inheritance, and this proposal is able to accommodate arguments from both sides. To substantiate this, I will first show how tax on inheritance can be seen from the perspective both of the giver and of the recipient, and then argue that the lifetime-based recipient tax can incorporate arguments for and against tax on inheritance.

Let us first consider this from a luck egalitarian perspective. Alstott and Rakowksi have discussed tax on inheritance based on the ideal of equality of opportunity. As Alstott sees it, it follows from the ideal of equality of opportunity that the perspective of the giver cannot be accorded any weight because what matters is to ensure everyone equal opportunities in life:

> [E]ach individual is a separate moral being, whose vision of the good life is entitled to equal respect. For opportunity to be equal for everyone – and not just for the first generation – the state must not permit individuals to act in ways that compromise equality.
>
> (Alstott 2007:488)

According to Alstott, what follows from the ideal of equality of opportunity is a 100% tax on inheritance. Rakowski provides an equivalent argument for confiscatory tax justified by the ideal of equality of opportunity (Rakowski 2000). He recognizes that the argument about the freedom to give and that one must be able to contribute to promoting the interests of one's family members as important arguments against such a tax. However, he does not analyse how these considerations could be incorporated and balanced against the other considerations.

Let us then look at this from the opposite point of view. To right libertarians, donors have full ownership over their own property, and an unlimited right to transfer assets to others. This element in libertarian thinking is implicit in

Nozick, and is explicitly expressed by Murrey Rothbard. In a discussion of whether inheritance taxes can be justified, he writes:

> The libertarian answer is to concentrate not on the recipient, but to concentrate on the giver, the man who bestows the inheritance. For if individuals have the right to their labor and property and to exchange the titles to this property for the similar property of others, they also have the right to give their property to whomever they wish. And of course most such gifts consist of the gifts of the property owners to their children – in short, inheritance.
>
> (Rothbard 2006:49–50)

Right libertarians insist that resources are not "manna from heaven" that awaits redistribution. Instead, they are something to which individuals have rights, and these rights include a complete freedom to transfer resources to others. It therefore follows that tax on inheritance is impermissible.

The proposal I defend here allows us to take both these perspectives into consideration. Seen from the perspective of the giver, one can appreciate that the giver is free to give as much as she wishes, provided that she distributes her wealth across several recipients. From the same perspective, one can also appreciate that the giver can transfer assets without any intervention up to the specified limit. From an egalitarian perspective, one can appreciate that the proposal ensures a significant degree of redistribution, depending on how one defines the limit as well as whether the limit is absolute or includes a progressive taxation of everything above the threshold. The proposal thus balances these two perspectives, and hence offers an interesting opportunity to unite conflicting concerns.

I thus argue that the proposal we are discussing offers a way of overcoming a deep disagreement on questions about inheritance tax. This is in line with one of the roles Rawls thinks political philosophy should fulfil, namely to "find common ground for political agreement" and contribute to resolving "deep and sharp conflict" (Rawls 2001:1–2). To show how, let us go back to the most important arguments for and against tax on inheritance. The following arguments are important reasons in favour of the tax:

1 Inheritance tax is important due to the difference of marginal utility of consumption among the rich and the worst off, given economic inequality
2 The inequality that follows from wealth transfers are undeserved compared to the inequality that follows from success in the market
3 Inheritance tax is important because it contributes to equality of opportunity
4 Inheritance tax is important because economic inequality can undermine democratic equality

Rawls' justification of the tax draws, as we have seen, primarily on 3 and 4. Mill employs, as we have also seen, 1 and 2. To defend my claim, I must however show how the proposal can also accommodate the most important arguments against inheritance tax:

1 Inheritance tax is problematic because it will reduce people's motivation to work and save (the incentive argument)
2 Inheritance tax violates the right to dispose of one's assets as one wants
3 Inheritance tax is problematic because people have the right to contribute assets to their family members

As we have seen, 1 is a justification for not imposing a confiscatory tax; 2 is, in my view, not convincing in itself. Inheritance creates large inequalities, and it is not in itself a good argument that one must be allowed to dispose of one's funds without any limitations. Both a consideration for political equality and a consideration of what is in the best interest of society speaks against giving this kind of *carte blanche* to dispose of one's own assets without any consideration of the negative consequences this might lead to. As we saw in Chapter 8, it also does not follow from private property rights that one must be given such a right. However, 3 is a narrowing of 2 with a special justification. Nagel argues that this is the most important reason to limit tax on inheritance (Nagel 2009–2010:120). However, he does not provide any good argument for why this is important. The way I see it, what we might call Nozick's identity and continuity argument hints at an answer. This argument, as we have seen, states that giving creates identity and continuity between parents and children, and I have argued that this argument must be accorded a certain weight.

Hence, there are good arguments for tax on inheritance and good arguments for limiting this tax. What can we say about the ability of the lifetime-based recipient tax to balance these concerns? First, we must recognize that even though the proposal gives donors the opportunity to give as much as they want provided that they spread their assets, it nevertheless entails a considerable limitation on their liberty. Most people who have large fortunes will want to transfer this wealth to a few, close relatives, usually their children. Their freedom to do so is therefore limited by the upper limit to how much can be transferred. One can therefore argue that the proposal puts an unjust limitation on what one may do with one's property. As Stephen Muntzer has pointed out in discussing Mill's proposal, if society limits what people can receive, this is also an indirect limitation of what someone can give (Munzer 1990:405).

This is an important counterargument. If I want to transfer €10 million to my daughter, and the upper limit is 1 million euro, this entails a limitation of my freedom. However, the right to transfer assets to one's family members is not an absolute right. Even right libertarians who are very concerned with rights should recognize this. As Braun has recently pointed out, the political rights will be undermined in a minimal state that allows unlimited transfers of wealth in the form of inheritance. Political rights must not be considered as formal rights; instead, they must be implemented in a context that allows people to see them as rights with real value (Braun 2016:385). To put it in Rawlsian terms: Tax on inheritance is necessary to ensure the fair value of the political liberties.

Note furthermore that my claim is not that the lifetime-based recipient tax ensures full freedom to give, but that it succeeds in balancing different considerations. When balancing different considerations, both sides must compromise. It is true that the proposal limits the right to give, but it does so in a way we should accept given the need to ensure social equality, which, among other things, is necessary to maintain political rights.

The incentive argument and the identity and continuity argument entail that we should exclude confiscatory tax on inheritance. This means that there are considerations of justice that speak both for and against tax on inheritance. These arguments do however not exclude a medium or even high tax on inheritance. I cannot here say exactly what rate the tax should have. However, notice that even with Atkinson's proposal to introduce progressive taxation that may exceed 65% marginal tax, the right to give to family members is protected.

However, inheritance tax can also be defended from a libertarian point of view. Even a minimal state must be financed somehow, and one must therefore ask oneself which kind of tax is most acceptable from a libertarian perspective. Halliday (2012) has shown that even if we see things from the perspective of the donor, as libertarians insist we do, the right conclusion can be to accept tax on testamentary goods. He claims that bequeaths are different to other uses of private property, in that it entails a lower opportunity cost. An opportunity cost is what we miss out on when choosing one option over another (Halliday 2012:626–631). If I buy a book that costs €10, the opportunity cost I incur is that I cannot buy something else for those €10. If I decide to bequeath my house to my daughter, I will still be able to live in the house until I die. In other words, I will still be able to use the house. This is a relevant difference compared to taxation of income, when the tax is taken away from me at once, without me having any use of the money. To Halliday, it follows that taxing inheritance is less of a forcible intervention into the lives of individuals compared to other taxes, and therefore something libertarians should have less qualms about.

Conclusion

If one cares about redistribution, inheritance tax is among the most important tax instrument to achieve that end. Inheritance tax has lower efficiency costs than other taxes, and the importance of broad tax bases also speaks in favour of having such a tax. Many will also see it as unjust to tax income while inheritance, with the current Norwegian tax system, is not taxed at all.

In other words, the state taxes your income—which is the result of your effort, and hence something you have earned—but does not tax inheritance—which is not the result of your effort, and hence not something you have earned.

The discussion of inheritance tax is made more complicated by the existence of arguments both in favour of the tax and in favour of limiting the tax. I have argued above that bequeaths may be expressions of love creating identity between donor and recipient. This argument speaks in favour of limiting the tax, and there are important incentive arguments that point in the same direction. Nevertheless, these arguments do not preclude a moderate or even high tax on inheritance. We should tax inheritance for the sake of democratic equality and equality of opportunity, but also to use the resources of society in the most efficient way possible, and finally, because inheritance is not something the recipient has earned.

Is it realistic for the inheritance tax to be reintroduced in the Norwegian context? The answer is yes. Compared to other suggested reforms to redistribute, reintroducing the inheritance tax would be easy. We know much more about the effects of inheritance tax than we do about, say, universal basic income. Reintroducing inheritance tax would not be a bold experiment with uncertain consequences.

A common objection to inheritance tax in the Norwegian public debate has been that the tax is not sufficiently precise. The Scheel committee has discussed this objection. The committee points out that the problem with the old inheritance tax was divergent valuations of different tax bases, so that there was too much room for adaptation. The conclusion is nevertheless that the tax should be reintroduced, albeit on a different basis:

> If the inheritance tax is to be reintroduced, this requires a thorough revision of the old rules so that market values are consistently used to establish tax bases, and that the opportunities for adaptation are limited as much as possible.
>
> (NOU 2014, Nr. 13:295)

The committee concludes that considerations of both efficiency and distribution speak in favour of reintroducing the inheritance tax.

A reintroduction of the inheritance tax will also be thoroughly grounded in expert opinion. The most important NOUs conclude that the inheritance tax should be an important part of the tax system. The Distribution committee, for example, made the following statement about the then-extant inheritance tax: "Today's inheritance tax normally has significant distributive effects, both because it is progressive, but also because people with high incomes and/or wealth normally also receive the most inheritance" (NOU 2009, Nr. 10:201).

Coupled to the fact that the most popular argument against inheritance tax, the argument about double taxation, is not valid, a reintroduction appears realistic, at least if one has faith in an enlightened public debate. Historically, there has been a continuous political struggle over the inheritance tax, with widely varying rates (NOU 2000, Nr. 8:23–26). Political moods shift, and there is no guarantee that the present appetite for tax cuts will remain insatiable forever.

Further reading

Much of what has been written about just inheritance tax in recent years belongs to the juridical literature. Here, I will limit myself to highlighting the most important philosophical works. Daniel Halliday's book *The Inheritance of Wealth: Justice, Equality, and the Right to Bequeath* is the first thorough political-philosophical treatment of inheritance tax for a long time. A symposium on the book will be published in the journal *LEAP* in 2020. Two anthologies that figure articles to which frequent references are made are Guido Erreygers and Toon Vandevelde's *Is Inheritance Legitimate?* and John Cunliffe and Guido Erreygers' *Inherited Wealth, Justice and Equality.* Among the most important articles published is Haslett's *Is Inheritance Justified?*, which defends the abolition of inheritance, and McCaffery's *The Political Liberal Case against the Estate Tax*, which argues against tax on inheritance.

Podcast: BBC Analysis 21.02.2016 has a podcast on inheritance.

Notes

1 Note the difference between an inheritance tax which is assessed on what the recipient receives, and an estate tax which is assessed on the wealth of the deceased (Piketty 2020:446). The UK taxes estates at 40% above the exemption level of 325,000 pounds (Institute of Fiscal studies 2016:25), whereas the US also taxes estates at a rate of 40%, but the exemption level was set at $5.43 in 2015 (Slemrod and Bakija 2017:68). For an interesting discussion of how the estate tax in the UK works, see Wolff (forthcoming).

2 This calculation presupposes that one inherits from the longest living and receives a standard deduction and 6% tax from both father and mother.

3 This seems to be a general trend. Piketty notes that this tax is unpopular in all surveys (Piketty 2020:978).

4 In Norway, the inheritance tax was replaced by a continuity principle that states that if you take over a property, you may be taxed based on the *appreciation* of the value of the property since the time when the people from whom you inherit bought the property. Clemet and Doksheim has argued that the continuity principle, over time, "will give a higher taxation of inheritance" (Clemet and Doksheim 2017:247). They reject on this basis that the removal of inheritance tax will contribute to increasing inequalities in Norway. I think this is a mistake, among other things, because a number of tax objects evade taxation with this continuity principle. Moreover, there is also the option (defended by Zimmer) of keeping the inheritance tax in combination with the continuity principle (see Zimmer 2013:305–306). A comprehensive discussion of the nuances of this question is outside the scope of my present inquiry.

5 Even though there are important distinctions between gifts and inheritance, I will in the following talk of transfers of inheritance and gifts as bequeaths, without including these distinctions.

6 This section builds on Pedersen (2018a).

7 Here, I must make a proviso. Think about Øystein's situation. He lost his mother at an early age. This means that he does not have the same opportunities that children with parents who live longer. For example, he will miss important knowledge, or does not have someone to babysit if he becomes a father. Therefore, one may argue that, even if the only ideal applied is equality of opportunity, then it does not follow that one should tax inheritance 100%. Øystein, who has been robbed of opportunities in losing his mother, should be taxed less to compensate for the loss incurred through his mother's premature death.

8 Nozick's proposal has clear similarities with Eugenio Rignano's defence of what has later become known as the Rignano principle. According to this principle, one can transfer what one has created oneself, but not what one receives from others; see Rignano (1924) or Pedersen (2018). For a recent attempt at applying this principle, see Halliday (2018), which is also the most accomplished philosophical defence of inheritance taxation in recent political philosophy.

9 When this should only be ascribed a limited worth, this is because there are many other ways to create identity and continuity between parents and children that do not have the same negative consequences as bequeaths. Spending time with one's children, talking with them about important questions are examples of this. For a more thorough discussion, see Pedersen and Bøyum (2020).

10 Jeremy Bentham, who was among the first philosophers to write on inheritance tax, was also early in formulating this explanation of the unpopularity of the tax; see Bentham (1795/1952:292).

11 See Cappelen and Pedersen (2018) for a more thorough discussion of the literature on different motives behind bequeaths.

12 In the survey, respondents were asked to consider five different arguments against inheritance tax. Seventy seven percent agreed fully or somewhat that the double taxation argument is an important argument against inheritance tax (Cappelen and Pedersen 2014).

13 For an excellent recent discussion, see White (2018:172–175).

14 The term death tax was first introduced by George W. Bush Jr., and in Norway, it has been fronted by the Progress Party in particular. Party leader Siv Jensen, for example, stated in a debate in 2013 that:

> we want to remove tax on death, what you call inheritance tax to make it sound less scary. An unreasonable tax that most people perceive as very unreasonable, and which is imposed on them by you when they are already dealing with grief and other challenges. Its going away and we are going to do that as fast as possible.
>
> (Jensen in Debatten, NRK 30.05.2013)

15 In this section, I draw on Cappelen and Pedersen (2018).

16 Mill used the terms "moderate independence" and "comfortable independence", and there may, of course, be a relevant difference between the two. However, moderate seems more in line with the general argument in Mill, and I have therefore chosen to use that formulation here.

17 Here, it might be objected that what follows from Rawls' two principles is wealth tax to avoid the concentration of wealth, and inheritance tax to ensure equality of opportunity. Analytically speaking, this distinction makes sense. However, that does not mean that the two ideals cannot be combined, and that is what Rawls does; see, for example, Rawls 1999:245.

18 In this section, I draw on Pedersen (unpublished).

11 Taxation of wealth

The Norwegian wealth tax was introduced at the end of the 19th century.[1] The only European countries, in addition to Norway, to levy a wealth tax are Belgium, Spain, and Switzerland (by the end of 2019). A number of European countries abandoned their wealth tax during the 1990s and 2000 (Glennerster 2012:235).[2] However, due to the growing attention on rising wealth inequality, there has recently been a renewed interest in wealth tax, and the tax is currently debated in a number of countries that has no experience with the tax (Saez and Zucman 2019b; Sandbu 2019). This interest is not only academic but also political. In the US, the presidential candidates Elizabeth Warren and Bernie Sanders both include proposals to tax wealth.[3]

We need to distinguish at least three different versions of wealth taxes. The kind of wealth tax that exists in Norway today is a national tax on wealth where the government calculates the wealth of each individual. This is the standard version of wealth tax. Another recently proposed wealth tax is based on self-evaluation. According to this radical proposal, it is up to the owners of wealth to decide the asset value of their house or business or whatever their wealth consists in. Based on that decision, the government will set a wealth tax. To ensure that the asset value is not set to low, the proposal is that the object is up for sale for the price set by the owner (Posner and Weyl 2018:55–62). A final version is the global wealth tax proposed by Thomas Piketty. The proposal is similar to the standard version when it comes to valuation, but Piketty's tax should ideally be levied worldwide (Piketty 2014:515–518). In the following, I will focus on the standard version of wealth tax and discuss it in the context of the Norwegian tax system.

I shall start with a brief description of the Norwegian wealth tax and then move to consider arguments in favour of the tax. I will try to show that a combination of the justifications found in Rawls and Piketty provides a robust justification for the tax. I then proceed to consider counterarguments. One important argument to be considered is that the wealth tax hinders job creation, another is that the wealth tax will lead to rich people moving abroad. Here, I will also briefly discuss the more general question of whether wealth "trickles down", for example, in cases of tax reductions. This argument holds that tax reductions are, in fact, in everyone's interests. This demonstrates the complexity of the issue, and partly explains why the tax is extremely controversial. However, given the high level of wealth inequality in Norway, I argue that these arguments are not decisive, and discuss a recent criticism at how wealth taxes have traditionally been designed in Europe. I show that the combined justification of the wealth tax and the criticism of the European model of wealth tax calls for increasing the exemption level and the rates and introducing a graduated rate schedule.[4] In the concluding section, I show that the Norwegian tax system has become less progressive, and argue that the inheritance tax and the wealth tax in the current context is necessary in order to deconcentrate wealth.

Arguments in favour of the wealth tax

Wealth tax is—as the name implies—a tax on wealth. In Norway, a person's wealth is calculated by deducing one's debt from one's wealth. All forms of wealth are included, and in principle, one is to use the market value of an object when evaluating how much it is worth (NOU 2009, Nr. 10:201).[5] In practice, the current rules are that the house one lives in (*primærbolig*) is valued at 25% of market value. Everything below kr1.5 million is exempt (150,000 euro). The tax rate varies, and has gradually been reduced from 1.1% in 2009 to 0.85% in 2017. The wealth tax is similar to tax on capital income. The difference is that the wealth tax must be paid independently of whether there has been any return on investment.

An important claim in Chapter 1 was that capitalist welfare states allow too much concentration of capital. This claim is supported by both Rawls and Piketty. According to Rawls, as we have seen, the background structure must be shaped to continuously intervene in the market to avoid too much concentration of capital. Such interventions are necessary to avoid the richest among us coming into a position where they can convert their economic power into political power. If this happens, the worst off may come to feel subordinate to the economic and political elite. This may compromise our fundamental ideals, in particular the ideal that all are free and equal and should be ensured equal opportunity to influence the political process. This may, in turn, make the indigent apathetic and bitter, and in the long run, undermine democracy.[6]

Tax on inheritance and wealth are measures that can be used to deconcentrate wealth. Inheritance tax was discussed in the previous chapter, and I will here say something about how we might see the division of labour between these two taxes in a Rawlsian perspective.[7] If the goal is to limit wealth, tax on inheritance is not sufficient on its own. We should also tax wealth directly; this, because inheritance taxation cannot stop someone from becoming so rich that they can buy political influence. In line with Rawls' argument, it is crucial that those who have become rich without inheriting any wealth must be prevented from becoming so rich that they can dominate and control others. Somewhat simplified, we can therefore say that it follows from the liberty principle that taxation of wealth is just if it is necessary to ensure citizens the status of free and equal, and to avoid the worst off being controlled and dominated by the super-rich.[8] Similarly, inheritance tax is just if it is necessary to realize the ideal of fair equality of opportunity.

How does this justification of the wealth tax connect to discussions about revenue from such a tax? As with the inheritance tax discussed in the previous chapter, the primary purpose of the tax is not to collect revenue, but to deconcentrate wealth. As Sugin puts it in her discussion of the Rawlsian justification of these taxes, "a wealth tax might not need to collect any revenue; it can operate as an insurance against the potential dangers of unequal concentrations of wealth" (Sugin 2004:2010). Thus, a Rawlsian justification of the tax does not have to enter the debate about revenue that has been so prominent in the recent debate between economists.[9]

From a luck egalitarian perspective, wealth tax is not a just form of tax. In this, then, the two dominant egalitarian theories disagree. In a Rawlsian perspective, wealth tax is justified in the need to protect a democratic practice. This practice requires us to limit the wealth of the very richest. According to the luck egalitarian ideal, one cannot justify putting limits on people's wealth by pointing to the fact that we are free and equal citizens in a constitutional democracy. To luck egalitarians, someone's wealth is just if it follows from choice, and unjust if it is due to factors outside of their control. In principle, therefore, and as argued above, the luck egalitarian ideal is compatible with very large inequalities in wealth.[10]

Rawls' comments on taxation are "illustrative and highly tentative" (Rawls 2001:136). He is primarily concerned with how taxes can be justified. It is not the task of the philosopher to give detailed advice on standard deductions and which rates a tax should be equipped with. Piketty is more detailed both about tax in general and when it comes to wealth tax in particular. Piketty emphasizes that tax on income, inheritance, and wealth are all necessary elements of a just tax system (Piketty 2014:524). Based on a normative ideal closely associated with Rawls', Piketty particularly emphasizes two arguments for wealth tax: An argument about the ability to pay and an argument about incentives.[11]

The first argument is that those with the greatest ability to pay must also pay the most, and that without a wealth tax, there is a danger that those who have the most will in effect pay no or very low taxes.[12] The logic, Piketty writes:

> is quite simple: income is often not a well-defined concept for very wealthy individuals, and only a direct tax on capital can correctly gauge the contributive capacity of the wealthy.
>
> (Piketty 2014:525)

This can be illustrated by those with the largest fortunes. They will often have a return on their capital of 6–7% per year, while at the same time only listing a fraction of this as taxable income. Their wealth will therefore rapidly increase because they can save most of what they make without breaking any laws. It simply does not help to tax reported income harshly so long as the reported income is only a fraction of the actual income:

> Effective tax rates (expressed as a percentage of economic income) are extremely low at the top of the wealth hierarchy, which is problematic, since it accentuates the explosive dynamic of wealth inequality, especially when large fortunes are able to garner larger returns. In fact, the tax system ought to attenuate this dynamic, not accentuate it.
>
> (Piketty 2014:526)[13]

This is a problem, Piketty thinks, in all developed economies, and the solution is progressive taxation of wealth. As an example, take the founder of Facebook, Mark Zuckerberg. In 2014, his wealth was estimated at $37.7 billion, while his reported income was approximately $600,000 (Fleischer 2017:270). If Zuckerberg was only to be taxed based on his income, I think many would agree that this would conflict with the principle of paying according to ability. Therefore, one may argue that income taxes must be supplemented by wealth tax in order to tax someone like Zuckerberg in a just way.[14] Let me also add that by supplementing the ideal of paying according to ability with the ideal of democratic equality, we have a still more robust justification for taxing the very largest fortunes.

Then, to the argument about incentives: Tax on wealth gives people incentives to maximize their return on investment. If there is a wealth tax of 1%, this incentivizes people to achieve a higher return on their investment in order for their wealth not to decrease.[15] This argument may seem unreasonable, and many will perceive it to be unfair that one has to pay wealth tax even if one's wealth decreases. Piketty acknowledges this, and argues that a just way of taxing wealth must be based in part on capital stock, and in part on the income generated by this capital stock. In this way, one can avoid the most problematic aspects of a "pure" wealth tax (Piketty 2014:527).

The argument about democratic equality and the ability to pay principle can be combined to provide a robust support for the wealth tax. Before proceeding to the arguments against the wealth tax, I shall discuss two possible objections against this way of justifying the tax. The first addresses the argument of democratic equality. Rakowski raises two issues. First, he argues that instead of a wealth tax which indirectly tries to solve the problem of disproportional power and influence of the wealthy, it would be better to limit influence directly. This can be done, according to Rakowski, through an insulation strategy: Regulating campaign spending, lobbying, and so on (Rakowski 2000:293). I discussed this objection in the Norwegian context in Chapter 7, and concluded that such a strategy is not likely to be sufficient given very large concentration of capital.

The second argument Rakowski puts forward is that many rich people do not have any political ambitions, and to impose a wealth tax on them justified on democratic equality would therefore be wrong:

> Even limited to a sliver of the top 1%, the tax inevitably would take from many wealthy people who had no designs on politics or markets but who quietly enjoyed their private holdings.
>
> (Rakowski 2000:292)

The wealth tax would, simply put, be unjust to all the rich people who have no desire to convert economic resources to political power.

I suggest that there are two ways to reply to this objection. The first is that, as I insisted in Chapter 7, it is the *opportunity* to convert economic resources into political power that must be restricted. The extremely rich will have this opportunity regardless of whether they have political ambitions. The second draws on the ability to pay principle: Extremely rich people with no ambition to convert their money into power and influence still have the ability to pay, and it is therefore just that they do so.

Arguments against the wealth tax

What about the counterarguments? Opponents of wealth tax claim that the tax prevents businesses from creating new jobs. Instead of being able to reinvest in new machines and new technology, businesses are drained of resources. The wealth tax must be paid also in years where a business has a negative result, and this can, it is claimed, be detrimental to companies' ability to grow and to create new jobs. Bjørn Kjos, owner of the low-cost airline Norwegian, gave an interesting example of how this argument is used. In 2015, Kjos appeared on the talk show Skavlan, together with Thomas Piketty. Kjos complained that he had to pay ten times more tax than his income. Piketty wanted to know how much Kjos was worth, but received no reply. Piketty's point was to show that Kjos owns a lot, and that he has potential power and ability to pay taxes in virtue of what he owns, and not only in virtue of what he earns. Kjos, however, wanted to show how unfair it was that he had to pay more in taxes than he earned in a year, and pointed out that he, in the previous year, suffered a net loss (NRK 2015).[16]

It is understandable that business owners do not want their wealth to decrease. However, Piketty's argument about the ability to pay rejects that taxing income alone is a viable option. Moreover, the Scheel committee notes that there are empirical studies demonstrating that drawing on one's wealth to pay taxes is in practice a very small problem (NOU 2014, Nr. 13:286).

Is it true that removing the wealth tax will be positive for job creation? It does not seem very persuasive that, as some have claimed, six out of ten business owners think that removing wealth tax would create more jobs (Olsen 2017). After all, they themselves have a lot to gain by removing the tax, and therefore may not be the right authority to judge on this issue. Moreover, there is no well-documented research supporting the claim that cutting wealth tax leads to more job creation.[17]

The Scheel report shows that the overall effect on saving through reduced wealth tax is uncertain, but also that most profitable projects in Norway will be able to secure financing also with a high wealth tax due to a well-functioning capital market (NOU 2014, Nr. 13:286–289). The report also points out that a reduction of the corporate tax is a more effective means if the goal is to stimulate investments:

> All in all, it is assumed that wealth tax only to a limited extent affects the overall scope of investment in Norway, but that it may have some impact on the access to capital for businesses that do not have access to an international market. The committee therefore thinks that a reduction in the corporate tax will be better targeted than a reduction in the wealth tax in strengthening the tax-based incentives to invest in Norway.
>
> (NOU 2014, Nr. 13:289)

Therefore, there is no sufficient basis to claim that the wealth tax has any significantly negative impact on investment and a resulting detrimental effect on job creation.

Another, common objection to wealth tax is that it harms Norwegian competitiveness. Many Norwegian businesses are export-oriented. Bjørn Kjos, for example, must compete in an international market, and if businesses are to compete internationally, having poorer competitive conditions will harm their ability to do so. This objection frequently cites the fact that Norway is one of few countries with a wealth tax. Looking at the wealth tax in isolation, this might make sense. However, ultimately, what matters are the combined effects of taxes and other conditions. Here, the World Bank holds that Norway ranks third among European countries when it comes to favourable tax conditions for the business community (Agenda 2016:9).

Furthermore, the wealth tax must be seen as one part of the taxation of capital stock, and in Norway, as we saw in figure 3 (Chapter 9), the taxes on capital stock are lower than in many other countries. In 2011, Norway was well below the OECD average (Figure 3). This is confirmed by more recent numbers showing that Norway has 3% tax rate on capital stock compared to the OECD average of 5.6%. The difference is largely explained by the fact that Norway has significantly lower property tax rates than most other OECD countries (NOU 2009:196; Agenda 2014:9; Sandvik 2017).

A related argument against the wealth tax is that it forces businesses that have insufficient returns on investment to withdraw their funds to invest them elsewhere. However, as Sandbu has demonstrated, this is not a good argument. The money will be taxed also if they are withdrawn from the business. Therefore, there is reason to think that a higher wealth tax would, in fact, lead investors to invest more of their money in businesses in order to increase the chances of growing their wealth (Sandbu 2014:8). This is a version of the incentive argument used by Piketty above. Furthermore, if the argument *was* correct, and investors redirected their investment into, for example, real estate, it would be better, as the Scheel committee argued (see Chapter 9), to increase taxation for real estate than to decrease the wealth tax.

Another objection to wealth tax is that it incentivizes people to move to other countries where this tax is smaller or non-existent. Tax lawyer Ernst Ravnaas claims that wealth tax makes a significant difference for the access to capital in Norway. Ravnaas' argument is based on his interviews of nine Norwegians with large fortunes who had moved abroad. Seven of these said they would move back to Norway if the wealth tax was removed. Ravnaas also showed that rich Norwegians who live abroad invest abroad, and that Norway therefore misses out on potential investments and jobs (Ravnaas 2016).

This, however, is a controversial claim. The Scheel report points out that the role of the wealth tax in determining where people settle should not be exaggerated, and thus that the argument about incentivizing people to move should not be accorded weight (NOU 2014:286). Furthermore, Saez and Zucman point out that there is some evidence that shows that the wealth tax might lead some to expatriate. However, they also argue that the "threat of expatriation is primarily a policy variable" (Saez and Zucman 2019b:25). Let me try to illustrate what that means.

If capital flight is a problem that arises because of the wealth tax, this still does not mean that removing the tax is the right thing to do. British philosopher Brian Barry has argued that one should rather increase the restrictions on those who are tax refugees (Barry 2005:192–193). Today, the Norwegian tax system allows those who have emigrated for tax reasons to spend up to 61 days a year in Norway. Hence, if you live in London with your fortune, you can still spend almost a sixth of your time back in Norway without having to pay wealth tax. Barry holds that tax refugees should be met with harsher restrictions. They should only be allowed to come to their country of origin under special conditions, such as in the event of serious illness or death in their close family. After all, tax refugees have chosen to emigrate to avoid having to pay tax, and one therefore does not do them any wrong by limiting their opportunity to spend time in their country of origin.[18]

Another policy option is to introduce an exit tax. The Warren proposal includes a suggestion for such a tax. It involves a 40% tax on net worth if you decide to expatriate for tax reasons (Saez and Zucman 2019b:27; Piketty 2020:571, 994). Piketty provides the following precise argument for why such a tax is just:

> The justification for an exit tax is that there is no natural right to enrich oneself by taking advantage of a country's legal and educational systems, and so on, and then extracting the wealth without returning part of it to the community.
>
> (Piketty 2020:994)

In sum, the exit tax and Barry's proposal shows that the threat of losing a large amount of capital due to tax refugees should not be considered decisive. Whether the tax actually has these consequences depends on a number of other choices of policy.[19]

Do tax reductions trickle down?

Is it true that tax reductions to the wealthiest will make everyone better off? In the Norwegian context, this way of justifying tax cuts has been very prominent. This assumption is often called trickle-down economics, and I shall briefly discuss this argument and frame it in the context of other broader macroeconomic debates. I cannot, however discuss these matters in depth here. Instead, my more modest aim is to present some important concepts and suggest how the trickle-down argument rests on some preconditions, and suggest how it can be problematized.

So-called trickle-down economics, then, is based on the assumption that tax reductions, for example, in the form of reduced corporate tax and tax on capital stock, will have positive effects on the economy, with the result that everyone is better off. By lowering taxes on corporations and investors, those who benefit from tax cuts will be able to create new jobs and raise the salaries of their employees, thus contributing to increased consumer demand.[20] At the same time, companies will buy more from each other. The assumption is that even though the worst off will have a smaller share of what the economy produces, they will still have more in absolute terms than without these tax cuts (Chang 2014:318–319).

Against this, one can object that tax cuts for corporations and investors can also lead to higher bonuses being paid to managers and larger dividends to shareholders. If this is the actual result, the tax cuts will improve the economy of those who are best off, without any trickle-down effect to those who are worse off. Such tax cuts would only reinforce inequality.

What actually happens is highly uncertain, and a matter of controversy also among economists. Whether trickle-down economics work or not matters a great deal. Trickle-down economics is, for example, the main justification for the tax cuts implemented by the Liberal Party Solberg government (2013–present). The argument from trickle-down economics seems to presuppose two things: First, businesses prior to the tax cuts do not have enough money to hire more people or pay their employees higher salaries. Second, businesses and business owners have a wish to hire new people and raise the salaries of their employees, if they receive more money through tax cuts. It is hard to see how tax cuts in themselves would act as an incentive to hiring new employees and raising their salaries. If this is true, then tax cuts will have the effect of making the rich richer without bettering the position of the worst off.

The argument from trickle-down economics is an empirical argument that can be partly evaluated by drawing on historical evidence. Is it the case that periods with large tax cuts to the rich have led to more economic growth, and that this growth has benefited everyone in society? If we use the US as example, the historical evidence contradicts the argument from trickle-down economics. From the 1950s to the middle of the 1970s, there was stable, high growth under a progressive tax regime that ensured the distribution of growth across society, improving everyone's condition. At the start of the 1980s, taxes for those with high incomes and wealth were drastically cut. At the same time, the economic growth no longer benefited everyone, but only those in the top percentiles of the income distribution. From 1979 to 2005, the worst off saw their real wages decline, while the middle class stagnated and could only maintain their real wages by working more (Greenwood and Holt 2010:404). This suggests that growth does not trickle down, but whether this fact can be attributed to other factors and whether this is also true of other countries are questions I cannot treat here.[21]

Even if trickle-down economics were right that tax cuts create more jobs, one would, in order to evaluate the policy, also have to take into consideration other possible solutions to the same problem. If the goal is to create jobs, it might, for example, be better to raise state spending. This is because large tax cuts—if they do, in fact, create more jobs—will also tend to create larger inequalities and this (as I have already noted in previous chapters) comes with negative consequences. Norwegian economist Einar Øverbye formulates the logic of trickle down in a precise way:

> The cake which is to be distributed might become bigger if the reforms work as they are intended, but it will most likely also increase inequality. The latter is more certain than the former. The question is whether increased inequality is a price worth paying, given these conditions.
>
> (Øverbye 2017b:252)

Now, the issue of increased state spending suggests that the state should take an active role through its fiscal policy. Traditionally, Keynesian economics have focused on fiscal policy such as government spending. Such measures should be employed, Keynesians argue, in order to counteract business cycles, unemployment, and recessions. In the macroeconomic debate, such arguments are often confronted by neoliberals arguing for privatization of state-owned enterprises, tax reductions, and deregulation as the better way to foster economic growth (Polillo and Guillen 2005:1768). I shall not enter this broader debate here. What this illustrates is how the issue of taxation and trickle-down effects are connected to broader issues of macroeconomics.

The issue of state spending is contentious. Another related issue involves how the government employs fiscal and monetary policy. The fiscal policy is controlled by the government who can increase the demand in the economy through increased spending and through changed tax rates. Monetary policy is currently controlled by central banks and involves altering interest rates and influencing the supply of money in order to ensure price stability and control inflation. Traditionally, as we have just seen, Keynesian economics have focused on fiscal policy such as government spending. However, monetary policy is also relevant in a distributive perspective. For example, it is normally assumed that the expansionary policies followed by many central banks after the financial crises have had the consequence of higher prices for real estates, which is primarily owned by the wealthiest (Fontan et al. 2016:335). In this way, monetary policies have had the effect of increasing inequality.

If this is correct, there is a potential tension between fiscal and monetary policy. Fiscal policy can involve measures to redistribute in order to reduce inequalities. Monetary policies might have the opposite effect and result in growing inequalities. Thus, some have argued that monetary policies should become more concerned with inequality. Rethinking the role of monetary policy involves questioning the mandates of central banks, which since the 1990s have become independent from national governments to an increasing degree (Polillo and Guillen 2005:1770; Fontan et al. 2016:322). One suggestion is that central banks should still primarily focus on inflation, but pick the inflation-reducing policies that produces the best consequences in terms of equality (Raa 2017:88; Fontan et al. 2016:341). A more radical proposal is that concerns for inequality should be met by monetary policies rather than by traditional tax measures (Fontan et al. 2016:346).[22]

I will not elaborate further on these distinctions here. What this shows is that questions of tax reductions and the broader issues of whether wealth will trickle down are complex and must be situated within a broader macroeconomic debate. In my view, the arguments against trickle-down economics suggest that one should be sceptical towards the assumptions discussed above, but I must stress that this is a controversial conclusion, and that the arguments I have given here cannot in themselves refute trickle-down economics.[23]

Therefore, we must ask to what extent wealth tax is a good instrument for redistribution. Here, the different official reports I have referred to (NOUs) and the economic expertise are in agreement. The Distribution committee concluded that "The wealth tax has a large distributional effect. For example, in 2006, about a sixth of the wealth tax was payed by the 1000 wealthiest in Norway" (NOU 2009:201). The Scheel committee conclude that "the wealth tax works as a progressive element in the tax system because it makes up a larger share of the income of high-income groups, where there is a large proportion of capital income" (NOU 2014:284–285). In fact, the wealth tax "makes up more than half of the taxes payed by those with the greatest taxable wealth" (NOU 2014:290).

A large majority of Norwegian economists share this view. In 2014, the national newspaper *VG* interviewed 25 of the foremost economists in Norway. The questions were on the topics of inheritance tax and wealth tax. Only 2 out of 25 thought that it would be right to remove the inheritance tax, while 3 were in favour of reducing or removing the wealth tax (Mosveen et al. 2014a). On the question of whether there were other taxes that could ensure the same redistribution, the doyen of Norwegian inequality research, Rolf Aaberge, replied that "I cannot see that there are realistic alternative taxes that will provide equally large redistributive effect (per tax krone/Euro) as the wealth tax; apart from the inheritance tax" (Aaberge in Mosveen et al. 2014a).

A reformed wealth tax

Recently, the European version of the wealth tax has been criticized. Saez and Zucman argue that there are three problems with the way the tax has been designed: Tax evasion, tax avoidance by rich people moving residence, and finally, the exemption levels in Europe have generally been too low (Saez and Zucman 2019b:25–30). I cannot discuss their proposal in detail here, but will simply sketch their criticism of the European wealth tax in order to provide a background to the reform of the Norwegian wealth tax that I will defend.

Take tax evasion first: Rich people can evade wealth taxes by moving their wealth to tax havens. These tax havens do not share information with foreign authorities.[24] Drawing on a paper by Alstadsæter et al. and Zucman and Saez show that there is "substantial tax evasion of the rich in Norway through offshore accounts" (Saez and Zucman 2019b:26). This first problem requires more coordination on an EU level, and Norway should take efforts to step up this work. In general, the authors argue that it is possible to avoid tax havens, but European governments have been half hearted in their effort to do so (Saez and Zucman 2019b:26).

Alternatively, rich people avoid the tax by moving residence to foreign countries (Saez and Zucman 2019b:25). The EU is, the authors argue, designed to foster such tax competition. Previously, with the wealth tax that existed in France, moving from Paris to London ensured that French citizens do not have to pay wealth tax. We looked at a main justification for such tax competition in Chapter 9 (the tax constitution approach). In my view, the problem of rich people moving residence can be met by the reforms suggested by Barry and Warren, as discussed above. Furthermore, Saez and Zucman argue that the US has led a much more proactive policy on both tax heavens and expatriation than have the EU (Saez and Zucman 2019b:27).

Finally, Saez and Zucman argue that the wealth tax in Europe fails because of low exemption levels. This fuels a concern for fairness. People argue that the wealth tax makes it necessary for middle-class families to sell their homes. Historically, this led to a lot of lobbying against the wealth tax, and many special exemptions where introduced. Thus, the tax base was eroded, and the legitimacy of the tax questioned (Saez and Zucman 2019b:28).

Again, the message from Saez and Zucman is that tax evasion and tax avoidance is not laws of nature. To what extent governments allow these phenomenon is down to policy choices (Saez and Zucman 2019b:30).[25] The EU should learn from the US on these matters:

> While countries in the EU generally have bigger governments, more social spending, and more regulations than the United States, it is the

> reverse with the EU super-structure that actually promotes policies that constrain governments more than what is done in the United States: this is true for tax competition, but also for government deficits and monetary policy.
>
> (Saez and Zucman 2019b:27)[26]

The lesson from this is that the EU should learn from the US, and that more cooperation is necessary. In the case of Norway, policy choices are available as a means to stop people from moving abroad, and the wealth tax should have much higher exemption level. However, Norway cannot, on its own, stop the rich from tax evasion. Nevertheless, this should not be seen as a decisive argument against the wealth tax. Instead, Norway should be in front when it comes to regulations on this issue.

How does the suggested increase of exemption level match with the combined justification for the wealth tax I suggested above? The ability to pay principle is an important justification for the wealth tax, and should be combined with the principle of democratic equality. What significance does this combined justification have for questions of standard deductions and tax rates? Fleischer has argued that if the primary justification for the wealth tax is democratic equality, then the tax should have a very high standard deduction (Fleischer 2017:274). A person with a wealth of €10 million suffers no distress, but also does not, under normal circumstances, have so much money that she can donate large sums to increase her political influence. This changes dramatically if that person has a €10 billion fortune. With such funds available, with a normal return on investment, the income alone will be too high to be spent through ordinary consumption. With such wealth, using one's funds to achieve political influence seem much more rational. The Scheel committee suggests increasing the standard deduction (NOU 2014, Nr. 13:297), but much less so than what would follow from Fleischer's logic. This is a consequence of Fleischer being concerned exclusively with justifying wealth tax on the basis of democratic equality, while the Scheel committee's justification is based on a more general and unspecified concern for distribution.

A combined justification for a progressive wealth tax that rests on both the principle of democratic equality and the ability to pay principle entails, in my view, a considerable raising of the standard deduction, but also a considerable raising of the rates and a graduated rate schedule. This provides a robust justification for the wealth tax, and a wealth tax with a much higher exemption level will also avoid the objection from fairness, as argued by Saez and Zucman. From a Rawlsian perspective, such taxation will, given the high level of wealth inequality in Norway, be an important step towards a more just tax system. Combined with a reformed and progressive inheritance tax, the wealth tax would be an important contribution to reducing the concentration of capital in Norway.

Concluding comments on the Norwegian tax system

In Norway, the income tax has become less progressive since the 1980s. In addition, the three other taxes most adapted to redistribution have either been removed (inheritance tax) or reduced (wealth tax and corporate income tax).[27] These taxes can be justified by their being effective tools to reduce the concentration of capital. Avoiding large concentration of capital is a main goal of *justice as fairness*. The NOUs I have discussed here, together with statements by the majority of Norwegian economists, show that the inheritance tax and the wealth tax are the most effective instruments of redistribution.

Removing wealth tax and tax on inheritance is problematic based on the following reasoning. We have seen that the inequalities that exist in Norway give those who have the most the opportunity to dominate and control others. We have also seen that this can have a number of other negative consequences tied to the self-respect of the worst off, with concomitantly servile and submissive behaviour. The inequalities are already at a level we should perceive as problematic. We can therefore say that the distribution is unjust in its present form, and that the tax system fails to correct this because it allows too great concentration of capital. In addition, the distribution is liable to become still more unfair in the nearest future, because we will then notice the consequences of the changes that have been made to the tax system in recent years as well as the developmental trends I pointed to in Chapter 9 (tax competition, robotification/automation, reduced degree of unionization). Note also that the NOUs we have looked at and a number of economic experts have reached the same verdict about the reduction of wealth tax and the removal of the inheritance tax. For these reasons, we must conclude that the Norwegian tax system does not sufficiently take care of justice.

The question then becomes how Norway should organize the tax system so that it can contribute to a fair distribution. The corporate tax and the income tax are, in my view, the most complicated taxes to evaluate. A reduction in corporate tax may be necessary to uphold competitiveness when other countries lower their corporate taxes. The danger of income shifting is an argument in favour of lowering the income tax. At the same time, there are considerations that pull in the opposite direction. The OECD report mentioned above concludes that increasing inequality in Norway has caused lower growth because the worst off cannot fully develop their abilities.[28] This is an argument to the effect that even egalitarian countries like Norway are not, in fact, ensuring equality of opportunity.[29] That is both unjust and bad for growth. This speaks in favour of limiting the cuts in the income tax and perhaps even increasing the rate for those with the highest income. Note also that *if* the corporate tax and the income tax are reduced, it is necessary to replace them with other taxes to ensure redistribution. This has not happened in the Norwegian context.

The wealth tax is less complex when considered from the perspective of *justice as fairness*. I have argued that Norway should raise the standard deduction, but also significantly raise the rates. This will result in a noticeably reduced concentration of capital. At the same time, it will probably cause an efficiency loss, even if the current wealth tax has no significant negative effects on efficiency. With higher rates for the richest, there is greater danger of more tax planning, and that some will move their fortunes abroad. The rates should therefore be raised gradually.

We should nevertheless raise the rates significantly, because there is a conflict between efficiency and redistribution, and considerations of efficiency have for a long time been given priority, something which requires a readjustment. If there is conflict between efficiency and redistribution, it is not given that efficiency should always be given priority, and to counter the tendency of increasing inequality, it is necessary to use more powerful instruments than those that have been used in recent years.

In conclusion, we should make note of a principle difference between the normative suggestions I defend here, and the suggestions put forth in the official reports (NOUs) on which I have based my description of the Norwegian tax system. The former are about drawing up long-term goals. Rawlsian defences of wealth tax and inheritance tax are long-term suggestions. They cannot simply be rejected because they may cause a loss of efficiency as a result of behavioural changes (wealth creation decreases if one increases income taxes). Rawls' hope is (as we have seen) that people will change how they think if we have just institutions. The hope is that a just background structure in time will lead to people being more willing to contribute to the community.

Let me illustrate with an example. One argument against my suggestion to significantly increase the wealth tax of the richest is that this will contribute to rich people moving abroad. We must therefore avoid increasing the wealth tax by too much. However, according to my argument here, there are three replies to this objection. First, it is possible to introduce an exit tax or stronger restrictions on tax refugees' ability to visit their home country. Second, the upwards adjustment of wealth tax must be gradual, and third, we must hope that people's preferences shift so that, in the long term, they are less motivated by self-interest and more by what is good for the community. If such a shift comes about, the richest people will be less disposed to move their wealth abroad, even if the tax on wealth increases. Such long-term changes in people's behaviour are not taken into account in the standard version of the Official Report (like the NOUs referred to here). The point is that normative political theory can allow itself more, let us call it ambitious reform proposals, than what is true of an official report. To a theory of justice inspired by Rawls, it is a matter of finding out what principles of justice we should use to regulate society, and then what implications this has for practical politics in the long term. To an official report like the NOU, the goal is to arrive at a reform of the tax system with minimal distorting effects given people's current preferences.

This example is meant to illustrate that the suggestion of an increase in the wealth tax should be considered as feasible, and that it cannot be rejected by claims that it will have negative effects on the economy.

Further reading

Eric Rakowski's *Can Wealth Taxes Be Justified* provides a rare philosophical discussion of the wealth tax. Piketty's *Capital in the Twenty-First Century* and *Capital and Ideology* are both important for the renewal of the interest for the wealth tax. Saez and Zucman's paper "Progressive Wealth Taxation" and their recent book *The Triumph of Injustice: How the Rich Dodge Taxes and How to Make Them Pay* has been much discussed in the US.

A critical discussion of trickle-down economics can be found in Ha-Joon Changs *23 Things They Don't Tell You about Capitalism.*

Podcasts: Planet Money episode 929, 24.7.2019: Could a wealth tax work?

Bloomberg Stephanomics, 06.11.2019: The Sanders or Warren Wealth Tax?

Notes

1 For a short history of the wealth tax in different countries, see Piketty (2020:560–577).

2 There has never been a wealth tax in the UK. However, the Labour Government of 1974 planned to introduce this tax, but failed to bring it through. For a history of the debate of wealth taxes in the UK, see Glennerster (2012) and Piketty (2020:573–574).

3 Warren's proposal is to tax wealth above $50 million at a marginal rate of 2% and at 3% above $1 billion (Saez and Zucman 2019b:2; Piketty 2020:570–571). Part of the political interests in this tax can be explained by the fact that "most people would prefer a mixed tax system based on both income and net worth" (Piketty quoting a survey by Fisman et al. 2017).

4 Compared to the vast amount of literature on inheritance tax, there is not much philosophical discussion of the wealth tax. Partly for that reason and partly for the complexity of the issue, this chapter is more tentative. For a philosophical discussion of the wealth tax, which I shall return to, see Rakowski (2000).

5 Wealth includes financial assets such as banking accounts/shares and non-financial assets such as real estate/land and buildings. For a more detailed definition of wealth that includes a discussion of durable goods and human capital, see Saez and Zucman (2019b:4).

6 Recall from Chapter 9 that Rawls' position on taxation is complex. The complexity is in part due to the fact that Rawls' discussion of tax is meant to apply to a property owning democracy. In a property owning democracy, capital is spread around through several mechanisms of predistribution (compare O'Neill and Williamson 2015:826–827). In less ideal contexts, where such mechanisms are not in place, it is still critical to ensure an equal distribution of property and wealth in order to protect the principle of equal liberty and the principle of fair equality of opportunity. Note also that Rawls explicitly argues in favour of inheritance tax, but does not discuss the wealth tax. What I say about a Rawlsian justification for wealth tax must therefore be understood as my interpretation of what follows from Rawls' position in a second-best context.

7 For additional discussion, see Halliday (2018:201–205) and Piketty (2020:978–979).
8 Sugin makes a similar point arguing that "a periodic wealth tax, which breaks up dangerous accumulations regularly during a person's lifetime" might be the most effective way of taxing wealth.
9 In the US, the debate on revenue has been fierce between Saez and Zucman, who advised the Warren proposal, and some of their critics, like Lawrence Summers; see Frank (2019).
10 If someone *chooses* to save, it follows that part of their wealth that is due to this choice is just, and not something that should be taxed. For an elaboration of this, see the discussion of Dworkin and wealth tax in Chapter 3. For a luck egalitarian critique of wealth tax, see Rakowski (2000).
11 As we have seen, Piketty's ideal solution is a global wealth tax. The arguments he gives for this kind of tax can, however, also be employed as a justification for a standard wealth tax, such as the one I am defending here. In his recent book, the arguments about the wealth tax concerns how it can be implemented at a national level (Piketty 2020).
12 Note that Murphy and Nagel are critical towards ability to pay principles. This is because ability to pay considers the tax burden, and according to Murphy and Nagel, the tax burden is morally irrelevant; see Murphy and Nagel (2002:28–30). I cannot address this concern in a proper way here; more work needs to be done in order to discuss this. I appreciate conversations with Preben Sørheim on this topic.
13 For a more detailed explanation of this problem, see Saez and Zucman (2019b:18–19).
14 For additional examples of how billionaires like Jeff Bezos and Warren Buffet pay very low taxes if not subject to a wealth tax, see Saez and Zucman (2019a:146). In the Norwegian context, the wealth tax constitutes a large part of the tax burden for the wealthiest people. In 2014, there were 28 billionaires in the country, and it has been estimated that 80% of their tax burden was due to the wealth tax (Sundberg 2014).
15 For a critique of this argument, see Rakowski (2000:295–296).
16 The clip can be seen on YouTube, see (Skavland 2015).
17 Prime Minister Erna Solberg, who has fronted the cuts in the wealth tax, admits that we cannot know with certainty that cutting the tax will create more jobs (Fossen 2017).
18 Whether such a change actually will stop people from becoming tax refugees depends on how important it is for them to be able to spend time in Norway. More knowledge is needed here about how potential tax refugees think. Moreover, a suggestion like this presupposes that one can distinguish between ordinary people and tax refugees, so that the arrangement does not impact ordinary persons who live abroad and who have not moved to avoid paying taxes. Barry also argues that tax refugees should not be given the same opportunity to donate money to political parties, own newspapers, and so on (Barry 2005:193).
19 There are other arguments against the wealth tax that I cannot discuss here. For example, some argue that the wealth tax is double taxation, others hold that such a tax is hard to implement due to valuation issues. Furthermore, in the US, some will simply say that the wealth tax is unconstitutional, and therefore not something to be considered. The argument about double taxation suffers from some of the weaknesses of the double taxation argument discussed in the previous chapter. The fact that the wealth tax has been part of the Norwegian system for a 100 years shows that valuation problems can be overcome. Finally, as Saez and Zucman have argued, the constitutionality of the wealth tax depends "on the make-up of supreme court" (Saez and Zucman 2019:22).

20 Let me add that the argument from trickle-down economics can also be used as an argument for lowered income taxes: Lower income taxes for the best off, and they will work harder so that the worst off become better off; the IMF report from 2014, mentioned above, shows that this assumption does not hold (Ostry et al. 2014:4, 7). This conclusion is supported by a 2019 study which concluded that "the positive relationship between tax cuts and employment growth is largely driven by tax cuts for lower-income groups and that the effect of tax cuts for the top 10 percent on employment growth is small" (Zidar 2019:1437).

21 Piketty argues in a similar manner but more generally, claiming that "strongly progressive taxation are clearly no obstacle to rapid productivity growth, provided that the top rates apply to sufficiently high levels of income and wealth" (Piketty 2020:543).

22 If this is a viable option, it would represent another mechanism to predistribute rather than to redistribute.

23 There are, as far as I can see, surprisingly few good discussions of this phenomenon. This is probably because, in order to assess this assumption, one would have to measure the effect of a tax cut on the whole economy in a long-term perspective, and this is very complicated. Moreover, the question has become ideological: The right and left have diametrically opposed opinions about trickle-down economics. For a review of the empirical literature in the field, see Akinci (2017). For a short, popular scientific treatment, see Chang (2014).

24 Saez and Zucman argue that moving wealth into tax havens is evasion and not "mere" tax avoidance. This is because wealth taxes "are based on the global wealth if citizens regardless of the location of the assets or the financial institutions managing the assets" (Saez and Zucman 2019b:25).

25 For a more nuanced defence of this claim, see Saez and Zucman (2019a).

26 For a similar point, see Piketty (2020:548–558).

27 Saez and Zucman argue that a similar trend goes for the US. "The three traditional progressive taxes – the individual income tax, the corporate income tax, and the estate tax – have weakened" (Saez and Zucman 2019b:1). As a remedy to the tax system becoming less progressive, they propose a wealth tax which would be "a powerful tool to restore progressivity" (Saez and Zucman 2019b:2, 20). Piketty argues that this trend towards lower progressivity is not limited to the US, but is instead a general trend: "progressivity has decreased significantly since the 1980s" (Piketty 2020:557).

28 See OECD (2014) presented in Chapter 9.

29 Redistributive taxes and offers of job training programmes that increase the skill level of those with little formal education are suggestions for specific measures.

Conclusion

In this book, I have discussed different theories of justice and defended *justice as fairness*. According to this theory, inequalities should be kept within strictly limited bounds in order to ensure that everyone has the same opportunity for political influence, and is offered the same chances in working life. If one allows inequalities beyond this ideal, it may have negative consequences in the form of submissive and servile citizens without self-respect. It can also detract from the sense of community in society and undermine social relations. In the following, I will briefly elaborate on a few important aspects of *justice as fairness*.

Rawls argues that capitalist welfare states are not just, and claims that property owning democracy is a better alternative. Is this criticism of the welfare state relevant to a society like the Norwegian? Some commentators have pointed out that the criticism fits the Anglo-Saxon form of welfare state better than it does the Nordic one (O'Neill 2012; Schemmel 2015). The Scandinavian welfare state offers generous schemes such as publicly funded health care, education, and access to child care for all. These are important schemes that make these countries clearly better positioned to achieve the goals identified in Rawls' theory. However, this is not enough to meet the requirements of *justice as fairness*. Property owning democracy requires a broad spectre of schemes to ensure dispersal of capital, and these schemes of dispersal must come in addition to, or on top of, a generous welfare state. Dispersion of capital is necessary because Norway—as we touched upon in the introduction—has more super-rich inhabitants per capita than the US. In Chapter 7, I argued that allowing a few to become extremely rich is a violation of justice because these super-rich citizens can achieve greater political power than others.

We should, as I mentioned in Chapter 5, distinguish between a short-term and a long-term goal that follow from Rawls' theory. The short-term goal is to deepen the welfare state and take measures to reduce the concentration of capital. The long-term goal is about larger reforms needed to realize property owning democracy.

To the short-term goal, I have argued that in spite of the fact that Norway comparatively speaking is a well-functioning welfare state, the economic structures allow too much concentration of capital. The richest citizens are given the opportunity to convert their economic resources into political power, and one does not succeed in giving everyone equal opportunities. This is problematic, not least because the inequalities can be expected to rise in the future.

An important reason for this injustice is that Norway does not use the opportunities present in its tax system. The abolition of the inheritance tax and the reduction of the corporate tax and the wealth tax mean that Norway does not ensure an equalization of problematic inequalities. In the last few years, the government has reduced the importance of some of the most important instruments that could have been used to redistribute. I have argued that a considerable strengthening of these taxes is compatible with private property rights and individual freedom, and that the problems associated with such strengthening are exaggerated. Piketty's analysis of the importance of the tax system to reduce inequalities provides an apt summary:

> The progressive tax is thus a relatively liberal method for reducing inequality, in the sense that free competition and private property are respected while private incentives are modified in potentially radical ways, but always according to rules thrashed out in democratic debate. The progressive tax thus represents an ideal compromise between social justice and individual freedom (Piketty 2014:505).

Taxes can change incentives, as we saw in Chapter 4. High taxes on the highest incomes makes it less attractive for the most capable to push for higher salaries. In the long term, institutions that are properly set up can also promote egalitarian attitudes.

The long-term goal is about a gradual move to a property owning democracy. The tax increases I have proposed will not be sufficient to realize this ideal. In order for property owning democracy to be fully realized, Norway would need a set of mechanisms that can ensure a capital ceiling and a capital floor. Such an ideal will entail societal changes away from the present system. It requires not only large institutional changes, but also a change in people's way of thinking and acting.

Let me say something about the institutional changes first. Together with a reformed tax system that limits what the richest can be allowed to earn and own, it requires schemes that provide capital to the worst off. This can be established by having a negative income tax, or special funds that pay money to anyone who is willing to work. Such schemes must be connected to egalitarian reforms of the welfare state (increased child/family allowances, support for poor children who want to participate in sport activity, and all-day schools with homework help and hot food).

To realize a well-functioning property owning democracy, it is also important to establish a form of predistribution, that is, mechanisms that sets limits to what people can receive in pre-tax income. An important example of predistribution is the legal framework for intellectual property (Scanlon 2018:102). If the patents or intellectual property rights of corporations did not have the same lifespan they have today, one would be able to reduce inequality. Widespread use of land value taxation is another example of predistribution (Kerr 2016). This is the taxation of limited natural resources that belong to the community. In Norway, there is already such a tax on the oil industry and on hydroelectric power. In addition, there is an ongoing debate on a similar tax for the aquaculture industry, and one can imagine that other uses of natural resources are similarly taxed (fisheries and wind power).

Another example is the importance of a pay structure that limits income inequality. Active measures to increase the bargaining power of wage earners have been highlighted as the best way of ensuring income equalization prior to taxation.[1] Research from OECD shows that this kind of measure efficiently equalizes income while not being detrimental to growth (OECD 2012; O'Neill and Williamson 2012c:5). IMF has also recently shown that a decreasing degree of unionization is strongly correlated with a rise in the highest incomes (Dabla-Norris 2015:21). Measures to strengthen unions are therefore very important to limit pre-tax income inequality.

Overall, it is necessary with new forms of predistribution and traditional forms of redistribution such as tax on income and wealth to realize property owning democracy. Predistribution can be seen as analogous to preventative strategies in health care, where one seeks to limit people's smoking and consumption of unhealthy food, so that fewer people will need treatment for COPD or obesity (Gregg 2012). Similarly, it is necessary to fight pre-tax inequalities because large inequalities are unhealthy, and because there are limits to how much one can reduce inequality with the help of tax mechanisms.[2]

More than today, people must also be motivated by egalitarian considerations of justice. More people need to think like Hans Olav Lahlum and Bill Gates. Lahlum, a successful author and representative for the socialist party, wants to pay more taxes, and states that his goal is to pay over kr1 million in taxes (Cosson-Eide and Sølhusvik 2017), while Gates states that billionaires like himself should pay significantly more taxes (NTB 2018). Fewer people must think like Bjørn Dæhlie, the Olympic skiing champion, who sees wealth tax as punishment, despite having a large fortune (Lien and Johansen 2017). Correspondingly, we need a change in motivation with regards to salaries. The salary of the head of the Norwegian state-owned oil company Equinor, Eldar Sætre, rose by 31% in 2017, up to kr14.9 million (or approximately €1.5 million) (Skarsaune 2018). The justification for these kinds of pay raises is usually that they are necessary to get executives to do their best. If executives and other especially capable people were motivated by doing their best for the community instead, these kinds of salaries would not be necessary, and one would experience much less inequality.

In other words, a shift to a property owning democracy requires an egalitarian ethos where people are not out to maximize what they themselves are left with, but instead are concerned with doing their best for the community.

Such a shift in people's way of thinking requires both that people more than today dedicate their lives to work for justice, but also that justice is understood in an egalitarian way, as we have seen Cohen and Rawls argue. Only in the long term, and only by changing institutions and attitudes, will it be possible to realize a society in line with a property owning democracy as defended by Rawls.

The most important objection to property owning democracy will be that it hurts productivity. Such an objection will point out that if one puts an upper limit to what the richest people can be allowed to control in terms of resources, then this will have negative effects on the economy. The wealthiest lose their incentives to make wise decisions, to save, and to work hard, if we limit the resources they can control.

This objection must be taken seriously. Economic growth can be important if the result of this growth is distributed in a just way.[3] However, the objection overlooks three things. First, it overlooks the fact that providing capital to the worst off may have positive effects on the economy. With a capital floor, even the worst off will be given the opportunity to develop their talents to the benefit of society. Furthermore, from the certainty that follows from everyone having some capital follows an increased willingness on the part of people to start new businesses. Everyone is given a larger degree of security, which will contribute to a greater willingness to take risk.

Second, the objection overlooks the fact that economic growth is not the only goal that should be given weight. As we saw in Chapter 7, there is a potential tension between democracy and maximizing economic growth if maximizing economic growth entails large inequalities. In other words, there is a potential tension between democracy and capitalism, and this entails that the concern for economic growth cannot be our only concern.

Third, the objection overlooks the fact that property owning democracy must be understood as a long-term ideal which presupposes a gradual shift to an egalitarian ethos. If a considerably larger share of the population think like Hans Olav Lahlum, those who are best off will see that they have more than enough to live good lives and still do their best. Only with just institutions and individuals who act and think on what is just can we hope to realize the ideal of a just society with free and equal citizens (see Chapter 4).

Another important objection is that there is little reason to think that an egalitarian ethos will come to dominate our thinking in the future. This is a complex objection that I am unable to fully discuss here. Instead, I have to limit myself to repeating the Rawlsian point that institutions shape how people think and act, so that egalitarian institutions may in the long term promote more egalitarian attitudes. Piketty's research presents an example of how such transformation might actually work.[4]

Compared to other countries, the Norwegian welfare state has been successful when it comes to creating good lives for its citizens. However, this does not mean that Norway is just and has done enough. If we go back 100 years, the welfare state of today would seem utopian. Norway has come a long way, but there is also much that remains to be done if the goal is a society without hierarchies where some are allowed to dominate and control others. Property owning democracy is a realistic utopian goal that all citizens should be afforded the same opportunity to be active and independent actors in the economic life of society. This is an ambitious goal, but in the long term, ambitious goals are what we need.[5]

Notes

1 Ahlquist (2017) has argued that strong unions contribute to both predistribution and redistribution. Predistribution because strong unions increase worker salaries and reduces executive salaries. Redistribution because union work gives people a form of political experience. Many are drawn into political work, and then often on the left, and a stronger left will normally result in more redistributive taxes. This example demonstrates that, as Martin O'Neill (2020) has recently shown, it is difficult to distinguish between predistributive and redistributive policies. This is because traditional redistributional measures such as top rate income taxes can have a predistributional effect. As we saw in Chapter 4, very high top tax rates can change how people think. With such measures in place, highly paid workers will be less focused on bargaining for higher salaries. Thus, a redistributive policy produces predistributive effects. Because of this difficulty of distinguishing between the two forms of distribution, O'Neill argues in favour of reconstructing the notion of predistribution. Instead of understanding it as different types of policies, it should be understood as different types of aims or effects of policies.

2 Recently, Piketty presented what is arguably the most detailed institutional structure to put in place something resembling a property owning democracy. The scheme includes progressive inheritance and income taxes, power sharing within firms, and perhaps most important, a progressive annual tax on wealth that can finance a capital endowment to be given to everyone at the age of 25. Such a scheme is designed to replace permanent private ownership with temporary private ownership (Piketty 2020:966–1034).

3 I will abstain from discussing whether economic growth is a good, and whether and how it might be balanced with sustainability.

4 In June 2020, as I am finishing this book, the world is in the midst of the COVID-19 pandemic. Although too early to conclude how the crisis will affect inequality and taxation, two trends deserve mention. The first is that research strongly suggests that pandemics prior to COVID-19 tended to increase inequality. Furthermore, government policies to address pandemics have tended to be regressive, indicating that the "rich are the major beneficiaries" (Furceri et al. 2020). As for tax policy, the crises might have effects on the relative importance of the income tax to wealth taxes. Most jurisdictions have high income taxes and low wealth taxes, and this might change, given that such a regime will be harder to justify in a situation where incomes are likely to be lower in the years following the crises. Thanks to an anonymous reviewer for making this point.

5 Compare the point about the role of political philosophy set out in Chapter 5.

References

Aaberge, Rolf and Stubhaug, Magnus E (2018): Formuesulikhet øker. SSB analyse 2018/18

Aarre, Einar (2016): "Han bygget cruiseanlegg til 250 millioner. Nå vil Oddvar Røysi rive alt". *BT magasinet* 15.10 Downloaded from: https://www.bt.no/btmagasinet/i/kG9Mk/Han-bygget-cruiseanlegg-til-250-millioner-Na-vil-Oddvar-Roysi-rive-alt

Agenda (2016): "Formueskatt og mulige endringer. Policy notat". https://tankesmienagenda.no/uploads/documents/post/Webversjon-Policynotat-En-ny-formuesskatt.pdf

Agenda (2018): «Våre eiere». https://tankesmienagenda.no/vare-eiere/

Agenda Perspektivnotat (2014): "Et rettferdig skattesystem". https://tankesmienagenda.no/uploads/documents/post/Perspektivnotat_Et_rettferdig_kattesystem_liten.pdf

Ahlquist, John S. (2017): "Labor Unions, Political Representation, and Economic Inequality". *Annual Review of Political Science*, 20, 409–432.

Akinci, Merter (2017): "Inequality and Economic Growth: Trickle-Down Effect Revisited". *Development Policy Review*, 36, 1, 1–24.

Alkire, Sabine (2002): *Valuing Freedoms. Sen's Capability Approach and Poverty Reduction*. Oxford. Oxford University Press.

Allingham, Michael (2014): *Distributive Justice*. London. Routledge.

Alsberg, Ola (2019): "Nordlandskommune med radikalt skattegrep. Kutter kraftig i formueskatten". *E 24*. https://e24.no/privatoekonomi/i/kJPVLL/nordlandskommune-med-radikalt-skattegrep-kutter-kraftig-i-formuesskatten

Alstott, Anne L. (2007): "Equal Opportunity and Inheritance Taxation". *Harvard Law Review*, 121 (2), 469–542.

Altinn (2019): "Tax for personal shareholders in private limited companies". https://www.altinn.no/en/start-and-run-business/direct-and-indirect-taxes/the-enterprises-tax/tax-for-personal-shareholders-in-private-limited-companies/

Anderson, Elizabeth (1999): "What Is the Point of Equality?" *Ethics*, 109 (2), 287–337.

Anderson, Elizabeth (2010a): *The Imperative of Integration*. Princeton. Princeton University Press.

Anderson, Elizabeth (2010b): "The Fundamental Disagreement between Luck Egalitarians and Relational Egalitarians". *Canadian Journal of Philosophy*, 40 (supp 1), 1–23.

Arneson, Richard (1989): "Equality and Equal Opportunity for Welfare". *Philosophical Studies*, 56 (1): 77–93.

Arneson, Richard J. (1990): "Liberalism, Distributive Subjectivism, and Equal Opportunity for Welfare". *Philosophy and Public Affairs*, 19 (2): 158–194.

Arneson, Richard J. (2000a): "Luck Egalitarianism and Prioritarianism". *Ethics*, 110 (2), 339–349.

Arneson, Richard J. (2000b) "Welfare should be the currency of justice". *Canadian Journal of Philosophy*, 30 (4), 497–524.

Arneson, Richard J. (2002): "Review of Sovereign Virtue". *Ethics*, 112 (2), 367–371.

Arneson, Richard J. (2005): "Disruptive Justice and Basic Capability Equality: "Good Enough" Is Not Good Enough". In Kaufman, Alexander (ed): *Capabilities Equality. Basic Issues and Problems*. London. Routledge, pp 17–43.

Arneson, Richard J. (2010): "Two Cheers for Capabilities". In Brighouse, Harry and Robeyns, Ingrid (eds): *Measuring Justice. Primary Goods and Capabilities*. Cambridge. Cambridge University Press, pp 101–128.

Arneson, Richard J. (Summer 2013 Edition): "Egalitarianism". In Zalta, Edward N. (ed): *The Stanford Encyclopedia of Philosophy*. http://plato.stanford.edu/archives/sum2013/entries/egalitarianism/.

Arneson, Richard J. (2018): "Dworkin and Luck Egalitarianism". In Olsaretti, Serena (ed): *The Oxford Handbook of Distributive Justice*. Oxford. Oxford University Press, pp 41–64.

Atkinson, Anthony (2015): *Inequality. What Can Be Done?* Cambridge. Harvard University Press.

Axelsen, David V. and Nielsen, Lasse (2014): "Sufficiency as Freedom from Duress". *Journal of Political Philosophy*, 23 (4), 406–426.

Bain, Alexander (1882): *John Stuart Mill: A Criticism with Personal Recollections*. London. Longmans Green and Co.

Bamford, Douglas (2015): "Ethical Taxation: Progressivity, Efficiency and Hourly Averaging". In Gaisbauer, Helmut P., et al. (eds): *Philosophical Explorations of Justice and Taxation*. Switzerland. Springer, pp 135–150.

Barry, Brian (2005): *Why Social Justice Matters*. Cambridge. Polity Press.

Barry, Christian and Halliday, Dan (podcast): Equality. In Dialogues, a Series of podcasts on Ethics. Downloaded from: https://ethicsmatterstvseries.com/dialogues/

Batchelder, Lily L. (2009): "What Should Society Expect from Heirs? The Case for a Comprehensive Inheritance Tax". *Tax Law Review*, 63 (1), 1–112.

Beckert, Jens (2008): *Inherited Wealth*. Princeton. Princeton University Press.

Bentham, Jeremy (1795/1952): "Supply Without Burthen. Escheat Vice Taxation". In Stark, W. (ed): *Jeremy Bentham's Economic Writings*. London. The Royal Economic Society, pp 283–367.

Bergens Tidende (2004): "Mektig gjennom rause gaver". *BT* 20.11 Downloaded from: https://www.bt.no/nyheter/okonomi/i/zl0A1/Mektig-gjennom-rause-gaver

Biron, Laura (2018): "Taxing or Taking? Property Rhetoric and the Justice of Taxation". In O'Neill, Martin and Orr, Shepley (eds): *Taxation. Philosophical Perspectives*. Oxford. Oxford University Press, pp 81–97.

Bøyum, Steinar (2016): *Utdanning, ulikskap og urettferd*. Bergen. Fagbokforlaget.

Bracewell-Milnes, Barry (1997) "The Hidden Costs of Inheritance Taxation". In Erreygers, Guido and Vandevelde, Toon (eds): *Is Inheritance Legitimate? Ethical and Economic Aspects of Wealth Transfers*. Berlin. Springer, pp 156–201.

Braun, Stewart (2016): "Liberty, Political Rights and Wealth Transfer Taxation". *Journal of Applied Philosophy*, 33 (4), 379–396.

Brennan, Geoffrey (2005a): "The Myth of Ownership". *Australian Journal of Legal Philosophy*, 30, 129–130.
Brennan, Geoffrey (2005b): "The Myth of Ownership. Liam Murphy and Thomas Nagel. A Review Essay". *Constitutional Political Economy*, 16, 207–219.
Brennan, Geoffrey (2018): "Striving for the Middle Ground. Taxation, Justice and the Status of Private Rights". In O'Neill, Martin and Orr, Shepley (eds): *Taxation. Philosophical Perspectives*. Oxford. Oxford University Press, pp 60–80.
Brennan, Jason (2014): *Why Not Capitalism?* New York. Routledge.
Brennan, Jason and Tomasi, John (2012): "Classical Liberalism". In Estlund, David (eds): *The Oxford Handbook of Political Philosophy*. Oxford. Oxford University Press, pp 115–132.
Brighouse, Harry and Swift, Adam (2009): "Legitimate Parental Partiality". *Philosophy & Public Affairs*, 37 (1), 43–80.
Brighouse, Harry and Swift, Adam (2014): *Family Values*. New Jersey. Princeton University Press.
Brülde, Bengt and Duus-Otterstöm, Göran (2015): *Klimatetik. Rettvisa, politik och individens ansvar*. Stockholm. Thales.
Burchardt, Tania, and Hick, Rod (2018): "Inequality, Advantage and the Capability Approach". *Journal of Human Development and Capabilities*, 19 (1), 38–52.
Calmfors, Lars and Roine, Jesper (2018): "Introduction". In Aaberge, Rolf et al. (eds): *Increasing Income Inequality in the Nordics*. Nordic Economic Policy Review, Nordic Council of Ministers. Copenhagen, pp 6–16.
Caney, Simon (2005): *Justice beyond Borders. A Global Political Theory*. Oxford. Oxford University Press.
Cappelen, Alexander, Hole, Astrid D., Sørensen, Erik Ø. and Tungodden, Bertil (2007): "The Pluralism of Fairness Ideals: An Experimental Approach". *American Economic Review*, 97 (3), 818–827.
Cappelen, Cornelius and Pedersen, Jørgen (2014): "Rettferdig arveavgift". *Tidsskrift for velferdsforskning*, 17 (2), 20–33.
Cappelen, Cornelius and Pedersen, Jørgen (2015): "Borgerlønn. En rettferdig reform?" *Tidsskrift for Samfunnsforskning*, 56 (3), 354–371.
Cappelen, Cornelius and Pedersen, Jørgen (2018): "Just Wealth Transfer Taxation: Defending John Stuart Mill's Scheme". *Politics, Philosophy & Economics*, 17 (3), 317–335.
Carens, Joseph H. (2015): "The Egalitarian Ethos as a Social Mechanism". In Kaufmann, Alexander (ed): *Distributive Justice and Access to Advantage*. Cambridge. Cambridge University Press, pp 50–78.
Caron, Paul L. and Repetti, James R. (2013): "Occupy the Tax Code: Using the Estate Tax to Reduce Inequality and Spur Economic Growth". *Pepperdine Law Review*, 1 (1), 1255–1290.
Casal, Paula (2007): "Why Sufficiency Is Not Enough". *Ethics*, 117 (2), 296–326.
Casal, Paula (2012): "Progressive Environmental Taxation: A Defence". *Political Studies*, 60, s419–433.
Chancel, Lucas and Piketty, Thomas (2015): "Carbon and Inequality: From Kyoto to Paris". *Paris School of Economics*, 3 November.
Chang, Ha-Joon (2014): *Economics: The User's Guide*. London. Pelican Books.
Chester, Ronald (1982): *Inheritance, Wealth and Society*. Bloomington. Indiana University Press.
Christiano, Thomas (2012) "Money in Politics". In Estlund, David (ed): *Oxford Handbook of Political Philosophy*. Oxford. Oxford University Press, pp 241–257.

Clemet, Kristin (2017): "Ulikhetsdebatten skjemmes av lavt presisjonsnivå og mange sleivspark. I". *Dagbladet* 05.05 Downloaded from: http://www.dagbladet.no/kultur/ulikhetsdebatten-skjemmes-av-lavt-presisjonsniva-og-mange-sleivspark/67541195

Clemet, Kristin and Doksheim, Marius (2017): "Underlige konklusjoner om ulikhet". *Tidsskrift for Velferdsforskning*, 20 (3), 246–250.

Cohen, G.A. (1989) "On the Currency of Egalitarian Justice". *Ethics*, 99 (4), 906–944.

Cohen, G.A. (1995a) *Self Ownership, Freedom and Equality*. Cambridge. Cambridge University Press.

Cohen, G.A. (1995b): "Robert Nozick and Wilt Chamberlain: How Patterns Preserve Liberty". In Cohen, G.A. (ed): *Self Ownership, Freedom and Equality*. Cambridge. Cambridge University Press, pp 19–37.

Cohen, G.A (2000): *If You're an Egalitarian, How Come You're So Rich?* Cambridge. Harvard University Press.

Cohen, G.A. (2008): *Rescuing Justice and Inequality*. Cambridge. Harvard University Press.

Cohen, G.A. (2009): *Why Not Socialism?* Princeton and Oxford. Princeton University Press.

Cohen, G.A. (2011): *On the Currency of Egalitarian Justice, and Other Essays in Political Philosophy*. Princeton. Princeton University Press.

Cohen, Joshua (2001): "Taking People as They Are?" *Philosophy & Public Affairs*, 30 (4), 363–386.

Cosson-Eide, Hans and Sølhusvik, Lilla (2017): "Lahlum vil gjerne betale en million i skatt". 03.07. NRK. Downloaded from: https://www.nrk.no/norge/lahlum-vil-gjerne-betale-en-million-i-skatt-1.13582806

Crisp, Roger (1997): *Mill on Utilitarianism*. London. Routledge.

Crisp, Roger (2003): "Equality, Priority and Compassion". *Ethics*, 113 (4), 745–763.

Cunliffe, John and Erreygers, Guido (eds) (2013): *Inherited Wealth, Justice and Equality*. Routledge. London and New York.

Dabla-Norris, Era et al. (2015): "Causes and Consequences of Income Inequality: A Global Perspective". IMF SDN 15/13. Downloaded from: https://www.imf.org/external/pubs/ft/sdn/2015/sdn1513.pdf

Dagens Næringsliv (14.05.2014): "OECD anbefaler Norge å gjeninnføre arveavgift". http://e24.no/makro-og-politikk/oecd-anbefaler-norge-aa-gjeninnfoere-arveavgift/22980351

Daniels, Norman (1975): "Equal Liberty and the Unequal Worth of Liberty". In Daniels, Norman (ed): *Reading Rawls. Critical Studies of a Theory of Justice*. Oxford. Blackwell, pp. 253–281.

David, Edmonds, Warburton, Nigel and Cohen, G.A. (2007): "G.A. Cohen on Inequality of Wealth". Interview on Philosophy Bites. http://philosophybites.com/2007/12/ga-cohen-on-ine.html.

Dietsch, Peter (2015): *Catching Capital. The Ethics of International Tax Competition*. New York. Oxford University Press.

Duff, David G. (2005): "Private Property and Tax Policy in a Libertarian World: A Critical Review". *Canadian Journal of Law and Jurisprudence*, XVIII (1), 23–45.

Duff, David G. (2016): "Tax Policy and the Virtuous Sovereign: Dworkinian Equality and Redistributive Taxation". http://commons.allard.ubc.ca/cgi/viewcontent.cgi?article=1120&context=fac_pubs

Dworkin, Ronald (1981a): "What Is Equality? Part 1: Equality of Welfare". *Philosophy & Public Affairs*, 10 (3), 185–246.

Dworkin Ronald (1981b): "What Is Equality? Part 2: Equality of Resources". *Philosophy & Public Affairs*, 10 (4), 283–345.
Dworkin, Ronald (2000): *Sovereign Virtue. The Theory and Practice of Equality*. Cambridge. Harvard University Press.
Dworkin, Ronald (2002): "Sovereign Virtue Revisited". *Ethics*, 113 (1), 106–143.
Dworkin, Ronald (2003): "Equality, Luck and Hierarchy". *Philosophy & Public Affairs*, 31 (2), 190–198.
Edmundson, William A. (2017): *John Rawls: Reticent Socialist*. Cambridge. Cambridge University Press.
Eia, Harald (2017): "Where in the World Is It Easiest to Get Rich?" Ted X Oslo. https://www.youtube.com/watch?v=A9UmdY0E8hU
Elford, Gideon (2017): Survey Article: Relational Equality and Distribution. *The Journal of Political Philosophy*, 25 (4), 80–99.
Erreygers, Guido and Vandevelde, Toon (eds): *Is Inheritance Legitimate? Ethical and Economic Aspects of Wealth Transfers*. Berlin. Springer.
Esping-Andersen, Gøsta (1990): *The Three Worlds of Welfare Capitalism*. Cambridge. Polity Press.
Estlund, David (ed) (2012): *The Oxford Handbook of Political Philosophy*. Oxford. Oxford University Press.
Farrelly, Colin (2004): "Taxation and Distributive Justice". *Political Studies Review*, 2, 185–197.
Fisman, Raymond et al. (2017): "Do Americans Want to Tax Capital. Evidence from Online Surveys". *NBER Working Paper* 23907.
Fleischer, Miranda Perry (2017): "Not So Fast: The Hidden Difficulties of Taxing Wealth". In Knight, Jack and Scwartzberg, Melissa (eds): *NOMOS LVI: Wealth. Yearbook of the American Society for Political and Legal Philosophy*. New York. New York University Press, pp 261–308.
Fontan, Clement, Claveau, Francois, and Dietsch, Peter (2016): "Central Banking and Inequalities: Taking Off the Blinders". *Politics, Philosophy & Economics*, 15 (4), 319–357.
Fosli, Halvor (2017): "Civitas tid har ennå ikke kommet". *Prosa*, 23 (2), 6–15.
Fossen, Cato Husabø (2017): "Erna Solberg innrømmer: Vet ikke om milliardkutt i formueskatt har effekt". *NRK* 31.07 Downloaded from: https://www.nrk.no/norge/erna-solberg-innrommer_-vet-ikke-om-milliardkutt-i-formuesskatten-har-effekt-1.13623807
Fourie, Carina et al. (eds): *Social Equality. On What It Means to Be Equals*. Oxford. Oxford University Press.
Frank, Robert (2019): "How Much Would a Wealth Tax Really Raise? Dueling Economists Reflect New Split in Democratic Party". *CNBC* 10.07 Downloaded from: https://www.cnbc.com/2019/07/10/dueling-economists-debate-how-much-a-wealth-tax-would-raise.html
Frankfurt, Harry (1987): "Equality as a Moral Ideal". *Ethics*, 98, 21–43.
Frankfurt, Harry (1997): "Equality and Respect". *Social Research*, 64 (1), 3–15.
Frankfurt, Harry (2015) *On Inequality*. Princeton. Princeton University Press.
Fraser, Nancy and Honneth, Axel (2003): *Redistribution or Recognition? A Political-Philosophical Exchange*. New York. Verso.
Freeman, Samuel (2007): *Rawls*. London. Routledge.
Freeman, Samuel (2013): "Property-Owning Democracy and the Difference Principle". *Analyse & Kritik*, 01, 9–36.

Fried, Barbara (1995): "Wilt Chamberlain Revisited: Nozick's "Justice in Transfer" and the Problem of Market-Based Distribution". *Philosophy & Public Affairs*, 24 (3), 226–245.

Fried, Barbara (1999): "The Puzzling Case for Proportionate Taxation". *Chapman Law Review*, 2 (157), 157–195.

Fried, Barbara (2003): "Proportionate Taxation as a Fair Division of the Social Contract Surplus: The Strange Career of an Idea". *Economics and Philosophy*, 19, 211–239.

Friedman, Milton (2002): *Capitalism and Freedom*. Chicago and London. The University of Chicago Press.

Furceri, Davide et al. (2020): "COVID-19 Will Raise Inequality If Past Pandemics Are a Guide". VOX CEPR policy Portal. https://voxeu.org/article/covid-19-will-raise-inequality-if-past-pandemics-are-guide

Gaisbauer, Helmut P. et al. (eds) (2015): *Philosophical Explorations of Justice and Taxation*. Switzerland. Springer.

Gale, William G. and Slemrod, Joel (2001): "The Impact of the Estate Tax on Wealth Accumulation and Avoidance Behaviour". In Gale, William G., Hines, James R., and Slemrod, Joel (eds): *Rethinking Estate and Gift Taxation*. Washington. Brookings Institution Press, pp 299–349.

Gibbard, Allan (1991): "Constructing Justice". *Philosophy & Public Affairs*, 20 (3), 264–279.

Glennerster, Howard (2012): "Why Was a Wealth Tax for the UK Abandoned? Lessons for the Policy Process and Tackling Wealth Inequality". *Journal of Social Policy*, 41 (1), 233–249.

Global Age Watch (2015): "Global Age Watch Index 2015". Downloaded from: http://www.helpage.org/global-agewatch/population-ageing-data/global-rankings-table/

Global Finance Magazine (2018): "Wealth Distribution and Income Inequality by Country". https://www.gfmag.com/global-data/economic-data/wealth-distribution-income-inequality

GOV.UK (2018): Home Ownership. Downloaded from: https://www.ethnicity-facts-figures.service.gov.uk/housing/owning-and-renting/home-ownership/latest

Greenwood, Daphne T. and Holt, Richard P.F. (2010): "Growth, Inequality and Negative Trickle Down". *Journal of Economic Issues*, 44 (2), 403–410.

Gregg, Paul (2012): "Predistribution Opens up a New Set of Policy Tools but Also a Key Constraint". *Policy Network*, 25 September.

Grihamar, Stine (2013): «Her er Civitas rike onkler. I VG 02.07. Downloaded from: https://e24.no/naeringsliv/i/WLP56L/her-er-civitas-rike-onkler

Grimen, Harald (2010): "Robert Nozick – den minimale staten". In Pedersen, Jørgen (ed): *Moderne Politisk Teori*. Oslo. Pax Forlag, pp 51–72.

Gruber, Jon and Saez, Emmanuel (2002): "The Elasticity of Taxable Income: Evidence and Implications." *Journal of Public Economics*, 84, 1–32.

Hacker, Jacob S. (2011): "The Institutional Foundations of Middle-Class Democracy". *Policy Network*, 06.05.

Halliday, Daniel (2012) "Is Inheritance Morally Distinctive?" *Law and Philosophy*, 32, 619–644.

Halliday, Daniel (2013): "Justice and Taxation". *Philosophy Compass*, 8 (12), 1111–1122.

Halliday, Daniel (2015): "Egalitarianism and Consumption Tax". In Gaisbauer, Helmut P. et al. (eds): *Philosophical Explorations of Justice and Taxation*. Switzerland. Springer, pp 119–133.

Halliday, Daniel (2018): *The Inheritance of Wealth. Justice, Equality and the Right to Bequeath*. Oxford. Oxford University Press.

Halvorsen, Marit Tronier (2012): "Meningsløs bruk av skatter og avgifter". *DN* 25.09 Downloaded from: https://www.dn.no/privat/privatokonomi/2012/09/25/-meningslos-bruk-av-skatter-og-avgifter

Halvorsen, Marit Tronier and Moene, Kalle (2015): "Hvordan bli rik? Lett å tjene penger i Norge". *Dagens Næringsliv* 14.03.

Hamlin, Alan (2018): "What Political Philosophy Should Learn from Economics about Taxation". In O'Neill, Martin and Orr, Shepley (eds): *Taxation. Philosophical Perspectives*. Oxford. Oxford University Press, pp 17–36.

Hansen, Marianne Nordli (2012): "Om konsentrasjonen av formue i Norge over tid". *Søkelys på arbeidslivet*, 29 (3), 213–223.

Haslett, D.W. (1986) "Is Inheritance Justified". *Philosophy and Public Affairs*, 15 (2), 122–155.

Haslett, D.W. (1997): "Distributive Justice and Inheritance". In Erreygers, Guido and Vandevelde, Toon (eds): *Is Inheritance Legitimate? Ethical and Economic Aspects of Wealth Transfers*. Berlin. Springer, pp 133–155.

Haugan, Bjørn (2018): "Høie anklager Støre for å ville ta penger fra pensjonistene". *VG* 07.05 Downloaded from: https://www.vg.no/nyheter/innenriks/i/l10gWM/hoeie-anklager-stoere-for-aa-ville-ta-penger-fra-pensjonistene

Haugan, Bjørn and Tjersland, Jon (2015): "Hagen gir en million til Høyre". *VG* 18.06 Downloaded from: https://www.vg.no/nyheter/innenriks/hagen-gir-en-million-til-hoeyre/a/23472624/

Hayek, Friedrich A. (1976): *The Constitution of Liberty*. London and Henley: Routledge & Kegan Paul.

Hirose, Iwao (2015): *Egalitarianism*. London. Routledge.

Hodgson, Louis-Philippe (2018): "Cohen's Community: Beyond the Liberal State". *Politics, Philosophy & Economics*, 17 (1), 23–50.

Hollander, Samuel (1985): *The Economics of John Stuart Mill: 2: Political Economy*. Oxford. Blackwell.

Holtug, Nils (2003): "Politisk Filosofi". In Lübcke, Poul (ed): *Engelsk og Amerikansk filosofi*. København. Politikens Forlag, pp 393–438.

Holtug, Nils (2006): "Prioritarianism". In Holtug, Nils and Lippert Rasmussen, Kasper (eds): *New Essays on the Nature and Value of Equality*. Oxford. Oxford University Press, pp 125–156.

Huseby, R. (2010): "Sufficiency: Restated and Defended". *Journal of Political Philosophy*, 18 (2), 178–197.

Huseby, Robert (2020): "Sufficiency and the Threshold question". *The Journal of Ethics*, 24, 207–223.

Institute for Fiscal Studies (2016): "A Survey of the UK Tax System". IFS Briefing Note, BN09.

Jackson, Ben (2012): "Property-Owning Democracy: A Short History". In O'Neill, Martin and Williamson, Thad (eds): *Property-Owning Democracy. Rawls and Beyond*. Malden. Blackwell Publishing, pp 33–52.

Jakobsen, Kjetil (2019): "Ulikhetens verdenshistorie. Thomas Piketty's 'Capital et Idealogie' forklart". *Agenda Magasin notat*. https://agendamagasin.no/wp-content/uploads/2019/12/Ulikhetenes-verdenshistorie_Agenda.pdf

Jensen, Siv (2013): "En enklere hverdag for folk flest". *Aftenposten* 08.08.

Johansen, Per Anders and Haug, Christine Spersrud (2013): "Øystein (19) fikk en regning på arveavgift på 450 000 kroner". *Aftenposten* 03.09.

Kanschik, Philipp (2015) "Why Sufficientarianism Is Not Indifferent to Taxation". *Kriterion –Journal of Philosophy*, 29 (2), 81–102.

Kerr, Gavin (2016): "Predistribution, Property-Owning Democracy and Land Value Taxation". *Politics, Philosophy & Economics*, 15 (1), 67–91.

Knight, Carl (2013): "Luck Egalitarianism". *Philosophy Compass*, 8 (10), 924–934.

Kristiansen, Bjørn Sand Wiederstrøm, Gunnar (2019): "Suksessforlakselobbyen". *Klassekampen* 12.11 Downloaded from: https://dagens.klassekampen.no/2019-11-12/suksess-for-lakselobbyen

Kymlicka, Will (2002): *Contemporary Political Philosophy*. Oxford. Oxford University Press.

Langvatn, Silje (2010): «Martha Nussbaum – I rettferdas nybrottsland». In Pedersen, Jørgen (ed): *Moderne Politisk Teori*. Oslo: Pax Forlag, pp 95–117.

Levy, Jacob T. (2019): "Libertarianism Without Locke". In Brennan, Jason, Van der Vossen, Bas and Schmidtz, David (eds): *The Routledge Handbook of Libertarianism*. New York. Routledge, pp 22–33.

Lien, Marte S. and Johansen, Eivind Linkvist (2017): "Dæhlie raser mot formueskatten: -Uforståelig for meg". *VG* 16.06 Downloaded from: https://www.vg.no/nyheter/innenriks/skatt/daehlie-raser-mot-formuesskatten-uforstaaelig-for-meg/a/24073745/

Lippert-Rasmussen, Kasper (2001): "Equality, Option Luck and Responsibility". *Ethics*, 111 (3), 548–579.

Lippert-Rasmussen, Kasper (2009): "Egalitarisme". In Kaspersen, Lars Bo and Loftager, Jørn (eds): *Klassisk og moderne politisk teori*. København. Hans Reitzels Forlag, pp 679–694.

Lippert-Rasmussen, Kasper (2015): "Luck Egalitarianism Versus Relational Egalitarians: On the Prospects of a Pluralist Account of Egalitarian Justice". *Canadian Journal of Philosophy*, 45 (2), 220–241.

Mack, Eric (2002): "Self Ownership, Taxation and Democracy: A Philosophical-Constitutional Perspective". In Racheter, Donald P. (ed): *Politics, Taxation and the Rule of Law. The Power to Tax in Constitutional Perspective*. Boston. Kluwer Academic Publishers, pp 9–31.

Mandle, Jon and Reidy, David A. (eds) (2015): *The Cambridge Rawls Lexicon*. Cambridge. Cambridge University Press.

McCaffery, Edward J. (1994): "The Political Liberal Case against the Estate Tax". *Philosophy & Public Affairs*, 23 (4), 281–312.

McCaffery, Edward J. (2002): "Fair Not Flat: How to Make the Tax System Better and Simpler". Chicago. University of Chicago Press.

Mead, James E. (1993): *Liberty, Equality and Efficiency*. New York. New York University Press.

Mill, John Stuart (1965): "Principles of Political Economy". In Robson, J.M. (ed): *The Collected Works of John Stuart Mill*. Toronto. University of Toronto Press, pp 3–971.

Mill, John Stuart (1970): "Utilitarianism". In Robson, J.M. (ed): *The Collected Works of John Stuart Mill*. Toronto. University of Toronto Press, pp 203–260.

Mill, John Stuart (1976): *Principles of Political Economy*. Fairfield. August M. Kelley Publishers.

Miller, David (1998): "Equality and Justice". In Mason, Andrew (ed): *Ideals of Equality*. Oxford. Blackwell Publishers, pp 21–36.

Miller, David (2015): "The Incoherence of Luck Egalitarianism". In Kaufmann, Alexander (ed): *Distributive Justice and Access to Advantage*. Cambridge: Cambridge University Press, pp 131–150.

Moene, Kalle (2014): "Forord". In Piketty, Thomas (ed): *Kapitalen i det 21. århundre*. Oslo. Cappelen Damm, pp 7–18.

Moene, Kalle (2015a): "De ekstremt rike". *Dagens Næringsliv*. 14.05. Downloaded from: https://www.dn.no/med-egne-ord/samfunn/debatt/skatt/de-ekstremt-rike/1-1-5330703

Moene, Kalle (2015b): "The Social Upper Class under Social Democracy". *Nordic Economic Policy Review*, 2, 245–262.

Moene, Kalle (2018): "Hvem skal arve verden?" *Dagens Næringsliv* 24.03. Downloaded from: https://www.sv.uio.no/econ/om/aktuelt/i-media/2018/2018-03-24-moene.html

Morris, Peter (2002): *Power. A Philosophical Analysis*. Manchester. Manchester University Press.

Moss, Jeremy (2014): *Reassessing Egalitarianism*. London. Palgrave Macmillan.

Moss, Jeremy (2015): "How to Value Equality". *Philosophy Compass*, 10 (3), 187–196.

Mosveen, Eirik et al. (2014a): "Se superøkonomenes dom. Derfor slakter de Erna og Siv". *VG* 24.10 Downloaded from: https://www.vg.no/nyheter/innenriks/solberg-regjeringen/derfor-slakter-de-erna-og-siv/a/23321988/

Mosveen, Eirik et al. (2014b): "Siv får skatteslakt av økonomiekspertene". *VG* 24.10 Downloaded from: https://www.vg.no/nyheter/innenriks/siv-faar-skatteslakt-av-oekonomi-ekspertene/a/23321538/

Munzer, Stephen (1990): *A Theory of Property*. Cambridge. Cambridge University Press.

Murphy, Liam (2005a): "Author's Introduction". *Australian Journal of Legal Philosophy*, 30, 122–128.

Murphy, Liam (2005b): "Author's Response to Commentators". *Australian Journal of Legal Philosophy*, 30, 147–154.

Murphy, Liam (2019): "How Not to Argue for Tax Justice". *Boston Review* 30.10 Downloaded from: http://bostonreview.net/class-inequality/liam-murphy-how-not-argue-tax-justice

Murphy, Liam and Nagel, Thomas (2002): *The Myth of Ownership. Taxes and Justice*. Oxford. Oxford University Press.

Nagel, Thomas (1975): "Review: Libertarianism Without Foundations". *The Yale Law Journal*, 85 (1), 136–149.

Nagel, Thomas (1991): *Equality and Partiality*. New York. Oxford University Press.

Nagel, Thomas (2009–2010): "Liberal Democracy and Hereditary Inequality". *Tax Law Review*, 63, 113–121.

Nagel, Thomas (2013) "Foreword by Thomas Nagel". In Nozick, Robert (ed): *Anarchy, State and Utopia*. New York. Basic Books, pp 1–5.

Nergaard, Kristine (2017): "Antall fagorganiserte og organisasjonsgrad i Norge". *Arbeidslivet.no*. http://www.arbeidslivet.no/Lonn/Fagorganisering/Antall-fagorganiserte-og-organisasjonsgrad-i-Norge/

Nicolajsen, Stian (2016): "Pappas penger teller mest". *Klassekampen* 15.10. Downloaded from: http://www.klassekampen.no/article/20161015/ARTICLE/161019972

Nielsen, Lasse (2014): "Kapabilitetsteorien og sosial retfærdighed". *Norsk filosofisk tidsskrift*, 49 (1), 17–30.

Norman, Richard (1998): "The Social Basis of Equality". In Mason, Andrew (ed): *Ideals of Equality*. Oxford. Blackwell Publishers, pp 37–51.

NOU (1984): *Skattekommisjonen*. Nr. 22.

NOU (1991): *Bedrifts- og kapitalbeskatningen*. Nr 17.

NOU (2000): *Arveavgift*. Nr. 8.

NOU (2003): *Skatteutvalget. Forslag til endringer i skattesystemet.* Nr 9.

NOU (2009): *Fordelingsutvalget.* Nr. 10.

NOU (2014): *Kapitalbeskatning i en internasjonal økonomi.* Nr. 13.

Nozick, Robert (1974): *Anarchy, State and Utopia.* Malden. Blackwell Publishing.

Nozick, Robert (1989/2000): "Parents and Children". In Vallentyne, Peter and Steiner, Hillel (eds): *Left-Libertarianism and Its Critics: The Contemporary Debate.* Basingstoke. Palgrave, pp 290–294.

NRK (2013) *Debatten.* 30.05. 2013.

NRK (2015): *Skavlan.* 13.03.2015.

NTB (2017): "Han gir mest i partistøtte og det er AP som får pengene". *VG* 08.08 Downloaded from: https://www.vg.no/nyheter/innenriks/arbeiderpartiet/han-gir-mest-i-partistoette-og-det-er-ap-som-faar-pengene/a/24113261/

NTB (2018): «Bill Gates: Milliardærer bør betale mye mer skatt». Downloaded from: https://www.bt.no/nyheter/utenriks/i/jPLngb/Bill-Gates-Milliardarer-bor-betale-mye-mer-skatt

Nussbaum, Martha (2006): *Frontiers of Justice: Disability, Nationality, Species Membership.* Cambridge. Harvard University Press.

Nussbaum, Martha (2011) *Creating Capabilities: The Human Development Approach.* Cambridge. Harvard University Press.

OECD (2010): "Tax Policy Reform and Economic Growth". OECD Publishing. http://dx.doi.org/10.1787/9789264091085-en

OECD (2012): *Going for Growth.* http://www.oecd.org/eco/public-finance/49421421.pdf

OECD (2014): *Focus on Inequality and Growth.* https://www.oecd.org/social/Focus-Inequality-and-Growth-2014.pdf

OECD (2018a): *Consumption Tax Trends 2018.* https://www.oecd.org/tax/consumption-tax-trends-19990979.htm

OECD (2018b): *Consumption Tax Trends 2018.* https://www.oecd.org/tax/consumption/consumption-tax-trends-united-states.pdf

OECD (2019): *Taxing Wages.* https://www.oecd.org/tax/tax-policy/taxing-wages-brochure.pdf

OECD Stat (2020): "Statutory Corporate Income Tax Rates". Downloaded from https://stats.oecd.org/Index.aspx?DataSetCode=CTS_CIT

Olsaretti, Serena (2004): *Liberty, Desert and the Market.* Cambridge. Cambridge University Press.

Olsaretti, Serena (ed) (2018): *The Oxford Handbook of Distributive Justice.* Oxford. Oxford University Press.

Olsen, Lars-Jørgen (2017): "Fjerning av formueskatt gir flere jobber". https://hoyre.no/aktuelt/nyheter/2017/fjerning-av-formuesskatt-gir-flere-jobber/

O'Neill, Martin (2007): "Death and Taxes. Social Justice and the Politics of Inheritance Tax". *Renewal,* 15 (4), 62–71.

O'Neill, Martin (2008): "What Should Egalitarians Believe?" *Philosophy & Public Affairs,* 36 (2), 119–156.

O'Neill, Martin (2020): "Power, Predistribution and Social Justice". *Philosophy,* 95 (1), 63–91.

O'Neill, Martin and Orr, Shepley (ed) (2018): *Taxation. Philosophical Perspectives.* Oxford. Oxford University Press.

O'Neill, Martin and Williamson, Thad (ed) (2012): *Property-Owning Democracy. Rawls and beyond.* Malden. Blackwell Publishing.

O'Neill, Martin, and Williamson Thad (2012a): "Introduction". In O'Neill, Martin and Williamson, Thad (eds): *Property-Owning Democracy. Rawls and Beyond.* Malden. Blackwell Publishing, pp 1–14.
O'Neill, Martin, and Williamson Thad (2012b): "Philosophical Foundations for "Good Capitalism". *Renewal. A Journal of Social Democracy*, 20, 1.
O'Neill, Martin, and Williamson Thad (2012c): "The Promise of Pre-Distribution". *Policy Network*, 28.09.
O'Neill, Martin, and Williamson, Thad (2015): "Taxation". In Mandle, Jon and Reidy, David A. (eds): *The Cambridge Rawls Lexicon.* Cambridge. Cambridge University Press, pp 825–827.
Ornitz, Jill and Struyk, Ryan (2015): "Donal Trump's Surprisingly Honest Lessons about Big Money in Politics". *ABC News.* 11.08 Downloaded from: http://abcnews.go.com/Politics/donald-trumps-surprisingly-honest-lessons-big-money-politics/story?id=32993736
Oslo Economics (2017): "Status og råd for etikkarbeid i kommunesektoren". OE-rapport 2017–61. http://www.ks.no/globalassets/vedlegg-til-hvert-fagomrader/utvikling/fou/fou-rapporter/status-og-rad-for-etikkarbeid-i-kommunesektoren.pdf
Ostry, Jonathan D., Berg, Andrew and Tsangarides, Charalambos D. (2014): Redistribution, Inequality and Growth. IMF SDN 14/02
Otsuka, Michael (2002): "Luck, Insurance and Equality". *Ethics*, 113 (1), 40–54.
Otsuka, Michael (2003): *LIBERTARIANISM Without Inequality.* Oxford. Clarendon Press.
Otsuka, Michael (2006): *How to Be a Libertarian Without Being Inegalitarian.* https://core.ac.uk/download/pdf/72941.pdf
Otsuka, Michael and Voorhoeve, Alex (2009): "Why it Matters That Some Are Worse of Than Others: An Argument against the Priority View". *Philosophy and Public Affairs*, 37 (2), 171–199.
Øverbye, Einar (2017a): "Likhet og ulikhet under Erna Solbergs regjering". *Tidsskrift for Velferdsforskning*, 20 (2), 164–170.
Øverbye, Einar (2017b): Likhet og ulikhet. *Tidsskrift for Velferdsforskning*, 20 (3), 251–253.
Page, E (2007) "Justice between generations. Investigating a sufficientarian approach". *Journal of global ethics*, 3 (1), 3–20.
Parfit, Derek (1997): "Equality and Priority". *Ratio*, 10, 202–221.
Paul, Jeffrey (1982): "Introduction". In Paul, Jeffrey (ed): *Reading Nozick: Essays on Anarchy, State and Utopia.* Oxford. Basil Blackwell, pp 1–23.
Pedersen, Jørgen (2018a): "Just Inheritance Taxation". *Philosophy Compass*, 13, 4.
Pedersen, Jørgen (unpublished) The Rawlsian Case for Wealth Transfer Taxation.
Pedersen, Jørgen and Bøyum, Steinar (2020): "Inheritance and the Family". *Journal of Applied Philosophy*, 37 (2), 299–313.
Persky, Joseph (2010): "Rawls's Thin (Millian) Defense of Private Property". *Utilitas*, 22 (2), 134–147.
Pettit, Philip (2012): *On the Peoples Terms: A Republican Theory and Model of Democracy.* Cambridge. Cambridge University Press.
Phipps, Shelley (2002): "The Well-Being of Young Canadian Children in International Perspective: A Functionings Approach". *Review of Income and Wealth*, 48 (4), 493–515.
Piketty, Thomas (2014): *Capital in the Twenty-First Century.* Cambridge. London. The Belknap Press of Harvard University Press.

Piketty, Thomas (2020): *Capital and Ideology*. Cambridge. The Belknap Press of Harvard University Press.

Piketty, Thomas and Saez, Emmanuel (2013): "A Theory of Optimal Inheritance Taxation". *Econometrica*, 81 (5), 1851–1886.

Platz, Jeppe von (2020): *Theories of Distributive Justice*. New York and London. Routledge.

Polillo, Simone and Guillen, Mauro F. (2005): "Globalization Pressures and the State: The Worldwide Spread of Central Bank Independence". *American Journal of Sociology*, 110 (6), 1764–1802.

Posner, Eric A. and Weyl, E. Glenn (2018): *Radical Markets*. Princeton. Princeton University Press.

Raa, Lasse Andre (2017): "Distribution Effects of Central Bank Independence". Master's thesis. Department of Comparative Politics, University of Bergen.

Rakowski, Eric (2000): "Can Wealth Taxes Be Justified?" *Tax Law Review*, 53, 263–375.

Ravnaas, Ernst (2016): Formuesskatteflukten. *Dagens Næringsliv* 20.01.

Rawls, John (1996) *Political Liberalism*. New York. Columbia University Press.

Rawls, John (1999a): *A Theory of Justice*. Cambridge. The Belknap Press of Harvard University Press.

Rawls, John (1999b): *The Law of Peoples*. Cambridge. Harvard University Press.

Rawls, John (2000): *Lectures on the History of Moral Philosophy*. Cambridge. Harvard University Press.

Rawls, John (2001): *Justice as Fairness. A Restatement*. Cambridge. The Belknap Press of Harvard University Press.

Rawls, John (2007): *Lectures on the History of Political Philosophy*. Cambridge. The Belknap Press of Harvard University Press.

Reich, Rob (2019): *Just Giving. Why Philanthropy Is Failing Democracy and How It Can Do Better.* Princeton and Oxford. Princeton University Press.

Rensin, Emmet (2014): *What America Can Learn from Norway's Success in Regulating Campaign Finance*. https://www.mic.com/articles/91111/what-america-can-learn-from-norway-s-success-in-regulating-campaign-finance

Rignano, Eugenio (1924): *The Social Significance of the Inheritance Tax*. New York. Alfred A Knopf.

Robeyns, Ingrid (2005): "The Capability Approach: A Theoretical Survey". *Journal of Human Development*, 6 (1), 93–114.

Robeyns, Ingrid (2006): "The Capability Approach in Practice". *Journal of Political Philosophy*, 14 (3), 351–376.

Robeyns, Ingrid (Winter 2016 Edition): "The Capability Approach". In Zalta, Edward N. (ed.): *Stanford Encyclopedia of Philosophy*. https://plato.stanford.edu/archives/win2016/entries/capability-approach/.

Robeyns, Ingrid (2017a): "Having Too Much". In Knight, J. and Schwartzberg, Melissa (eds): *NOMOS LVI: Wealth. Yearbook of the American Society for Political and Legal Philosophy*. New York. New York University Press, pp 1–44.

Robeyns, Ingrid (2017b): *Wellbeing, Freedom and Social Justice. The Capability Approach Re-Examined*. Cambridge. Open Book Publishers

Robeyns, Ingrid (2018): "The Capability Approach". In Olsaretti, Serena (ed): *The Oxford Handbook of Distributive Justice*. Oxford. Oxford University Press, pp 109–128.

Roemer, John E. (1996): *Theories of Distributive Justice*. Cambridge. Harvard University Press.

Ronzoni, Miriam (2012): "Life Is Not a Camping Trip – On the Desirability of Cohenite Socialism". *Politics, Philosophy & Economics*, 11 (2), 171–185.

Rothbard, Murray N. (2006): *For a New Liberty. The Libertarian Manifesto*. Auburn. Ludwig Von Mises Institute.

Ruud, Solveig (2018): "Slik er det privatiserte drømmesamfunnet til Siv Jensens ungdomsorganisasjon". *Aftenposten* 05.09 Downloaded from: https://www.aftenposten.no/norge/politikk/i/9mAdx9/Slik-er-det-privatiserte-drommesamfunnet-til-Siv-Jensens-ungdomsorganisasjon

Saez, Emmanuel and Zucman, Gabriel (2019a): *The Triumph of Injustice. How the Rich Dodge Taxes and How to make Them Pay*. New York. W.W Norton & Company.

Saez, Emmanuel and Zucman, Gabriel (2019b): "Progressive Wealth Taxation". Brooking Papers on Economic Activity. https://www.brookings.edu/wp-content/uploads/2019/09/Saez-Zucman_conference-draft.pdf

Sandbu, Martin (2014): "Thomas Piketty: Kapitalen i det 21.århundre. Piketty i annerledelseslandet". *Nytt Norsk Tidsskrift*, 31 (4), 477–486.

Sandbu, Martin (2019): "Hvis Sveits kan beskatte formue kan Norge også". *Aftenposten* 04.08.

Sandvik, Rasmus Haugen (2017): "Sju myter om formueskatten". I *Agenda Magasin* 25.06.

Scanlon, Thomas (2003): "The Diversity of Objections to Inequality". In Scanlon, Thomas (ed): *The Difficulty of Tolerance. Essays in Political Philosophy*. Cambridge. Cambridge University Press.

Scanlon, Thomas (2018): *Why Does Inequality Matter?* Oxford. Oxford University Press.

Scheffler, Samuel (2003): "What Is Egalitarianism". *Philosophy & Public Affairs*, 31 (1), 5–39.

Scheffler, Samuel (2015) "The Practice of Equality". In Fourie, Carina et al. (eds): *Social Equality. On What It Means to Be Equals*. Oxford. Oxford University Press, pp 21–44.

Schemmel, Christian (2015): "How (Not) to Criticise the Welfare State". *Journal of Applied Philosophy*, 32 (4), 393–409.

Schmidtz, David and Freiman, Christopher (2012): "Nozick". In Estlund, David (ed): *Oxford Handbook of Political Philosophy*. Oxford. Oxford University Press, pp 411–428.

Schoenblum, Jeffrey A. (1995): "Tax Fairness or Unfairness? A Consideration of the Philosophical Bases for Unequal Taxation of Individuals". *The American Journal of Tax Policy*, 12 (2), 221–271.

Schokkaert, Erik and Devooght, Kurt (2003) "Responsibility-Sensitive Fair Compensation in Different Cultures". *Social Choice and Welfare*, 21 (2), 207–242.

Sen, Amartya (1979): *Equality of What?* The Tanner Lecture on Human Values. http://tannerlectures.utah.edu/_documents/a-to-z/s/sen80.pdf

Sen, Amartya (1985): *Commodities and Capabilities*. Amsterdam. North Holland.

Sen, Amartya (1993): "Capability and Well-Being". In Nussbaum, Martha and Sen, Amartya (eds): *The Quality of Life*. Clarendon Press. Oxford, pp 30–53.

Sen, Amartya (2004): "Capabilities, Lists, and Public Reason: Continuing the Conversation". *Feminist Economics*, 10 (3), 77–80.

Sen, Amartya (2005) "Development as Capability Expansion". In Fukuda-Parr, Sakiko and Shiva Kumar, A.K. (eds): *Readings in Human Development*. Oxford. Oxford University Press, pp 41–58.

Sen, Amartya (2006): "What Do We Want From a Theory of Justice". *Journal of Philosophy*, CIII (5), 215–238

Sen, Amartya (2009a): *The Idea of Justice*. New York. Penguine Books.

Sen, Amartya (2009b): "Utvikling som frihet". In Svendsen, Lars (ed): *Liberalisme. Politisk frihet fra John Locke til Amartya Sen*. Oslo. Universitetsforlaget, pp 503–524.

Shields, Liam (2012): "The Prospects for Sufficientarianism". *Utilitas*, 1 (24), 101–117.

Simmons, A. John (2010): "Ideal and Nonideal Theory". *Philosophy & Public Affairs*, 38 (1), 5–36.

Skarsaune, Erlend (2018): "Statoil sjefen økte lønnen med 31 prosent". *Bergens Tidende* 24.03 Downloaded from: https://sysla.no/offshore/statoil-sjefen-okte-lonnen-med-31-prosent/?utm_source=bt&utm_medium=webwidget&utm_campaign=promo

Skarvøy, Lars Joakim and Henden, Harald (2017): "Erna åpner for flere nullskatteytere:- Bekymrer meg ikke". *VG* 01.08 Downloaded from: http://www.vg.no/nyheter/innenriks/skatt/erna-aapner-for-flere-nullskattytere-bekymrer-meg-ikke/a/24108033/:

Skavland, Fredrik (2015): *Thomas Piketty Full Interview*. https://www.youtube.com/watch?v=YMrEqceUF5

Slemrod, Joel and Bakija, Jon (2017): *Taxing Ourselves*. Cambridge. The MIT Press.

Spinner-Halev, Jeff (2012): Historical Injustice. In Estlund, David (ed): *The Oxford Handbook of Political Philosophy*. Oxford. Oxford University Press, pp 319–335.

Spence, Thomas (2017): "Christen Sveaas gir seks millioner kroner til de borgerlige og er valgkampens mest gavmilde enkeltperson». In Aftenposten 28.07. Downloaded from: https://www.aftenposten.no/norge/politikk/i/22vGl/christen-sveaas-gir-seks-millioner-kroner-til-de-borgerlige-og-er-valg

SSB (2017a): *Økonomisk utsyn over året 2016*. http://www.ssb.no/inntekt-og-forbruk/artikler-og-publikasjoner/_attachment/299065?_ts=15ad8858368#page=11

SSB (2017b): *Stort flertall eier boligen*. https://www.ssb.no/bygg-bolig-og-eiendom/artikler-og-publikasjoner/stort-flertall-eier-boligen

SSB (2018): *Finansiering av politiske partier*. https://www.ssb.no/valg/statistikker/partifin

Statista (2020): "Homeownership Rate in the United States from 1990–2019". Downloaded from: https://www.statista.com/statistics/184902/homeownership-rate-in-the-us-since-2003/

Steiner, Hillel and Vallentyne, Peter (2009): "Libertarian Theories of Intergenerational Justice". In Gosseries, Axel and Meyer, Lukas (eds): *Intergenerational Justice*. Oxford. Oxford University Press, pp 50–76.

Stemplowska, Sofia and Swift, Adam (2012): "Ideal and Nonideal Theory". In Estlund, David (ed): *Oxford Handbook of Political Philosophy*. Oxford. Oxford University Press, pp 373–389.

Stewart, Miranda Perry (2005): "Taxes and Justice in Context". *Australian Journal of Legal Philosophy*, 30, 133–142.

Sugin, Linda (2004) "Theories of Distributive Justice and Limitations on Taxation: What Rawls Demands from Tax systems". *Fordham Law Review*, 72 (5), 1991–2014.

Sundberg, Johan D. (2014): "Uten formueskatt ville 28 milliardærer betalt 80 prosent mindre i skatt". *E24* 17.10 Downloaded from: https://e24.no/privatoekonomi/i/QogE28/uten-formuesskatt-ville-28-milliardaerer-betalt-80-prosent-mindre-i-skatt

Svåsand, Lars (2001): "Statlig finansiering av politiske partier. Intensjonene og utfallet". *NOU* 3. Downloaded from: https://www.regjeringen.no/no/dokumenter/nou-2001-03/id143453/sec22

Tan, Kok-Chor (2012): *Justice, Luck and Institutions. The Site, Ground and Scope of Equality*. New York. Oxford University Press.

Temkin, Larry (2002): "Equality, Priority and the Levelling Down Objection". In Clayton, Matthew and Williams Andrew (eds): *The Ideal of Equality*. New York. Palgrave Macmillan, pp 126–161.

Thomas, Alan (2017) *Republic of Equals. Predistribution and Property-Owning Democracy*. New York. Oxford University Press.

Tungodden, Bertil (2003): "The Value of Equality". *Economics & Philosophy*, 19 (1), 1–44.

UNCTAD (2012): *Trade and Development Report 2012*. New York and Geneva. United Nations.

United Nations (2019): *World Happiness Report*. https://worldhappiness.report/news/finland-again-is-the-happiest-country-in-the-world/

Valentini, Laura (2012): "Ideal vs. Non-Ideal Theory: A Conceptual Map". *Philosophy Compass*, 7 (9), 654–664.

Vallentyne, Peter (1997). "Self-Ownership and Equality: Brute Luck, Gifts, Universal Dominance, and Leximin Real Freedom for All by Philippe Van Parijs". *Ethics*, 107 (2), 321–343.

Vallentyne, Peter (2007) "Distributive Justice". In Goodin, Robert E., Pettit, Philip and Pogge, Thomas (eds): *A Companion to Contemporary Political Philosophy*. Oxford, Wiley-Blackwell, pp 548–562.

Vallentyne, Peter (2012): "Left-Libertarianism". In Estlund, David (ed): *The Oxford Handbook of Political Philosophy*. Oxford. Oxford University Press, pp 152–168.

Vallentyne, Peter (2018): "Libertarianism and Taxation". In O'Neill, Martin and Orr, Shepley (eds): *Taxation. Philosophical Perspectives*. Oxford. Oxford University Press, pp 98–110.

Vallier, Kevin (2018): "Rawls, Piketty and the Critique of Welfare-State Capitalism". *The Journal of Politics*, 81, 1.

Volacu, Alexandru, and Dumitru, Adelin Costrin (2018): "Assessing Non-Intrinsic Libertarianism." *Philosophia*, 47, 249–264.

Waldman, Paul (2014): "How Our Campaign Finance System Compares to Other Countries". *The American Prospect* 04.04 Downloaded from: https://prospect.org/power/campaign-finance-system-compares-countries/

Waldron, Jeremy (1988): *The Right to Private Property*. Oxford. Clarendon Press.

Wangberg, Ida Søraunet and Moene, Kalle (2015): "Fagbevegelsen gjør arbeidslivet mer produktivt". *Manifest Tidsskrift*. http://www.manifesttidsskrift.no/fagbevegelsen-gjor-arbeidslivet-mer-produktivt/

Wenar, Leif (Winter 2013 Edition): "John Rawls". In Zalta, Edward N. (ed): *The Stanford Encyclopedia of Philosophy*. http://plato.stanford.edu/archives/win2013/entries/rawls/.

White, Stuart (2018): "Moral Objections to Inheritance Tax". In O'Neill, Martin and Orr, Shepley (eds): *Taxation. Philosophical Perspectives*. Oxford. Oxford University Press, pp 167–184.

Wiborg, Øyvind N. (2017): "Hvor er formuene i Oslo? Gylne ghettoer og deres utvikling over tid". In Ljunggren, Jørn (ed): *Oslo. Ulikhetens by*. Oslo. Cappelen Damm Akademisk, pp 105–120.

Williamson, Thad (2012a): "Is Property-Owning Democracy a Politically Viable Aspiration?" In O'Neill, Martin and Williamson, Thad (eds) *Property Owning Democracy. Rawls and Beyond.* Malden. Wiley Blackwell, pp 287–306.
Wilkinson, Richard G and Pickett, Kate (2009): *The Spirit Level.* New York. Bloomsbury Press.
Wolff, Jonathan (1991): *Property, Justice and the Minimal State.* Cambridge. Polity Press.
Wolff, Jonathan (1998): "Fairness, Respect and the Egalitarian Ethos". *Philosophy & Public Affairs,* 27 (2), 97–122.
Wolff, Jonathan (2007): "Equality: The Recent History of an Idea". *Journal of Moral Philosophy,* 4 (1), 125–136.
Wolff, Jonathan (2010) "On John Rawls': A Theory of Justice". *Philosophy Bites.* http://philosophybites.com/2010/02/jonathan-wolff-on-john-rawls-a-theory-of-justice.html
Wolff, Jonathan (2015a): "Social Equality and Social Inequality". In Fourie, Carina et al. (eds): *Social Equality. On What It Means to Be Equals.* Oxford. Oxford University Press, pp 209–225.
Wolff, Jonathan (2015b): "Equality and Social Justice". In McKinnon, Catriona (ed): *Issues in Political Theory.* Oxford. Oxford University Press, pp 99–120.
Wolff, Jonathan (forthcoming): "Family Fortunes". *Law, Ethics and Philosophy.*
Wolff, Jonathan and De-Shalit, Avner (2007): *Disadvantage.* Oxford. Oxford University Press.
Young, Robert (2005): "Everyday Libertarianism, Consequentialism and Income Tax". *Australian Journal of Legal Philosophy,* 30, 143–146.
Zelenak, Lawrence (2003): "The Myth of Pretax Income". *Michigan Law Review,* 101, 2261–2274.
Zidar, Owen (2019): "Tax Cuts for Whom? Heterogeneous Effects of Income Tax Changes on Growth and Employment". *Journal of Political Economy,* 127 (3), 1437–1472.
Zimmer, Fredrik (2013): "Arveavgift ut, kontinuitetsprinsipp inn". *Skatterett,* 32 (4), 305–326.

Index

Note: Bold page numbers refer to tables; italic page numbers refer to figures and page numbers followed by "n" denote endnotes.